# Use this book and pass it on

| Date | Name | Course / University |
|------|------|---------------------|
|      |      |                     |
|      |      |                     |
|      |      |                     |
|      |      |                     |
|      |      |                     |
|      |      |                     |
|      |      |                     |
|      |      |                     |
|      |      |                     |
|      |      |                     |
|      |      |                     |
|      |      |                     |
|      |      |                     |
|      |      |                     |
|      |      |                     |
|      |      |                     |

# CONTENTS

# Foreword

Having been involved for some decades with those considering Oxbridge, I can sympathise with the anxieties and hopes that prospective applicants face. Some sixth formers feel that the odds are stacked against them; they suspect that there is some hidden key or secret formula which is denied to them and that only those with some privileged access to this formula can ever be successful. This misconception means some good applicants with a lot of potential give up before they even begin.

These challenges and uncertainties have intensified in recent years as even more hurdles seem to have been placed before prospective applicants. The grades which Oxford and Cambridge ask for have risen – two A*s and an A at A Level have become standard requirements for Science subjects and an A* and two As for Arts and Humanities subjects. Changes to the A Level system, including the decoupling of the AS Level from the A Level, have increased uncertainty, meaning that more Admissions Tests have been introduced to help assess an applicant's aptitude. Tests have become required by roughly fifty courses across Oxford and Cambridge at the time of going to press and more can be expected. Requests for written work to be submitted are also on the increase. Finally, there is the interview, which many find to be the most daunting aspect of the admissions process. One thing remains clear: the competition has never been fiercer.

It is important to ask one essential question: 'what are the real qualities that the universities are looking for in a successful applicant?' Applicants must understand that the universities are placing these extra demands on the admissions process in order to try to reveal these qualities. The first thing to realise is that the universities are not looking for some pre-determined template which all applicants should fit into. In fact, it is quite the opposite: they are looking for individuality and not conformity. There is no hidden agenda. Anyone with the right qualifications has an equal chance of success and what, to the outsider, may seem to be a system slanted in favour of those who can buy success is in fact a system designed to select the best applicants regardless of their background. If you want to apply and have the appropriate grades you have as good a chance as anyone else. Background is irrelevant.

The biggest problem which the universities face is the fact that so many applicants have identical qualifications. How can they make a judgement between those with equal grades, who on paper look as good as each other? The answer is to look beyond the simple statistics which the UCAS form records, and to try and find the 'best' applicants. And by 'best', they don't just mean the person who has accumulated the most knowledge – they are looking for all-round intellectual ability, alongside academic curiosity and commitment. Nobody can obtain these things overnight: applicants who prepare long-term and are prepared to stretch themselves to the limit and aim for the highest in terms of intellectual and academic achievement are the most successful.

The various tests and extra written submissions are designed to try and pin-point these qualities. It is highly significant that many of the tests are described in terms of 'aptitude' tests or assessments of 'thinking skills'. The question is, 'is this applicant really suited intellectually to this particular subject? Can this applicant show creative and logical thought, outside of what they've been taught in school?'

If the applicant has managed to successfully overcome these hurdles, then they are ready for the final assessment of the interview. The interview gives applicants the chance to show their individual qualities in a verbal way. The same vital qualities of motivation and potential are being tested at interview, as well as how the applicant responds to unexpected academic and intellectual challenges. You need to show that you are a committed and engaged applicant who will excel in the Oxbridge academic environment.

All applicants (and parents), however, will of course ask themselves 'how can I prepare for these extra hurdles?' It is clear that at one level, the answer is that you can't and nor should you be able to. That is, you cannot suddenly improve your academic ability and potential overnight. What you can do is consult those whose experience can help you to show yourself to your best possible advantage. This is what the educational consultancy Oxbridge Applications and the authors of this book are aiming to do. What is on offer is a wide range of experience and expertise to help you play to your strengths and avoid the pitfalls into which so many students fall, which prevent the interviewer from getting a true impression of the applicant's abilities.

'Oxbridge Applications' is not a conveyor belt, nor is the admissions process. There is no coaching or any attempt to 'beat the system' – that would be as unethical as it is impossible. What is possible is for you to develop your academic capabilities through helpful advice. Remember: anyone can offer you advice, but only you can turn it into success."

Barry Webb
Former Oxbridge Admissions Tutor
Member of the Oxbridge Applications' Advisory Board
June 2016

# Introduction

An offer from Oxbridge is the result of a long academic journey, designed to assess your suitability for Oxbridge and ensure the best candidates receive a place. While the Oxbridge application process is not faultless, at each stage, Admissions Tutors seek to unveil the potential of applicants to become successful Oxbridge students.

The purpose of this book is to demystify the process and to help you approach each stage of the application to the best of your ability. We give you an overview of the process and in-depth advice on the key stages of the application, including specific advice for international applicants and students considering a reapplication.

In our 16 years working with Oxbridge applicants, we have frequently experienced misconceptions about what students need to do in order to be successful. Below, we address these and give some insight into what Admissions Tutors are looking for:

### DO I NEED TO COME FROM A CERTAIN BACKGROUND?

Despite the stereotype that Oxford and Cambridge are universities of the elite, wealthy, and well-educated, a little over half of successful students to both universities come from non-fee paying schools. Equally, you are at no disadvantage applying from an independent school. Students also worry that they will only be considered if they have a family member who has previously attended the university, but again, this is not something Admissions Tutors are interested in. Although Oxbridge will take your educational background into account to some extent, they are assessing you as an individual candidate for your subject, not merely as a product of your schooling and background. Of course you need to have a certain ability in your subject, but the tutors are much more interested in the way you think than in where you come from or the school you attended.

## DO I HAVE TO FIT A CERTAIN ACADEMIC MOULD?

Oxford and Cambridge are looking for the best and brightest applicants, and this means considering more than just your grades. They will, of course, consider your academic achievements so far, but this is just one aspect through which they assess your ability and potential. Having perfect grades is not enough to guarantee you a place.

Chapters three to seven will draw your attention to other crucial elements of the application, from your personal statement to the interview. These elements of the process exist to provide Admissions Tutors with further opportunities to assess your motivation and potential to study the subject at university level, as well as to differentiate between applicants who all have excellent grades.

One way of demonstrating these attributes is to show an interest in your subject outside of your school work. Students often feel they have to read a particular book, or show an interest in a particular area of the subject, whereas in fact you should use your extra reading to prove your genuine interest in the course you are applying for. Exploring your personal interests in the subject will make you much more likely to come across as a positive, enthusiastic and motivated student in your interview. Admissions Tutors are not expecting students to be the finished product or to know everything there is to know about the subject – they are looking for someone who is engaged, interested, and proactively willing to learn more.

## DO I NEED TO HAVE A CERTAIN PERSONALITY?

Shyer students often worry that the nature of the interview process means that they need to be outgoing and extroverted in order to succeed at this stage. All that is really important is that you are able to express yourself and your ideas coherently and clearly to your interviewer so that they can see your potential and ability in your subject. Remember that the tutors interviewing you are very experienced in assessing a student's suitability for studying their chosen course at Oxbridge and will try and look past nerves and shyness to gauge your ability.

The interview is also your opportunity to demonstrate your teachability. Admissions Tutors are looking for applicants with good knowledge and an aptitude for their subject, who can apply new information to a familiar situation, or apply existing knowledge to the unknown. They are looking for students who are willing to learn and who can think for themselves, even when put on the spot. Chapters six and seven of this book explore the interview in more depth, including example questions answered by our Oxbridge graduates and fifty real-life past interview questions to help you practice.

Many students, teachers, and parents believe there is a secret formula to gaining a place at Oxbridge. The purpose of this book is not to reveal this formula – not because it is secret, or because it is reserved for those who have the right credentials and knowledge, but because there is no formula. Rather, there is the opportunity to educate yourself as to what Admissions Tutors look for in applicants and how to make informed decisions at each stage of your application.

*So you want to go to Oxbridge? Tell me about a banana...* has been compiled by Oxbridge graduates with personal experience of the application process. In this book, we take you through each stage, providing guidance and tips on how to put forward the best possible application. This book is just a starting point for the journey ahead – it is a spring-board from which to begin researching your course and college, reading around your chosen subject, taking mock admissions tests, and practicing your answers to even the most 'off-the-wall' interview questions. It is by proactively taking your application into your own hands that you will realise your potential and develop knowledge and skills that will remain invaluable, whatever the outcome.

# YOUR OXFORD APPLICATION 2016-17

# YOUR CAMBRIDGE APPLICATION 2016-17

# Oxbridge Application Timeline

The main stages of the application will be expanded on in-depth in their respective chapters. This chapter outlines information about the smaller aspects of the application which are nevertheless still important if they are relevant to you.

**UCAS FORM**

Applicants to Oxford and Cambridge must submit their UCAS form by 15th October. On the form, you need to specify which college and course you wish to apply to. You can find the UCAS form on the UCAS website: www.ucas.com. Universities will not be told where else you have applied. You can also submit your application to your other three or four choices later than October 15th by logging back into your UCAS form and selecting your other choices before the January deadline. You won't be able to edit your application – you will be submitting exactly the same application as you did to Oxbridge, just slightly later.

**OFFER**

In the January following your interview, your college or department will send you a letter or email informing you of the outcome of your application. If you have been successful, the letter will make you an offer and these usually have academic conditions attached, e.g. A Level results or STEP requirements. Oxford usually set a date on which applicants will receive their offers (in 2016 this was 6th January), but Cambridge are less specific, although they guarantee you will hear either way by the end of January.

**GRADES**

You must achieve the grades set out in your conditional offer in order to secure your place. If you do miss your grades but are close to meeting your offer, get in contact with your college as soon as possible to see whether they might still be able to accept you. If something happens in the lead up to or during exams that may affect your performance, it is advisable to inform the college of this before your results come out, so they are prepared for the possibility of you missing your offer. There is no set rule on this; it really depends on the college and the circumstances.

## EXTENUATING CIRCUMSTANCES

If you have extenuating circumstances surrounding your application which have caused educational disruption or disadvantage, both universities have systems in place to take this into account when considering your application. Extenuating circumstances could include serious illness or significant caring responsibilities, but if you are unsure, contact the admissions office.

If you are applying to Cambridge, there is an Extenuating Circumstances form which must be completed by your school or college and submitted by the deadline of 15th October. If your school is unaware of your circumstances, a doctor or social worker can submit the form on your behalf.

If you are applying to Oxford, your teachers will need to include details of any special circumstances in your main UCAS application as part of your reference.

## MUSIC AWARDS AND SCHOLARSHIPS – CAMBRIDGE

ORGAN SCHOLARSHIPS

You will need to submit your Cambridge Online Preliminary Application (COPA) by 1st September. Although you should wait until after the results of your Organ Trial before submitting your UCAS form, you will need to submit at least a draft of your personal statement with your COPA form. Following the submission of your COPA, you should submit a final version of your personal statement and reference before your Organ Trial. If the colleges judge that you are not of the required academic standard, they will no longer consider your scholarship application. Auditions are held in Cambridge in mid-to-late September and academic interviews happen at the same time. You should be ready to submit your written work (if required) when you apply. Organ scholarship offers and academic places are then confirmed before the UCAS deadline. You must accept any scholarship offer you are made by a college, even if it wasn't your first choice. Offers will then be made formally through UCAS. In some cases, you may be asked to return in December for a further interview. Organ Scholars can apply to both Oxford and Cambridge and to more than one college, but must specify only one choice on their UCAS form. The university recommend that you put down any college from which you would be prepared to accept an offer on your form. For more information on which colleges are offering scholarships and to download the application form, visit the Cambridge website.

CHORAL AWARDS

You only apply for a Choral Award once you have been offered an academic place at the university, although you can attend Vocal Assessment Days in September before you apply to gain an informal assessment of whether you are suitable for the college choirs you are interested in. You can mention your interest in becoming a Choral Scholar on your Supplementary Application Questionnaire (SAQ), but there is no disadvantage if you only declare your interest after your offer in January. You need to submit the Choral Award application form by 15th February of the year that you're planning to begin your course. You can apply for a Choral Award at as many colleges as you wish (providing you're eligible) and the university encourage you to list several, but your first choice must be the college that has offered you the academic place. If your application is successful, you will be invited to a choral audition by the end of March. The audition will involve singing a prepared piece, sight-reading, and ear tests. You can find out more on the Cambridge website, which also has sample tests. If you are offered a Choral Award by a college other than the one which has offered you an academic place, you can either apply for an academic transfer to the college which offered you the Choral Award, or you can remain at your original college and sing at another choir. If you are pooled, you can still be considered for a choral place at the college you originally applied to, but you will not be able to transfer academically to this college.

INSTRUMENTAL AWARDS

If you are not a singer or organist, you can still apply for the Instrumental Awards for Chamber Music scheme. The scheme is only open to certain instruments (the full list of which can be found on the Cambridge website) and you apply after you have received an academic place at the university. The deadline to submit your application is 28th February and if you meet the conditions of your offer, you will be invited to audition at the end of September, before you take up your place.

## MUSIC AWARDS AND SCHOLARSHIPS – OXFORD

ORGAN SCHOLARSHIPS

The deadline for the Organ Scholarship Application Form is 1st September. Although you should wait until after the results of your Organ Trial before submitting your UCAS form, you will need to submit at least a draft of your personal statement along with an academic and musical reference. If your application is judged suitably strong academically, you will be invited to audition. Auditions usually take place in Oxford towards the end of September, and you will have your academic interview at the same time. This means that you should be ready to submit your written work when you apply as it will be requested soon afterwards. Organ scholarship offers and academic places are then confirmed before the UCAS deadline. You must accept any scholarship offer you are made by a college, even if it wasn't your first choice. Offers will then be made formally through UCAS. Organ Scholars can apply to both Oxford and Cambridge and to more than one college, but must specify only one choice on their UCAS form. The university recommend that you put down any college from which you would be prepared to accept an offer on your form, including for deferred places at the same college if they are available. For more information on which colleges are offering scholarships and to download the application form, see the Oxford website.

CHORAL AWARDS

The deadline for the Choral Award application form is 1st September and you will need to submit a musical reference at the same time. You are able to choose up to ten colleges in order of preference, and the university recommend you nominate at least three. The choral trials usually take place in late September. You won't have an academic interview during this time – this takes place in December with all other applicants. Even if you're successful in your Choral Award application, you're not guaranteed an academic place – both successful and unsuccessful applicants should submit their UCAS application before 15th October, after the choral trials. Unsuccessful applicants for the Choral Awards may still gain an academic place. If you're unsuccessful with your application for a Choral Award, but receive an academic offer, there may be an opportunity when you arrive to re-apply to a particular choir when you're at Oxford.

INSTRUMENTAL AWARDS

If you are not a singer or organist, many colleges at Oxford also offer Instrumental Awards. If you are interested in these, auditions take place after you have begun your studies, but a list of colleges that offer awards is available on the Oxford website.

# International Applicants

## Guidance on navigating the application process as an overseas applicant.

You are classed as an international or overseas applicant if you are domiciled outside of the UK or EU. It does not matter where you hold a passport as your status depends solely on your country of permanent residence. If you are unsure about whether you are an international or home applicant, the university admissions office can clarify your status. Importantly, if you will be living overseas at the time of your application, you will still need to complete the Cambridge Online Preliminary Application (COPA), discussed later on in this chapter, even if you will not be paying international fees.

Applying to Oxford or Cambridge as an international student can be very competitive. In 2014, 27.8% of all Cambridge applicants and 34.7% of Oxford applicants applied from outside the UK. The success rate for non-UK Cambridge applicants in the same admissions cycle was 12.1% versus 26.5% for UK applicants, and 9.5% for non-UK Oxford applicants compared to 23% for UK applicants. If you are an overseas applicant applying to Oxbridge, beginning preparation early and familiarizing yourself with the application process can help you to overcome the barriers between you and a place at Oxbridge.

In this chapter, we discuss the application process for an international applicant, including information on language requirements, accepted qualifications, and visas.

### English language requirements

As Oxford and Cambridge courses are taught in English, all applicants must have a good verbal and written grasp of the language. If English is not your first language, but you have been in full-time education in the English language for the past two years, you will not need to sit a test. Otherwise, you may be asked to complete a formal qualification such as the IELTS or TOEFL, a list of which can be found on each university's website.

## Country-specific qualifications

Many international qualifications are recognised by both Oxford and Cambridge, but not all are accepted by the university. It is important to visit the university websites to ensure that your qualification type makes you eligible to make an application.

For the more popular international qualifications, we have outlined the standard grade requirements for Oxford and Cambridge below:

- INTERNATIONAL BACCALAUREATE – Cambridge requires 40-41 with 7,7,6 in your higher level subjects; Oxford requires 38-40 with 6s and 7s in your higher level subjects

- EUROPEAN BACCALAUREATE – Cambridge require 85-90% overall, with 90% in the subjects most relevant to your course; Oxford requires an average of 85% or above, with 8 or 9s in relevant subjects

- SATS/ADVANCE PLACEMENTS/ACTS – Cambridge requires 5 APs at grade 5 in relevant subjects, and although they say they will judge SAT/ACT scores on an individual basis, they usually require 2100 or above combined score in SAT Critical Reading, Mathematics and Writing or an ACT score of at least 32 out of 36. Oxford requires either a combined score of 2100 in the SAT Critical Reading, Mathematics and Writing, or an ACT score of at least 32, plus 3 APs at grade 5 or 3 SAT subject tests at 700 or more.

## UCAS (Universities and Colleges Admissions Service)

Every student applying to Oxford or Cambridge must submit their application through UCAS. From mid-September, you can apply to Oxford and Cambridge (and other UK universities) online. You can use UCAS anywhere in the world and can find out more information about it and applying online at www.ucas.com.

Your application does not have to be completed all at once; you can return to it later and change or add information before you submit it. However, you will need to mark every section of the form as complete before you can send your application to UCAS. The application deadline for Oxbridge and all UK medical courses is 15th October, but this may be earlier if you are applying to Cambridge and would like to be interviewed overseas (more information on this topic is available later in the chapter).

## Academic reference

As part of your application, you will need a reference highlighting your academic and personal suitability for your chosen course. This will usually be written by a teacher from your current school who knows you well and can provide an accurate account of your abilities. A full written reference is required (name and address are not sufficient), and your reference must be written in English. If you are applying through a school, college or other organisation, you will not have access to your reference; it will be completed on your behalf by your referee and sent directly through UCAS to your chosen universities.

If you are applying as an individual, you need to ensure that the reference section is completed in good time as you will not be able to send your application to UCAS without it. If you are applying independently but would like your reference to be written by a registered school, college or other organisation, you can request that the centre completes the reference for you in the 'Apply' section of the UCAS website. For more information on the reference, please refer to the UCAS website.

## Admissions Tests and written work

For some courses, you may be asked to sit an Admissions Test (see Chapter 4) or submit essays written in English (see Chapter 5). If you are applying for a course that requires you to sit an Admissions Test, you will need to register to sit the test.

This registration must take places before 15th October for most tests, and so you will need to find an approved test centre to register with. You cannot register yourself, but must apply to a test centre which is usually your school. If your school is not an approved test centre, a list of approve centres worldwide is available on the Admissions Testing Service's website which can help you find a local centre. Furthermore, dates and costs for taking Admission Tests can be found on the Admissions Testing Service's website.

## The Cambridge Online Preliminary Application (COPA)

The COPA is an online form you will need to complete if you are applying to Cambridge from overseas, irrelevant of your fee status or citizenship, or if you are applying for an Organ Scholarship. This includes applicants from Iceland, Liechtenstein, Monaco, Norway and Switzerland. The COPA provides Cambridge with comprehensive information on all applicants, and also helps them to make arrangements for overseas interviews. The important dates for overseas interviews are discussed later in this chapter. A detailed guide to completing your COPA form can be found on the Cambridge website.

**Supplementary Application Questionnaire (SAQ)**

If you are applying to Cambridge, you will also need to complete the SAQ online. The SAQ is a form applicants submit after their UCAS application, which, similarly to the COPA, provides Cambridge with more comprehensive information on each applicant. However, as you have already completed the COPA form, the only information you will need to provide on the SAQ is your UCAS ID number and COPA Reference Number.

**The interview**

As an international student, you may have different interview options available to you, depending on your home country, university, college and course choice. Cambridge suggest that applicants for Architecture, History of Art, Classics, and Music apply to be interviewed in Cambridge, but otherwise say that where you are interviewed has no effect on your application. If possible, we recommend that students have a face-to-face interview in order to have the same experience and opportunity as other applicants.

For those who cannot be interviewed in Cambridge, the university conducts a number of interviews overseas in September and October. In 2016, overseas interviews will be held in Canada, China, Hong Kong, Malaysia and Singapore. Please note that eligibility for these interviews is restricted and deadlines can be earlier – you can find full information on the countries where interviews will be offered and the restrictions on the Cambridge website.

In some cases, Oxford can arrange interviews over the telephone, video conference or Skype but this is not guaranteed and is subject to certain restrictions, which can be found on the Oxford website. In particular, all short-listed applicants for Medicine at Oxford, or students applying from the European Economic Area (EU, Norway, Iceland and Lichtenstein) and Switzerland, must attend interviews at Oxford in December to be considered.

## Earlier deadlines for Cambridge international applicants

If you are an international applicant who will be travelling to the UK for your interview in December, the usual UCAS deadline of 15th October will apply to you. However, if you would like to be interviewed in China, Malaysia or Singapore, different deadlines will apply to your application. Please note the following deadlines are for 2017 entry. They remain roughly the same each year, but for 2018 entry and beyond please refer to the Cambridge website to confirm:

| | |
|---|---|
| 20th September 2016 | Students applying to Cambridge who would like to be interviewed in China, Malaysia or Singapore must have submitted their UCAS application and COPA by this date. |
| 15th October 2016 | Students applying to Cambridge who would like to be interviewed in Cambridge, Canada and Hong Kong must have submitted their UCAS application. All students applying to Oxford must have submitted their UCAS application by this date. |
| 19th October 2016 | International students applying to Cambridge who would like to be interviewed in Cambridge, Canada and Hong Kong must have submitted their COPA by this date. |

Admissions tests and interviews will take place between September and December, and you will be notified of the university's decision in the January after you apply.

## Visas

If you are offered a place at Oxbridge but you are not a national from the European Economic Area or Switzerland, you will need to apply for a Tier 4 student visa in your home country before you begin your studies.

The UK Border Agency requires you to be formally sponsored by a licensed UK higher education institution. Oxford or Cambridge will sponsor you, but only once your offer becomes unconditional. This means you must have gained a place and met all the academic and financial conditions before you can apply for a visa.

As circumstances for individuals vary, please visit the Oxford or Cambridge website in order to find out the full requirements. Visa details for interviews in the UK can be also found on the universities' websites.

## Quotas for international Medicine applicants

While not a part of the application process, international Medicine applicants should note the high competition for places when considering their course choice. International applicants for Oxbridge Medicine courses must contend with quotas on the number of applicants the universities accept from overseas:

- Oxford has 14 places for international (non-EU) medicine applicants across both the standard and Graduate Entry medicine courses each year.

- Cambridge has 21 places for international (non-EU) medicine applicants for the undergraduate course each year.

If you are an international applicant interested in becoming a doctor, it is worth considering applying for a different undergraduate course, such as Biomedical Sciences, Biochemistry, Biological Sciences or Biological Natural Sciences, before applying for a Graduate Medicine course.

# 1 CHOOSING A COURSE

**EXPLORE THE UNDERGRADUATE COURSES
ON OFFER AT OXFORD AND CAMBRIDGE**

# Explore the undergraduate courses on offer at Oxford and Cambridge

Both Oxford and Cambridge agree that a student's most important decision should be their course choice, more so than the university they apply to. With over 75 courses on offer at Oxford and Cambridge, there is a vast range of disciplines and course combinations to choose from, some of which you may not have previously considered. Even if you know you want to study a certain subject already, it's worth taking the time to understand the course structure and options at both universities, and establish which course you are most suited to. If you are successful, you will be studying your subject for at least three years, so it is important to select a course which best suits your academic interests and ambitions.

Applicants need to be able to demonstrate an interest not only in the subject area, but in the specific course offered by the universities – if you are applying for Philosophy, Politics and Economics (PPE), for example, you need to demonstrate an interest in Philosophy, Politics and Economics as you will have to study all three in your undergraduate career, rather than one or two elements of the course. Admissions Tutors assess the applications of hundreds of applicants over the years and it can quickly become apparent when an applicant is not interested or motivated to study the course.

When deciding which course you want to study, take some time to consider the following questions:

What am I enjoying about my current studies? What topics do I love studying in class to the extent that I carry on exploring ideas and reading outside of school?

Interest is the first step to demonstrating real motivation and potential for your chosen subject. If you want to secure a place, your interviewer will need to know that you already enjoy interacting with your subject and that you'll continue to do so in tutorials and supervisions.

"Physics applies maths, logic and experience to help understand the universe and all its machinations. Why wouldn't you want to study that? Beyond its intrinsic value, studying Physics is also a great way to train your mind to formulate creative solutions to quantitative puzzles. Almost everything that can be measured can also be modelled using insights from Physics."

Tom, Physics at Oxford

### DO I UNDERSTAND THE COURSE I'M APPLYING FOR?

Your interviewers will expect you to have a clear understanding of what the course entails. For example, you might have an interest in Philosophy at Cambridge, but may not be prepared to grapple with the mathematical nature of logic which will come up in the first year of study and likely during the admissions process. If you don't have a core understanding of what logic is or how to approach it, you may find the application difficult. Likewise, if you apply for Economics & Management (E & M) at Oxford and Economics at Cambridge, you will need to be able to solve mathematical problems confidently, and be expected to have an understanding of the macro-economic situation in Britain. In previous years, applicants have been asked to prove Pythagoras' Theorem algebraically, as well as explain quantitative easing and discuss GDP growth. Be sure to read the full course prospectus so that you can see what you will potentially be studying each year.

"I chose English because I love the process of teasing out the depth of meaning in a text through close reading. It fascinates me to see how much more there is to understanding a sentence than just reading words – how structure, tradition and association, rhythm, metre, mimesis – a million elements all contribute to a writer communicating complex thoughts."

Olivia, English at Oxford

## AM I GOOD ENOUGH ACADEMICALLY?

The enjoyment factor is not the only thing to consider – you need to be good at your subject too. As two of the top universities in the world, Oxford and Cambridge are looking for the best and brightest students. All-round academic achievement is extremely important, and you need to have the grades on paper (at GCSE and A Level or equivalent) to complement your desire to study the subject. Cambridge often put more weight on UMS scores or predicted grades, while Oxford like to see excellent grades at GCSE. To put forward a strong application to either, however, you will need strong results at both GCSE and A Level. Make sure you know the grade requirements for the courses you are considering – as well as the subjects different courses require you take at school – so you are aware of the specific grades you will need to achieve to meet the conditions of your offer.

## HAVE I CONSIDERED A SUBJECT I HAVEN'T STUDIED BEFORE?

Many university courses apply academic skills that you've already developed at school to different subject disciplines, such as Engineering, which includes elements of both Mathematics and Physics. If you enjoy History, Classical Civilisation or Human Geography, for example, you may enjoy learning about the development of society and culture in the Archaeology & Anthropology course at Oxford or Human, Social, and Political Sciences (HSPS) at Cambridge. Alternatively, if Physics, Chemistry and Maths are your preferred subjects, you might consider studying their application to our planet which is taught in the Earth Sciences course at Oxford. The interviewers are looking for students who have taken the initiative to explore their chosen subject independently.

## HAVE I COMPARED SIMILAR COURSES AT OXFORD AND CAMBRIDGE?

While there are obvious similarities between the two universities, there are key differences between the courses at each institution. Cambridge courses generally allow students more flexibility and the chance to explore less traditional areas of the subject. At Cambridge, courses are split into Parts I and II. Part I allows you to gain a broad knowledge and understanding of your subject, before choosing your own modules in Part II, which gives you the opportunity to devise your own course of study.

Oxford courses tend to be more rigidly structured with a traditional approach. Undergraduates usually engage with their subject in more depth from the outset. If you compare Natural Sciences (Physical) at Cambridge with its nearest equivalent Physics at Oxford, for example, Oxford Physicists get an earlier induction into the specifics of their chosen subject. In contrast, Cambridge Physical Natural Scientists gain a wide view of the available options in their first year before honing their interests in the second year.

Both universities are world-renowned for their teaching across all subjects, so the decision is more a personal one, dependent on your preferences and interests, rather than on the quality of teaching.

## WILL MY SUBJECT AT UNIVERSITY BE THE SAME AS MY SUBJECT AT SCHOOL?

The style of learning and the topics that you will cover at university will be different than what you studied at school. Research the course contents to ensure your ability and enjoyment of your subject will translate to university study, as often the course contents at university differs from what many applicants expect. Mathematics at school, for example, is more similar to an undergraduate Physics course in many ways than it is a Mathematics course.

## WHAT DO I WANT TO DO AFTER UNIVERSITY?

It's worth bearing in mind that you don't necessarily need a vocational undergraduate degree to go into certain fields. Many applicants feel compelled to apply for courses such as Law and Medicine because they fear that, if they don't, they will miss out on the option of those careers. If you feel this pressure, you should remember that a Law conversion course only takes one year longer than the equivalent qualification for a Law student, and that Magic Circle firms now take almost half of their trainees from non-Law backgrounds. Some recruiters actually prefer to take graduates in different subjects such as English, History or Languages, who have completed a Law conversion, so that they can bring a different approach to the profession. There is also a graduate fast-track programme for Medicine, reducing the five-year training to four years for those with the relevant Science at A Level. Similarly, many applicants believe that without an Economics-based degree, a career in the City will be beyond reach. Bear in mind there are many successful graduates from disciplines as varied as History, Engineering, Maths and Land Economy, who are now excelling in the financial world.

If you already know you want to be a heart surgeon or a chemical engineer, you should look to choose the most suitable course to give you the necessary qualifications and experience to achieve that goal. Our advice, however, is that you should only apply if you feel absolutely certain about your choice. Not only are these courses often among the most competitive, Admissions Tutors are likely to test your total commitment and understanding of the profession at interview.

## HOW CAN I BEGIN RESEARCHING COURSE CHOICE?

Having read this chapter, you should now have an idea of what factors are important to consider when deciding your course. To help you understand the range of courses available at Oxford and Cambridge, we have compiled profiles of courses currently available at Oxford and Cambridge, with input from graduates who studied each course. These pages will give you a taster of the key elements of the course, as well as past interview questions and reading recommendations. You can also find suggestions of similar courses you might like to consider at the bottom of each course page. Once you have narrowed down your course choice, Chapter 7: Approaching Questions shows you example interview questions for your subject. We've enlisted recent graduates to talk you through how best to approach these.

Outside of the information provided in this book, it is often useful to start with the university prospectuses and the university and course Open Days. These days give you the opportunity to meet with tutors and current students to discuss your subject with those who have experienced the course first-hand. A faculty tour will also grant insight into the workings of the department, and many will host a lecture to give you a taste of the working life of a student. There is also a wealth of information on the Oxford and Cambridge websites. You can also try reading books or articles related to subjects you are considering, as this will give you an idea of whether you will enjoy studying the subject at university level. For some suggestions, see our course profiles later in this chapter.

# Anglo-Saxon, Norse, and Celtic (ASNAC)

**COURSE LENGTH:** Three years

**PAST INTERVIEW QUESTIONS:**

- How could you go about dating an unknown manuscript?
- What is the difference between history and literature, especially in the context of the Anglo-Saxon period?
- How will your choice of A Levels benefit your study of ASNaC?

The ASNaC course combines the study of literature, language and history of the early medieval period. It is unique to Cambridge, and allows students to work on a range of disciplines in great depth. No specific subjects are required, but language and humanities A Levels are preferred. You will be required to sit a writing and comprehension based assessment before the interview. Most colleges will require you to submit written work to demonstrate your ability to structure material and argue your point of view.

**"The amount of choice is amazing – essentially you can design your own degree, and the dissertation allows you to contribute towards the field of scholarship."**

Harriet, ASNaC graduate

**INTERESTED? WHY DON'T YOU EXPLORE...**

Beowulf translation by Seamus Heaney – one of the most important works of Anglo-Saxon literature and a set text on the course.

The Sagas of Icelanders: A Selection by Robert Kellogg – a particularly good introduction to Old Norse literature.

Anglo-Saxon England by Frank Stenton – a core history text covering the period prior to the Norman Conquest.

**NOT THE COURSE FOR YOU?** Consider Classics, English or History at Cambridge or Oxford.

# Archaeology

**COURSE LENGTH:** Three years

**EXAMPLE INTERVIEW QUESTIONS:**
- What is the role of archaeologists and museums?
- How would you define an archeological layer?
- What is civilisation and how is it different to a society or culture?

The Archaeology course is new for students applying in 2016 and encompasses archaeology, Assyriology, Egyptology and biological anthropology. The flexible nature of the course allows you to specialise from the first year, or gain a broad understanding of all of the disciplines before focusing on up to two subjects from the second year. Field work is included in the course, and if you choose to study Assyriology or Egyptology you will take a relevant language. There are no required subjects for this course, but Classics, Geography, History, a language, science or social science subject are considered useful preparation. You will be required to sit a written assessment at interview, and some colleges ask you to submit written work.

**INTERESTED? WHY DON'T YOU EXPLORE...**

The Archaeology of Britain by John Hunter and Ian Ralson – a concise and up-to-date overview of the archaeological record of Britain

In Small Things Forgotten: An Archaeology of Early American Life by James Deetz – a look at how small objects can fill in the gaps between large historical events and daily life.

Archaeology: Theories, Methods and Practice by Colin Renfrew and Paul Bahn – a thorough introduction to archaeology, including the most recent developments in the practice of this discipline.

**NOT THE COURSE FOR YOU?** Consider HSPS (Human, Social, and Political Sciences) or History or consider the Archeology and Anthropology course at Oxford.

# Architecture

**COURSE LENGTH:** Three years

**PAST INTERVIEW QUESTIONS:**
- What would you say is the most important building of the 20th Century?
- What are your views on the combination of modern and historical architecture?
- What are the social implications of architecture?

The course provides a wide-ranging education in the principles of architectural design and its theoretical background. It is one of the few subjects that combines the intellectual challenge of a Cambridge Tripos with the opportunity for creative design. All applicants are expected to show a portfolio of recent work at interview but this needn't be of an architectural nature. You will be required to sit a written and practical assessment at interview and some colleges may ask you to submit written work. Mathematics, Physics or Art A Levels are preferred, but no specific subjects are required.

"The course is a great mix of science and design. I liked having the flexibility to study many sub-topics alongside the design, and I found the studio projects challenging and exciting."

Chloe, Architecture graduate

**INTERESTED? WHY DON'T YOU EXPLORE...**

Invisible Cities by Italo Calvino – a novel comprising fantastical description of cities from the perspective of Marco Polo.

Towards a New Architecture by Le Corbusier – a classic modernist architectural text.

The Timeless Way of Building by Christopher Alexander – proposes a new theory of architecture that relies on the understanding of design patterns.

**NOT THE COURSE FOR YOU?** Consider the Engineering and History of Art courses at Oxford and Cambridge, or Materials Science or Fine Art at Oxford.

# Asian and Middle Eastern Studies (AMES)

**COURSE LENGTH:** Four years (with the third year spent abroad)

**PAST INTERVIEW QUESTIONS:**
- How would life in the Gulf be transformed if its oil supplies ran out?
- What are the advantages of studying a foreign culture from an outsider's perspective?
- Why did the Cultural Revolution not happen in England?

Asian & Middle Eastern Studies is not only a language course. It also covers history, philosophy, literature and current affairs, and the course works towards a complete understanding of Asian and Middle Eastern culture and tradition. You can choose to study Arabic, Chinese, Hebrew, Japanese or Persian. It is possible to study an Asian and Middle Eastern Language alongside a Modern Language in some cases. All Asian and Middle Eastern languages are taught ab initio, so no specific subjects are required, but a modern or ancient language A Level is desirable. You are required to sit writing and comprehension-based assessments before the interview. Most colleges will require you to submit written work.

**"The sense of achievement you get from studying a completely new language and culture from scratch certainly makes the course worthwhile."**

Andrew, Asian & Middle Eastern Studies graduate

**INTERESTED? WHY DON'T YOU EXPLORE...**

The Rise of Civilization in East Asia by Gina L. Barnes – charts the development of China, Korea and Japan.

Wild Swans: Three Daughters of China by Jung Chang – a compelling account of three generations of women living in 20th century China.

A History of the Arab Peoples by Albert Hourani – a comprehensive history covering Arab culture, society and politics.

**NOT THE COURSE FOR YOU?** Consider MML (Modern & Medieval Languages) at Cambridge or Modern Languages or Oriental Studies at Oxford.

# Chemical Engineering

**COURSE LENGTH:** Four years

**PAST INTERVIEW QUESTIONS:**

- What do you understand by the term 'activation energy'? Has it any relation to enthalpy of reaction?
- Explain boiling points at different atmospheric pressures.
- How does the equation of force between two charges apply to the hydrogen atom?

If you wish to study Chemical Engineering, you will spend your first year studying either Engineering or Natural Sciences. Both are considered good preparation for pursuing Chemical Engineering and are equally taken up by students. From second year, you will begin studying the core disciplines of the subject before specializing in fourth year. Projects and practical work are assessed throughout the course. For both routes, Chemistry and Mathematics at A Level or equivalent is required, with Physics essential for the Engineering route and highly recommended for Natural Sciences. Depending on the route you take, you will be required either to take the assessment for Natural Sciences or Engineering before interview (see the respective course pages for more information).

**INTERESTED? WHY DON'T YOU EXPLORE...**

Introduction to Chemical Engineering: Tools for Today and Tomorrow, by Kenneth A. Solen and John Harb – a relatively short and easy read outlining the discipline and giving examples of relevant calculations.

Perry's Chemical Engineers' Handbook by Don W. Green and Robert H. Perry – a complete and updated guide to the principles and processes of chemical engineering.

Elementary Principles of Chemical Processes by Richard Felder and Ronald Rousseau – an informative guide to formulating and solving material and energy balances in chemical process systems.

**NOT THE COURSE FOR YOU?** Consider the general Engineering courses at Cambridge or Oxford, Physical Natural Sciences at Cambridge, or Physics or Chemistry at Oxford.

# Classics

**COURSE LENGTH:** Three years (four if you don't already have Latin or Greek A Level)

**PAST INTERVIEW QUESTIONS:**

- How civilised was the Roman world?
- Are history and myth compatible?
- Is the ending of the Iliad useful?

The course encompasses the study of the literature, history, culture, philosophy and language of the classical world. Less traditional than the Oxford course, Classics at Cambridge gives you the opportunity to explore a rich and expansive volume of Latin and Greek texts. For the three-year course, a Latin A Level or equivalent is essential. However, if you haven't studied a classical language before, you can opt for the four-year degree, which begins with a preliminary year developing language skills. You will be required to sit a written assessment at interview, involving a translation or language exercise. Most colleges will require you to submit written work.

"Very few courses offer you the opportunity to study two languages to a very high standard whilst also studying the history and culture of the people whose language you are learning."

May, Classics graduate

**INTERESTED? WHY DON'T YOU EXPLORE...**

The Iliad – Homer's works are the bedrock of all Classical literature.

Classics: A Very Short Introduction by Mary Beard & John Henderson – this is an excellent book for understanding the breadth of Classics.

The Latin Love Poets from Catullus to Horace by R.O.A.M. Lyne – surveys the poetry of the major Latin practitioners.

**NOT THE COURSE FOR YOU?** Consider Classics at Oxford, ASNaC (Anglo-Saxon, Norse, and Celtic) at Cambridge or CAAH (Classical Archaeology & Ancient History) at Oxford.

# Computer Science

**COURSE LENGTH:** Three years, with an optional fourth year

**PAST INTERVIEW QUESTIONS:**

- What is the fundamental difference between a spreadsheet and a database?
- What factors contribute to the accuracy of the Global Positioning System (GPS)?
- How would you ensure security between two people, A and B?

The course is partly mixed with other sciences, making it very flexible, with a wide range of project and practical work. There are two routes through the course, one of which combines Computer Science with Mathematics. Cambridge was the first university to offer a Computer Science course, and the world's first fully programmable computer, EDSAC, was built there. A Level Mathematics is essential, and Further Mathematics is highly desirable. You will be required to take a mathematics based assessment at interview, and students wishing to combine Computer Science with Mathematics will need to take the STEP exams.

"I enjoyed mastering something that is so fundamental, but which few people really take the time to investigate."

Alexandra, Computer Science graduate

**INTERESTED? WHY DON'T YOU EXPLORE. . .**

The Mythical Man-Month by Fred Brooks – this book is focused on quite a bit in first year lectures.

The Emperor's New Mind by Roger Penrose – this book uses the physics of computing to explore the concept of artificial intelligence.

Computer Science: A Modern Introduction by Les Goldschlager & Andrew Lister – an introductory overview.

**NOT THE COURSE FOR YOU?** Consider Computer Science at Oxford, or Mathematics or Engineering at Oxford or Cambridge.

# Economics

**COURSE LENGTH:** Three years

**PAST INTERVIEW QUESTIONS:**

- What is the point of privatisation?
- Why is climate change Economics and not Chemistry?
- Compare Keynesian and classical macroeconomics.

The course will give you a solid understanding of the core features of Economics, both pure and applied, with compulsory micro- and macroeconomics papers. It also allows considerable breadth, giving you the opportunity to consider topics from an inter-disciplinary perspective, taking in history, sociology, mathematics, statistics and philosophy. A Level Mathematics is essential, and Economics and Further Mathematics are desirable. You will be required to sit a mathematics and comprehension based assessment before interview. Some colleges will ask you to submit written work, and/or sit the STEP exams.

"The course offers a lot of variety, which enabled me to focus on the specific aspects of Economics that most interested me."

Rebecca, Economics graduate

**INTERESTED? WHY DON'T YOU EXPLORE. . .**

Black Swan by Nassim Nicholas Taleb – a very good book on the current, flawed economic system.

The Ascent of Money by Niall Ferguson – an accessible history of money, banking and credit systems.

Too Big to Fail: Inside the Battle to Save Wall Street by Andrew Ross Sorkin – widely regarded as the definitive history of the banking crisis.

**NOT THE COURSE FOR YOU?** Consider Land Economy, History or Mathematics at Cambridge or PPE (Philosophy, Politics and Economics) or E&M (Economics & Management) at Oxford.

# Education

**COURSE LENGTH:** Three years

**PAST INTERVIEW QUESTIONS:**

- What are the current issues facing educational practitioners today?
- What makes a good teacher?
- What should be the government's involvement in education?

The course aims to provide an understanding of education through in-depth study of a particular field of interest, alongside wider social and educational issues. There are three tracks available: Education, Psychology and Learning; Education, Policy and International Development; and Education, English, Drama and the Arts. You will be required to sit a written test at interview and some colleges will require you to submit written work and/or have taken an A Level in a subject relevant to your chosen track.

**"The course provides an excellent basis not only for teaching, but also for further academic study."**

Debra, Education Studies graduate

**INTERESTED? WHY DON'T YOU EXPLORE. . .**

Fifty Modern Thinkers on Education ed. by Joy Palmer – accessible summaries of great educators and their impact and influence.

Philosophy of Education: The Key Concepts by John Gingell & Christopher Winch – a good reference book.

How Children Think and Learn by David Wood – an important study in developmental psychology.

**NOT THE COURSE FOR YOU?** Consider the specialist subjects (Biological Sciences, Classics, English, Geography, History, Mathematics, Modern Languages, Music or Theology) on their own at either Oxford or Cambridge.

# Engineering

**COURSE LENGTH:** Four years

**PAST INTERVIEW QUESTIONS:**

- Explain one of the following to someone with no knowledge of Physics: force, momentum, power.
- Sketch a velocity time graph for a skydiver jumping out of a plane.
- Why does a bullet spiral?

Year one provides a broad education in Engineering and furnishes you with the necessary analytical, design and computing skills to take on your specialisation in Part II. There are 10 possible specialization areas including aerospace and aerothermal engineering, bioengineering, civil and structural engineering, and energy, sustainability and the environment. You're required to complete eight weeks of industrial experience by the end of your third year. A Level Mathematics and Physics are essential, while Further Mathematics is strongly encouraged. You will be required to sit a mathematics and engineering-based admissions test before interview.

"The practical side of the course gives a real-life understanding of what you learn. I loved being able to explain the results that were generated through theory in lab sessions."

Charlie, Engineering graduate

**INTERESTED? WHY DON'T YOU EXPLORE. . .**

Mathematical Methods for Science Students by George Stephenson – this is the main set text for the course.

Cats' Paws and Catapults by Steven Vogel – an introduction to biomechanics.

The New Science of Strong Materials: Or Why You Don't Fall Through the Floor by J. E. Gordon – explores the general properties of all materials.

**NOT THE COURSE FOR YOU?** Consider Natural Sciences (Physical) or Mathematics at Cambridge, or Engineering, Materials Science or Physics at Oxford.

# English

**COURSE LENGTH:** Three years

**PAST INTERVIEW QUESTIONS:**

- Why do you think English is important?
- When reading a novel or poem, how important is its historical context?
- Can a play just be read, or must it be seen on stage to be understood?

First and second year papers are broad in their scope and you can generally choose what you want to study within a given period. Third year offers students a lot of freedom to study literature from around the world, other art forms, and related intellectual traditions. The backbone of the course is Practical Criticism, which is the close analysis of unseen texts. You can be quite creative with this, and will usually be asked to discuss an unseen passage at interview. Writing style is incredibly important, which is why most colleges will ask you to submit written work before coming up to interview. You will also be required to sit the ELAT before interview. An English A Level or equivalent is required.

**"English is such a discursive subject, so it really helps having intelligent people around who challenge your ideas and force you to think more deeply and creatively."**

Claudia, English graduate

**INTERESTED? WHY DON'T YOU EXPLORE. . .**

The Wheel of Fire by G. Wilson Knight – classic critical essays on Shakespeare's tragedies which will help prepare you for the compulsory Shakespeare paper.

The Poetry Handbook by John Lennard – this will arm you with the necessary vocabulary to approach unseen texts.

Literary Theory: An Introduction by Terry Eagleton – a good place to start learning about English as an academic discipline.

**NOT THE COURSE FOR YOU?** Consider English at Oxford, Philosophy at Cambridge or Modern Languages, History or Classics at Oxford or Cambridge.

# Geography

**COURSE LENGTH:** Three years

**PAST INTERVIEW QUESTIONS:**

- Is climate change a man-made phenomenon?
- What is the role of maps in a modern-day society?
- Define the term 'globalisation'.

The first year covers topics from globalisation through to environmental economics and Quaternary climate change. You will also take the Geographical Skills and Methods paper to equip you with numerical and spatial data analysis skills, survey and fieldwork techniques. Specialisation into human or physical geography is possible from second year. You will need strong analytical skills and a good writing style, so most colleges will require you to submit written work. You will be required to sit a thinking skills, comprehension and data based assessment before interview, and some colleges require an A Level or equivalent Geography or another essay-based subject.

"The Geography course prompted me to question why humans consider our world, society and landscape the way we do. It was a transformative course for me as I began to look at everyday problems more analytically."

Jim, Geography graduate

**INTERESTED? WHY DON'T YOU EXPLORE. . .**

Human Geography: an Essential Anthology ed. by John Agnew – a vital resource.

Glaciers and Glaciation by Douglas Benn & David Evans – a comprehensive overview of the nature and history of glaciers.

The City in History by Lewis Mumford – this award-winning book traces the origins of the sprawling cities we know today.

**NOT THE COURSE FOR YOU?** Consider Land Economy, Economics or Natural Sciences (Physical) at Cambridge or Geography or PPE (Philosophy, Politics and Economics) at Oxford.

# History

**COURSE LENGTH:** Three years

**PAST INTERVIEW QUESTIONS:**
- What is the difference between modern history and modern politics?
- Do you think that all of history is a history of thought?
- Is it a historian's job to look for cycles in history?

History at Cambridge offers the chance to study a hugely diverse range of topics from British Economic History, to Ancient Greece, the History of the USA or even the History of Political Thought. The compulsory Themes and Sources paper allows you to take on a broad theme in comparative history and trace its changes over time (e.g. gender). You will be required to take a writing and comprehension based assessment before interview and most colleges will ask you to submit written work. Some colleges will also require you to have an A Level or equivalent in History or another essay-based subject.

"I loved the freedom to pursue my own interests. I was never told to stick to a certain topic, but always encouraged to go beyond reading lists and go beyond traditional approaches."

Esther, History graduate

**INTERESTED? WHY DON'T YOU EXPLORE. . .**

A Little History of the World by E.H. Gombrich – a classic piece of historical writing, chronicling human development through the ages.

The Art of War by Sun Tzu – this razor-sharp ancient Chinese treatise gives an interesting insight into military strategy and, on a more fundamental level, how humans make decisions.

Guns, Germs and Steel by Jared Diamond – an engaging book on human history, which takes into account environmental factors in the development of societies.

**NOT THE COURSE FOR YOU?** Consider ASNaC (Anglo-Saxon, Norse, and Celtic) or HSPS (Human, Social, and Political Sciences) at Cambridge, or Classics or History of Art at Oxford or Cambridge.

# History and Modern Languages

**COURSE LENGTH:** Four years

**EXAMPLE INTERVIEW QUESTIONS:**

- What is the role of fiction in history?
- Is national character a useful concept in history?
- What is the role of a translator?

A new course in 2016, the History and Modern Languages course offers you the chance to study French, German, Russian or Spanish alongside History, providing an insight into the cultures of other countries and an understanding of both past and present events in an international context. The two disciplines are studied side by side throughout, with the third year spent abroad. Unless you are applying for Russian, you must have the language you intend on studying at A Level or equivalent, and some colleges also require History. You will be required to take a History assessment before interview, and a Modern Languages assessment at interview (see Cambridge History and Modern Languages pages respectively). Some colleges will also ask you to submit written work.

**INTERESTED? WHY DON'T YOU EXPLORE...**

The Russian Language in the Twentieth Century by Bernard Comrie and Gerald Stone – an interesting look at how social change can affect language change, with Russia as the example.

Spain: A History, by Raymond Carr – an overview of the political, economic, social, and intellectual factors that have shaped Spanish history over the last two thousand years.

German Thought and Culture: From the Holy Roman Empire to the Present Day by H.J. Hahn – an introduction to the complexities of the German identity, from a cultural, historical, philosophical and literary perspective.

**NOT THE COURSE FOR YOU?** Consider Cambridge's Modern Languages, Asian and Middle Eastern Studies and History courses, or consider combining a language with English, Philosophy, Classics or History at Oxford.

# History and Politics

**COURSE LENGTH:** Three years

**EXAMPLE INTERVIEW QUESTIONS:**

- In a democracy, can the majority impose its will on the minority?
- Is society based on the political system, or did the political system evolve from society?
- Who writes history?

Introduced in 2016, the History and Politics course gives students a strong grounding in the two subjects and a chance to explore the ways in which historical and political understanding can interlink and provide insight into the modern world. The first year introduces you to historical knowledge, intellectual history, political science and international relations, and from second year you can choose more specialised papers, allowing you to explore conceptual political issues, quantitative methods and a wide ranging knowledge of world history. Some colleges require History or another essay-based subject at A Level or equivalent and you will be required to sit a writing and comprehension test before interview. Most colleges will also ask you to submit written work.

**INTERESTED? WHY DON'T YOU EXPLORE...**

The Politics, Aristotle – a central text to the study of political science.

The Age of Extremes by Eric Hobsbawn – a historical and political look at the short twentieth century.

The Great Sea: A Human History of the Mediterranean – a history of one of the great centres of world civilization, with an emphasis on human activity.

The English National Character by Peter Mandler – an interesting study of what it has meant to be 'English' over the last 200 years.

**NOT THE COURSE FOR YOU?** Consider History or History and Modern Languages or HSPS at Cambridge, or explore History and its joint honours courses or PPE at Oxford.

# History of Art

**COURSE LENGTH:** Three years

**PAST INTERVIEW QUESTIONS:**

- How does art reflect its society?
- How would you account for there being such a vast quantity of art based on religious subject matter?
- What do you believe makes something a piece of art?

History of Art is for students interested in studying works of art and understanding them in their historical and social context. The course makes first-hand use of the wealth of resources found in Cambridge such as the excellent Fitzwilliam Museum, which houses illuminated manuscripts, stained-glass windows, and sculptures by distinguished artists such as Henry Moore. You will be required to take a written assessment at interview and most colleges will ask you to submit written work. Some colleges will ask you to have taken an A Level or equivalent in an essay-based subject.

"The course develops your understanding of the world and art. I spent a great deal of my time learning about history and literature, the other two areas that I would have really enjoyed studying."

Jade, History of Art graduate

**INTERESTED? WHY DON'T YOU EXPLORE. . .**

The Story of Art by E.H. Gombrich – this gives a very good overview of the history of art.

Studies in Iconology by Erwin Panofsky – a useful introduction to symbolism and how to look at works of art.

This is Modern Art by Matthew Collings – another good introductory book, this time to the world of contemporary art.

**NOT THE COURSE FOR YOU?** Consider History of Art at Oxford. You might also wish to consider Fine Art at Oxford, or History at Oxford or Cambridge.

# Human, Social, and Political Sciences (HSPS)

**COURSE LENGTH:** Three years

**PAST INTERVIEW QUESTIONS:**

- What is class?
- What aspect of the US government is not democratic?
- How is Trafalgar Square a symbol?

This is one of two newer courses available since 2012, broadly replacing Politics, Psychology & Sociology and Archaeology & Anthropology. The course is huge in its scope, allowing you to explore a variety of subjects (such as International Relations or Social Anthropology), before tailoring the course to suit your specialised area of interest in the second and third years. You will be required to sit a writing and comprehension based pre-interview assessment and most colleges will ask you to submit written work. Some colleges will ask that you have an essay-based subject at A Level or equivalent.

"I chose the course because it encapsulated my interest in studying people through a theoretical and practical lens. The combination of disciplines allowed me to look at the lived reality of people at a micro-level, as well as studying broader political and social themes at a macro-level, providing an academically rigorous grounding across the social sciences."

Olivia, HSPS graduate

**INTERESTED? WHY DON'T YOU EXPLORE. . .**

Setting the People Free: The Story of Democracy by John Dunn – traces the Ancient Greek roots of democracy through to the modern age.

Why Humans Have Cultures by Michael Carrithers – a firm foundation for the study of culture, society and history.

The Culture of the New Capitalism by Richard Sennett – looks at the social implications of the new-economy model.

**NOT THE COURSE FOR YOU?** Consider PPE (Philosophy, Politics and Economics), Archaeology & Anthropology or EP (Experimental Psychology) at Oxford. Or try History and Politics, Economics, PBS (Psychological and Behavioural Sciences) or Philosophy at Cambridge.

# Land Economy

**COURSE LENGTH:** Three years

**PAST INTERVIEW QUESTIONS:**

- Why is the USA a country when Europe isn't?
- How do towns grow?
- Why are wages higher in London?

The course is predominantly a mix of Law and Economics, and looks at how these disciplines interact and are applied to the built and natural environment. Less theoretical than an Economics degree, Land Economy gets to grips with solving real-world issues, such as sustainable housing and rural conservation. No particular A Levels are required, but Economics, Mathematics and Geography are desirable. You will be required to take the Thinking Skills Assessment at interview and some colleges will require you to submit written work.

**"The course offers a wide range of paper choices, and there's a lot of freedom to make Land Economy into your own subject."**

Henry, Land Economy graduate

**INTERESTED? WHY DON'T YOU EXPLORE. . .**

Economics by John Sloman – a comprehensive introduction, particularly useful for those without an Economics A Level.

Economics: Principles and Policy by William J Baumol & Alan S Blinder – a vital guide to land law and economics.

The World is Flat by Thomas Friedman – examines the influences shaping business in the technological age.

**NOT THE COURSE FOR YOU?** Consider Geography or Economics at Cambridge or Geography, E&M (Economics & Management) or PPE (Philosophy, Politics and Economics) at Oxford.

# Law

**COURSE LENGTH:** Three years

**PAST INTERVIEW QUESTIONS:**

- How do you think the House of Lords should be reformed?
- What do you think is more important, actions or motives?
- Is international law the first step to a single legal system, and would such a system be possible?

Law students are challenged to think in a deeply analytical way, approach problems from a logical position, and defend their arguments against criticism. Although you will primarily study English law, there are opportunities to study other legal systems, including EU and international law. You will be required to sit the Cambridge Law Test at interview and most colleges will ask you to submit written work. There is no expectation for you to have studied Law before applying, but some colleges will require that you have an essay-based subject at A Level or equivalent.

> **"I enjoyed learning the set rules of law and then exploring the room for interpretation within them."**
>
> Cara, Law graduate

**INTERESTED? WHY DON'T YOU EXPLORE. . .**

The Times Law Supplement – essential reading as it helpfully summarises all the week's legal events and issues.

Learning the Law by Glanville Williams – an accessible introduction to the basics of law.

Discipline and Punish by Michel Foucault – evaluates the changes in western penal systems in the modern age.

**NOT THE COURSE FOR YOU?** Consider Land Economy at Cambridge. Law (Jurisprudence) is also available at Oxford, with the option to take Law with Law Studies in Europe.

# Linguistics

**COURSE LENGTH:** Three years

**PAST INTERVIEW QUESTIONS:**

- Discuss the ambiguities in this sentence: 'I bumped into a woman carrying flowers'.
- Do you agree with the Chomskyan theory of a 'universal grammar'?
- How do you think babies learn languages differently to older people?

Linguistics is the systematic study of human language, through both the diverse characteristics of individual languages and the properties which all languages share. The course is interdisciplinary, drawing on methods and knowledge from a wide range of subjects, such as philosophy, biology and psychology. You will be required to take a writing and analysis based assessment at interview and most colleges will ask you to submit written work. No specific A Level subjects are required, although a language or English, or even Mathematics, does serve as good preparation.

"The study of different accents and dialects is to me the most interesting part of the course."

Sarah, Linguistics graduate

**INTERESTED? WHY DON'T YOU EXPLORE. . .**

The Language Instinct by Steven Pinker – lucidly explains everything you need to know about language learning.

The Articulate Mammal by Jean Aitchison – an excellent introduction to the field of psycholinguistics.

Syntactic Structures by Noam Chomsky – a key text in linguistics, and Chomsky's first published book.

**NOT THE COURSE FOR YOU?** Consider English or MML (Modern & Medieval Languages) at Cambridge. Or check out PPL (Psychology, Philosophy & Linguistics) or Modern Languages & Linguistics at Oxford.

# Mathematics

**COURSE LENGTH:** Three years, with an optional fourth year

**PAST INTERVIEW QUESTIONS:**

- Is mathematics a language?
- Describe a complex number to a non-mathematician.
- How many ways are there of arranging 'n' objects and why?

In your first year, you will choose between two paths: Pure and Applied Mathematics or Mathematics with Physics. Both will teach you the fundamentals of higher mathematics. There is the chance to specialise as you progress, with optional computational projects in your second and third years. You may be invited to complete a fourth year of study if you achieve a first or high II.i at the end of third year. A Level Mathematics is essential and AS or A Level Further Mathematics is strongly advised. A Level Physics or an A Level in a second science/mathematics subject are required by some colleges. All colleges will require you to sit the STEP and some will set an additional test at interview.

"The thing that I enjoyed most about my course was how challenging it was, and there is no doubt that the Cambridge Tripos is the most challenging mathematical undergraduate degree in the country."

Tahar, Mathematics graduate

**INTERESTED? WHY DON'T YOU EXPLORE. . .**

The Mathematical Tourist by Ivars Peterson – a journey through important mathematical concepts, told in accessible language.

Alice in Numberland by J Baylis & R Haggerty – this is recommended by tutors as preparation for the course.

Fermat's Last Theorem by Simon Singh – an interesting read on one of the most notorious mathematical problems.

**NOT THE COURSE FOR YOU?** Consider Mathematics at Oxford, which offers several joint course degrees, or Computer Science or Engineering at either university.

# Medicine

---

**COURSE LENGTH:** Three years pre-clinical, followed by a three-year clinical degree

**PAST INTERVIEW QUESTIONS:**

- What are the challenges to be faced by the NHS in the near future?
- What would life be like without enzymes?
- What do you know about Parkinson's disease and its treatment?

The course involves a combination of intensive scientific teaching and practical training to equip you with the skills to deal with patients effectively. The pre-clinical years are taught through lectures, practical classes and supervisions, with emphasis shifting during the clinical years to learning practically in clinical environments such as hospitals. You will need to have a solid scientific understanding to succeed in Medicine, which is why A Level Chemistry and a further two of the following subjects are required: Biology/Human Biology, Physics, and Mathematics. You will be required to sit the BMAT and how well you do in this is an important factor in the selection process.

"The first three years are essentially an academic biological sciences degree, which gave me a good grounding in pre-clinical concepts."

Jules, Medicine graduate

**INTERESTED? WHY DON'T YOU EXPLORE. . .**

Human Physiology by Gillian Pocock & Christopher Richards – covers most of the major physiological systems in a clinically relevant way.

Principles of Evolutionary Medicine by Peter Gluckman, Alan Beedle & Mark Hanson – a good review of advances in the field of evolutionary biology.

The Man Who Mistook His Wife for a Hat by Oliver Sacks – details the strangest neurological conditions Sacks has treated as a clinical neurologist.

**NOT THE COURSE FOR YOU?** Consider Natural Sciences (Biological) at Cambridge or Medicine or Biomedical Sciences at Oxford.

# Modern and Medieval Languages (MML)

**COURSE LENGTH:** Four years (with the third year spent abroad)

**PAST INTERVIEW QUESTIONS:**
- Why do some languages have genders when others don't?
- Can you only understand or analyse a text properly in its original language?
- What is the role of a translator?

You'll study two languages, one of which you can learn from scratch. Languages available are French, German, Italian, Portuguese, Russian, and Spanish. These languages can also be combined with Classical Latin and Greek. If you wish to study one of these languages alongside Arabic, Hebrew or Persian, you apply for the Asian and Middle Eastern Studies course. The course is very literary in its focus, although slightly more balanced with language work in your first year. By the second year, you'll be expected to be fluent in your language and the focus will change to the culture and literature of your chosen language, with less emphasis on oral skills. You'll get the chance to develop further your verbal skills during the compulsory third year abroad. An A Level in at least one of your chosen languages is essential and you will be required to take a written assessment in English and a foreign language at interview. Most colleges will also ask you to submit written work.

> "I got to try so many new things, from language exchanges and foreign film nights, to living and working abroad."

Steph, Modern & Medieval Languages graduate

**INTERESTED? WHY DON'T YOU EXPLORE. . .**

Through the Language Glass by Guy Deutscher – an extremely readable study of how language influences the way we view the world.

Foreign newspapers, such as Le Monde, El Pais, Die Welt – it's a good idea to keep up-to-date with current affairs in the languages you're applying for. Reading the headline articles of the major newspapers of that language will be helpful and may provide content for discussion at interview.

**NOT THE COURSE FOR YOU?** Consider History and Modern Languages, English, Linguistics or Classics at Cambridge. Or Consider the selection of Modern Languages joint school degrees on offer at Oxford.

# Music

**COURSE LENGTH:** Three years

**PAST INTERVIEW QUESTIONS:**
- Is an awareness of context necessary to appreciate a composer's works?
- Why do you think the jazz tradition branched off from popular music?
- Is music an art incomparable to history in that history cannot be performed?

The Music course is highly regarded amongst academic musicians for the advanced level of training it offers in harmony, counterpoint, fugue and analysis. Although largely academic in its scope, there is now a growing emphasis on performance skills within the Cambridge course, with a recital examination now an option for second and third year students. A Level Music is essential for some colleges, although some accept ABRSM Grade 8 Theory. Most colleges will ask you to submit written work and take a written assessment at interview.

"The course gave me a broad awareness of chronology, as well as a detailed knowledge of my specific areas of interest. It also provides great training for practical skills."

Joanna, Music graduate

**INTERESTED? WHY DON'T YOU EXPLORE. . .**

The Norton Anthology of Western Music by J. Peter Burkholder & Claude V. Palisca – extremely readable and a good starting point to exploring western music.

The Dynamics of Harmony by George Pratt – a short book packed full of information on tonal composition and harmony.

A Guide to Musical Analysis by Nicholas Cook – an important introduction to analytical processes and terminology.

**NOT THE COURSE FOR YOU?** Consider Music at Oxford.

# Natural Sciences (Biological)

**COURSE LENGTH:** Three years, with an optional fourth year

**PAST INTERVIEW QUESTIONS:**

- What evidence is there to suggest that humans are still evolving?
- How could you prove chloroplasts used to be free-living organisms?
- Why is carbon of such importance in living systems?

The course (also known as NatSci B) offers a wide range of science subjects for you to choose from., covering everything concerned with living things: Zoology, Plant Sciences, Molecular Biology, Physiology and Pharmacology, as well as less obvious subjects like Geology or Psychology. There is also the option to take modules in physical sciences alongside. The breadth of the course reflects the increasingly multi-disciplinary nature of modern scientific research. At least two sciences/mathematics A Levels are essential, and a third is required by some colleges. You will be required to take a science and maths based test before interview. Students should indicate on their Supplementary Application Questionnaire (SAQ) whether they wish to pursue the Biological or Physical route of Natural Sciences, although this choice isn't absolute.

"Few universities offer the breadth and depth of the Natural Sciences course. It was an added bonus that we only specialised in our third and fourth year, allowing us the first two years to figure out what area of science was our passion."

Henry, Natural Sciences (Biological) graduate

**INTERESTED? WHY DON'T YOU EXPLORE. . .**

The Greatest Show on Earth: The Evidence for Evolution by Richard Dawkins – a popular and controversial read, which should help you to form your own opinions on evolution.

How Animals Work by Knut Schmidt Nielson – a good analysis which will help you to grasp comparative physiology.

The Diversity of Life by Edward O. Wilson – a great overview of biodiversity.

**NOT THE COURSE FOR YOU?** Consider Biomedical or Biological Sciences, Biochemistry or EP (Experimental Psychology) at Oxford.

# Natural Sciences (Physical)

**COURSE LENGTH:** Three years, with an optional fourth year

**PAST INTERVIEW QUESTIONS:**

- Explain Schrödinger's cat.
- How does sound come from a flute?
- What is the photoelectric effect?

Natural Sciences (Physical) includes modules in Physics, Chemistry, Earth Sciences and Materials Science and also allows you to combine with some biological science options. There is a more practical focus in the second and third year, with significantly more lab work. If the option of combining several different scientific disciplines appeals to you, then this is a great course choice, as it is much more varied and multidisciplinary than a combined honours degree at another university. This is why at least two sciences/mathematics A Levels are essential, and a third is required by some colleges. You will be required to take a science and mathematics based test before interview. Students should indicate on their Supplementary Application Questionnaire (SAQ) whether they wish to pursue the Biological or Physical route of Natural Sciences, although this choice isn't absolute.

"I loved being able to discuss science across the board with friends, from chatting about semiconductors with engineers to discussing primate behaviour with anthropologists."

Matthew, Natural Sciences (Physical) graduate

**INTERESTED? WHY DON'T YOU EXPLORE. . .**

Warped Passages: Unravelling the Universe's Hidden Dimensions by Lisa Randall – an accessible read on theoretical physics.

A Brief History of Time by Stephen Hawking & Leonard Mlodinow – this gives a good overview of physical cosmology, whilst explaining some difficult mathematics.

Why Chemical Reactions Happen by James Keeler & Peter Wothers – a good overview of chemical processes, to help you think like a chemist.

**NOT THE COURSE FOR YOU?** Consider the many science courses available at Oxford, such as Physics, Chemistry, Materials Science or Engineering Science.

# Philosophy

**COURSE LENGTH:** Three years

**PAST INTERVIEW QUESTIONS:**

- Is happiness a basis for morality?
- How would you define consciousness?
- Give an example of an argument with false premises but a true conclusion.

The Philosophy course considers 'ultimate' problems such as the nature of reality and purpose of our existence. In your first year, you'll acquire the reasoning skills to enable you to tackle general philosophical problems, in addition to taking a compulsory logic paper. The main emphasis of the current undergraduate course continues in the analytic tradition of previous Cambridge philosophers, Bertrand Russell and Ludwig Wittgenstein. No particular subjects are required at A Level, however, a combination of arts and science subjects is considered useful. You will be required to take a logic and writing-based assessment at interview and some will require you to submit written work.

"The Cambridge Philosophy Tripos was an excellent choice for me, largely because it's so intense that you manage to learn an extraordinary amount of philosophy over the course of three years."

Jamie, Philosophy graduate

**INTERESTED? WHY DON'T YOU EXPLORE. . .**

Ethics and the Limits of Philosophy by Bernard Williams – a must read for those interested in broadening their understanding of moral philosophy.

Meditations by Descartes – Descartes is hugely influential, and easy to read.

Practical Ethics by Peter Singer – an excellent and accessible introduction to the field of applied ethics.

**NOT THE COURSE FOR YOU?** Consider the many joint school Philosophy degrees on offer, or PPE (Philosophy, Politics and Economics) at Oxford. You might also like to consider Theology at either university.

# Psychological and Behavioural Sciences (PBS)

**COURSE LENGTH:** Three years

**PAST INTERVIEW QUESTIONS:**

- Do you know why we have two eyes and two ears?
- What do you believe is the best parenting strategy?
- Design an experiment to test the effect of cortisol on healing time.

Introduced in 2012, PBS offers a broad degree covering all aspects of psychology, from social relations to neurological processes. There are two compulsory papers in your first year, which will give you a solid grounding in psychology and psychological research methods. From here you will be able to choose which direction you want to go in, and how much lab and project work you would like to do. Mathematics, science and humanities subjects are considered useful and some colleges require Biology or Mathematics at A Level or equivalent, or two mathematics/sciences subjects. You will be required to take a thinking skills, writing and comprehension based assessment before interview and most colleges will ask you to submit written work.

**INTERESTED? WHY DON'T YOU EXPLORE. . .**

Psychology: The Science of Mind and Behaviour by Richard Gross – a key reference book which covers all the main areas of psychology across 50 chapters.

Developmental Social Psychology by Kevin Durkin – provides a good introduction to the subject and the themes and topics that will come up in lectures.

The Language Instinct by Steven Pinker – lucidly explains everything you need to know about language learning.

**NOT THE COURSE FOR YOU?** Consider EP (Experimental Psychology) or PPL (Psychology, Philosophy & Linguistics) at Oxford.

# Theology, Religion, and Philosophy of Religion

**COURSE LENGTH:** Three years

**PAST INTERVIEW QUESTIONS:**

- How would you define faith?
- Would having a personal faith help or hinder the study of theology?
- What did Kant say about proving God's existence?

As well as covering a broad range of religions, you will have the opportunity to explore contemporary and historic thought, and the culture and practice of religion, drawing on philosophy, ethics, history, literature, sociology and classics. The course offers you the chance to branch out at an early stage. One of the four scriptural languages (Greek, Hebrew, Sanskrit or Arabic) must be studied in the first year, though no prior knowledge is required. No specific A Levels are required, but English, Religious Studies, History or languages are considered useful and some colleges require an essay subject at A Level or equivalent. You will be required to take a writing and comprehension assessment before interview and most colleges will ask you to submit written work.

"Theology at Cambridge is taught as an inter-disciplinary and dynamic subject within the modern world."

Misbah, Theology graduate

**INTERESTED? WHY DON'T YOU EXPLORE. . .**

The Puzzle of Evil and The Puzzle of God by Peter Vardy – these books offer an interesting and accessible introduction to theology and philosophy.

Christian Theology: An Introduction by Alister McGrath – an introduction to important theological concepts.

Genealogy of Morality by Friedrich Nietzsche – a key text on ethics.

**NOT THE COURSE FOR YOU?** Consider Philosophy, History, English or Classics at Cambridge. Theology is also available at Oxford.

# Veterinary Medicine

**COURSE LENGTH:** Six years

**PAST INTERVIEW QUESTIONS:**
- How are diseases able to spread between species?
- Why do 80% of racehorses have stomach ulcers?
- Explain the oxygen dissociation curve.

During the three-year pre-clinical course, you will undertake a thorough scientific programme of study, with the option to pursue an interest in a specialised topic in your third year, from pathology to philosophy. This opportunity is unique to the Cambridge vet school. The final three years focus more on the practical application of knowledge and the sixth year has no lectures to maximise the time students have for hands-on learning. You will need to have a solid scientific understanding, which is why Chemistry to at least AS Level and a further two of the following subjects are required: Biology/Human Biology, Physics, and Mathematics. You are required to sit the BMAT and how well you do in this is an important factor in the selection process.

"I liked that we were thoroughly schooled in the fundamentals before we were let loose on the clinical course."

Freya, Veterinary Medicine graduate

**INTERESTED? WHY DON'T YOU EXPLORE. . .**

The Textbook of Veterinary Anatomy by Dyce, Sack and Wensing – this is known as 'the Vets' Bible' and it's a crucial read.

Getting into Veterinary School by John Handley – useful guide which includes application tips and interview advice.

Veterinary Ethics: An Introduction by Giles Legood – this book will help you to frame opinions on ethical issues.

**NOT THE COURSE FOR YOU?** Consider Natural Sciences (Biological) at Cambridge, Biomedical Sciences at Oxford, or Medicine at either Oxford or Cambridge.

# Archaeology and Anthropology

**COURSE LENGTH:** Three years

**PAST INTERVIEW QUESTIONS:**

- Some people say that in 100 or 200 years we will have one global culture. What do you think about this?
- What is the point of archaeology?
- How would you define 'ritual'?

Commonly referred to as Arch and Anth, the course will give you a broad overview of past and contemporary human societies. This is through social, biological and material perspectives, covering almost every aspect of human behaviour. No specific A Level subjects are required, although a combination of arts and sciences is useful. You will be asked to submit two pieces of written work, plus a 500-word essay in response to a question given on the Oxford website (e.g. 'what can we learn about people past and present from their material culture?'), so that the Admissions Tutors can assess your understanding of, and passion for, the subject.

"The course has the perfect combination of science (biological anthropology) and social science (social and cultural anthropology) for me."

Tom, Archaeology and Anthropology graduate

**INTERESTED? WHY DON'T YOU EXPLORE. . .**

On the Origin of Species by Charles Darwin – this text is central to evolutionary biology.

The Selfish Gene by Richard Dawkins – an excellent complementary text for The Origin of Species, to get you up to speed with a more modern look at evolution.

Orientalism by Edward Said – this classic text about definition through opposition sets up some of the major themes of anthropology.

**NOT THE COURSE FOR YOU?** Consider Classical Archaeology and Ancient History (CAAH) or Human Sciences at Oxford and Archaeology or Human, Social, and Political Sciences (HSPS) at Cambridge.

# Biochemistry (Molecular and Cellular)

**COURSE LENGTH:** Four years

**PAST INTERVIEW QUESTIONS:**
- When does science become technology?
- What is the significance of the human genome project?
- Why are there only twenty amino acids?

Biochemistry is the study of living things at a molecular level. The course involves a lot of essay writing in a way that other science degrees such as Physics or Chemistry do not, in addition to many practical requirements. An important aspect of the Oxford Biochemistry course is its fourth-year project (lasting 18 weeks full time), which allows you to explore both laboratory-based research and specific recent advances in biochemistry in detail. A Level Chemistry, with another science or Mathematics, is essential.

**"I enjoyed the fact that Biochemistry is such a fast-moving subject with so many advances being made all the time."**

Padma, Biochemistry graduate

**INTERESTED? WHY DON'T YOU EXPLORE. . .**

Genome by Matt Ridley – this will give you short introductions to various areas of genetics and evolution.

Foundations of Organic Chemistry by Michael Hornby and Josephine Peach – a short book, which covers some important concepts really well.

Power, Sex, Suicide: Mitochondria and the Meaning of Life by Nick Lane – a very interesting read on the subject of cell biology.

**NOT THE COURSE FOR YOU?** Consider Biological Sciences, Biomedical Sciences, Chemistry or Human Sciences at Oxford. You might also want to take a look at the Natural Sciences (Biological) course at Cambridge.

# Biological Sciences

**COURSE LENGTH:** Three years

**PAST INTERVIEW QUESTIONS:**
- What are the arguments for preserving biodiversity?
- How does the immune system recognise invading pathogens as foreign cells?
- Discuss ways in which plants are adapted to dry conditions.

Biological Sciences is a rapidly developing subject area. It is an immensely diverse subject, and you will be studying cutting edge topics from evolutionary biology to molecular genetics. There is a lot of essay writing required, but the main emphasis is on practical laboratory work, preparing you for your third-year research project. There is the option to carry out your project in the field, either in the UK or in the tropics. A Level Biology is essential and another science or Mathematics is considered helpful.

"The course is very well designed – it allows you to get a solid foundation in the first year, start specialising in the second year and then really immerse yourself in your chosen specialisations in the third year."

Sally, Biological Sciences graduate

**INTERESTED? WHY DON'T YOU EXPLORE. . .**

The Single Helix by Steve Jones – a witty and engaging writer, this is a collection of his essays on popular science.

The Secret Life of Trees by Colin Tudge – everything you need to know about trees, covering botany, reproductive techniques and their historical importance.

The Beak of the Finch by Jonathan Weiner – an account of a 20-year study of Darwin's finches, which shows how we can watch evolution happen in real-time.

**NOT THE COURSE FOR YOU?** Consider Biochemistry or Biomedical Sciences at Oxford. Alternatively, take a look at the Natural Sciences (Biological) course on offer at Cambridge.

# Biomedical Sciences

**COURSE LENGTH:** Three years

**PAST INTERVIEW QUESTIONS:**
- Why is the heart on the left-hand side of the body?
- Why is Physics less relevant to Biomedical Sciences than Chemistry?
- How does immunisation work?

The smallest of the three Biology courses on offer at Oxford in terms of intake, Biomedical Sciences is for students fascinated by the human body and how it works. Understanding how cells, organs and systems function within the human body promotes your understanding of human diseases, and students study a range of areas from molecular biology to neurophysiology. The course enables you to study human biology from a medical perspective, without having to commit to a medical career. Two of the following A Levels are essential to apply: Biology, Chemistry, Physics or Mathematics, and all colleges will require you to sit the BMAT.

"I considered Experimental Psychology before deciding on Biomedical Sciences – I chose the latter because it enables the in-depth study of more than one organ."

Rena, Biomedical Sciences graduate

**INTERESTED? WHY DON'T YOU EXPLORE. . .**

Biomedicine and the Human Condition by Michael G. Sargent – traces developments in biomedicine, and how they have improved human life.

Incognito by David Eagleman – an engaging popular science book, which explores the unconscious workings of the mind.

The Man Who Mistook His Wife for a Hat by Oliver Sacks – details the strangest neurological conditions Sacks has treated as a clinical neurologist.

**NOT THE COURSE FOR YOU?** Consider Medicine at either university. Or take a look at Biochemistry, Biological Sciences or Experimental Psychology (EP) at Oxford. You may also be interested in Natural Sciences (Biological) at Cambridge.

# Chemistry

**COURSE LENGTH:** Four years

**PAST INTERVIEW QUESTIONS:**
- What happens to the mobility of Group 1 elements going down the periodic table?
- What makes some chemicals explosive?
- How does a glow stick work?

The focus of the first year is on three core areas of chemistry: organic, inorganic and physical. If you have a scientific approach, and Chemistry is your favourite subject, this course is ideal, with far less emphasis on essay writing than the Biochemistry course. What makes this course unique is the inclusion of a compulsory fourth year, entirely dedicated to original research, which will enable you to develop your critical awareness of developments in the field and your ability to carry out independent research. A Levels in both Chemistry and Mathematics are essential. Another science or Further Mathematics is considered helpful. You will be required to take the Thinking Skills Assessment before interview.

> **"The course enabled me to develop my analytical skills and to continue with the mathematical concepts of science."**
>
> Clemmie, Chemistry graduate

**INTERESTED? WHY DON'T YOU EXPLORE. . .**

Chemistry Review – this quarterly review, edited by academics at the University of York, is a great resource covering A Level topics and beyond.

Foundations of Organic Chemistry by Michael Hornby and Josephine Peach – a short book, which covers important concepts clearly.

The Periodic Table: A Very Short Introduction by Eric R. Scerri – an engaging history of the evolution of the periodic table.

**NOT THE COURSE FOR YOU?** Consider Biochemistry, Biomedical Sciences, Earth Sciences (Geology) or Materials Science. You might also like to consider the Natural Sciences courses on offer at Cambridge.

# Classical Archaeology and Ancient History (CAAH)

**COURSE LENGTH:** Three years

**PAST INTERVIEW QUESTIONS:**

- Why do you think ancient history is important?
- When would you start a book about the history of England?
- What are the advantages and disadvantages of removing artefacts?

The course looks at the societies and cultures of the ancient world, centered on Greece and Rome, through their written texts, visual art and material remains. Although it is primarily a historical and non-linguistic degree, there is the chance to study ancient languages as part of the course. Designed to give an integrated, interdisciplinary approach to the topics studied, this combination is unique to Oxford. No specific A Levels are required, but a classical language, Classical Civilisation or Ancient History can be helpful. You will be asked to submit two pieces of written work.

"My favourite module was the museum or site report, which gives you complete freedom to choose the topic you research."

Harry, CAAH (Classical Archaeology and Ancient History) graduate

**INTERESTED? WHY DON'T YOU EXPLORE. . .**

Love, Sex and Tragedy; How the Ancient World Shapes Our Lives by Simon Goldhill – very readable, with good ideas on why the classical era is relevant today.

The Roman World by Martin Goodman – an illuminating view of the Roman world and its people.

The Archaeology of Ancient Greece by James Whitley – a thoroughly researched overview of Ancient Greece.

**NOT THE COURSE FOR YOU?** Consider Archaeology and Anthropology, Classics and its joint honours or History and its joint honours at Oxford, or Archaeology, Classics or History at Cambridge.

# Classics

**COURSE LENGTH:** Four years

**PAST INTERVIEW QUESTIONS:**

- What were Plato's and Aristotle's views of women?
- Did the Romans or the Greeks leave a more notable impression on the culture of today?
- What are the gods' main roles in the Iliad?

Classics is a varied and interdisciplinary subject, enabling you the opportunity to study the literature, philosophy, linguistics, history and archaeology of ancient Greek and Roman civilisations. You will also develop a good reading knowledge of Latin and Greek. In order to fit in such a broad range of study, the Oxford Classics course lasts four years, and is split into two. If you have studied Ancient Greek or Latin, you are admitted into Course I. However, if you will be studying these languages from scratch, you should apply for Course II. You will be required to sit the Classics Admissions Test and you will be asked to submit two pieces of written work.

"I loved the challenge of deciphering ancient texts, in particular Greek comedy."

Jack, Classics graduate

**INTERESTED? WHY DON'T YOU EXPLORE. . .**

The Iliad – Homer's works are the bedrock of all classical literature.

Classics: A Very Short Introduction by Mary Beard and John Henderson – this is an excellent book for understanding the breadth of Classics.

The Latin Love Poets from Catullus to Horace by R.O.A.M. Lyne – surveys the poetry of the major Latin practitioners.

**NOT THE COURSE FOR YOU?** Consider Archaeology and Anthropology or Classics, History or Philosophy and their joint honours at Oxford. Classics is also offered at Cambridge.

# Classics and English

**COURSE LENGTH:** Three years (four if you don't have Latin or Greek A Level)

**PAST INTERVIEW QUESTIONS:**

- What role did the chorus have in Greek plays and how well do they translate into a modern context?
- Is it fair that Ted Hughes won a literary prize for a translation of an Ovid poem?
- What is tragedy?

Classics and English is as much a degree in comparative literature as it is a joint honours degree and the course is unique in this approach. English may be taken with Latin or Greek or both. If you already have Latin or Greek A Level, this is a three-year course (Course I). If you do not have either language, you can take Course II, which involves a preliminary year learning either Latin or Greek, with some study of classical literature. An English A Level is essential for applicants for this course. You will sit two tests, both the ELAT and the CAT, and you will be asked to submit two pieces of written work.

> "I loved the variety of being able to switch between different disciplines, including translation, commentary, research and essay writing."
>
> Mike, Classics and English graduate

**INTERESTED? WHY DON'T YOU EXPLORE. . .**

I, Claudius by Robert Graves – a modern novel written in the form of Claudius' biography.

The Classical World: An Epic History from Homer to Hadrian by Robin Lane Fox – an excellent overview of the classical era.

The Bible – so much of English literature draws on ideas and language from the Bible. Read sections to understand the themes which might be applicable to literature e.g. Revelations, Job, the Gospel, Genesis, and Exodus.

**NOT THE COURSE FOR YOU?** Consider Classics or English at Oxford or Cambridge. Alternatively, you might be interested in Anglo-Saxon, Norse, and Celtic (ASNaC) at Cambridge.

# Classics and Modern Languages

**COURSE LENGTH:** Four years (five if you do not have Latin or Greek A Level. The third year is spent abroad in both cases)

**PAST INTERVIEW QUESTIONS:**

- How does the literature you have read affect your opinion of that society?
- What is the difference between historical books and books written in the past?
- Can you think of examples in poetry or in literature where tone or meaning has been lost in translation?

The Classics and Modern Languages course provides the opportunity to study one language (Czech, French, German, Modern Greek, Italian, Portuguese, Russian or Spanish), along with Latin and/or Ancient Greek. The main focus of both parts of the course is on literature and language, and as you progress you will get the opportunity to study linguistics and ancient history as well. You may need an A Level in your chosen language, depending on which language you choose. You will have to sit both the CAT and the MLAT and will be asked to submit written work.

"The joy of the course is the opportunity it affords to study a diverse range of subjects in one degree."

Amy, Classics and Modern Languages graduate

**INTERESTED? WHY DON'T YOU EXPLORE. . .**

Classics: A Very Short Introduction by Mary Beard and John Henderson – this is an excellent book for understanding the breadth of Classics.

Greek Tragedy by Albin Lesky – a masterful overview of tragic theatre in Greece.

Through the Language Glass by Guy Deutscher – an extremely readable study of how language influences the way we view the world.

**NOT THE COURSE FOR YOU?** Consider Classics and Modern Languages on their own, or Classics and Oriental Studies at Oxford. You may also be interested in Modern and Medieval Languages (MML) or Classics at Cambridge.

# Classics and Oriental Studies

**COURSE LENGTH:** Four years (three if you opt out of spending the third year abroad and Oriental Studies is your main subject)

**PAST INTERVIEW QUESTIONS:**

- What links can be drawn between ancient Egyptian and other ancient languages?
- What underlying cultural differences separate Japan from the West?
- If Bach is conducted by an Arab person, is it Western or Eastern music?

This course allows you to combine the study of an Oriental language – Akkadian, Arabic, Armaic and Syriac, Armenian, Coptic, Egyptian, Hebrew, Old Iranian, Pali, Persian, Sanskrit or Turkish – and culture with Latin or Greek and the study of the ancient world. There are two options: Classics with Oriental Studies and Oriental Studies with Classics. In each case the first subject becomes the main focus, comprising approximately two thirds of the degree and the second subject forms the remaining third. Latin and/or Greek at A Level are also essential for candidates hoping to study Classics Course I. You will be required to sit the CAT and some candidates must also sit the OLAT, depending on which language you decide to focus on. You will also be required to submit two pieces of written work.

**"Studying Classics with Oriental Studies allowed me to focus on the aspects of each course I enjoyed."**

Olivia, Classics and Oriental Studies graduate

**INTERESTED? WHY DON'T YOU EXPLORE. . .**

Orientalism by Edward Said – this classic text explores the concept of definition through opposition.

The Location of Culture by Honi Bhabha – a difficult but interesting study in culture and national identity.

The Ancient Orient by Wolfram von Soden – a comprehensive presentation of ancient Near Eastern civilisation.

**NOT THE COURSE FOR YOU?** Consider both Classics and Oriental Studies on their own, or Classics and its other joint honours. You might also like to consider Asian and Middle Eastern Studies (AMES) or Classics at Cambridge.

# Computer Science

**COURSE LENGTH:** Three years, with an optional fourth year

**PAST INTERVIEW QUESTIONS:**
- Tell me about binary searches and their efficiency.
- What are the possible ways of making a secure transfer?
- What is the fundamental difference between a spreadsheet and a database?

Computers are among the most complex products created by humans. Computer Science is about understanding their programs, networks and systems. The course, largely theoretical in its approach, will develop your understanding of the underlying principles of programming. Oxford offers two courses in Computer Science: a 3-year BA degree and a 4-year Masters degree, though there is no distinction between them on applying. A Level Mathematics is required, and Further Mathematics or a science is recommended. You will also be required to sit the MAT.

**"The Computer Science course at Oxford is highly regarded in the industry that I have gone on to work in."**

Jenny, Computer Science graduate

**INTERESTED? WHY DON'T YOU EXPLORE. . .**

An Introduction to Algorithms by Thomas H. Cormen et al. – this is quite tricky, but getting your head around the content is likely to impress.

Programming in Haskell by Graham Hutton – an introduction for one of the leading languages in teaching functional programming.

Computer Science: A Modern Introduction by Les Goldschlager and Andrew Lister – an introductory overview.

**NOT THE COURSE FOR YOU?** Consider the Computer Science and Philosophy course at Oxford. Alternatively, try Computer Science at Cambridge, or Mathematics or Engineering at either university.

# Computer Science and Philosophy

**COURSE LENGTH:** Three years with an optional fourth year

**PAST INTERVIEW QUESTIONS:**

- What is the relevance of philosophy in science as opposed to everyday life?
- Write an algorithm to find all factors of a number.
- How would you define infinity?

Computer Science and Philosophy overlap in many areas, including Artificial Intelligence, logic, robotics and virtual reality, as well as sharing skills such as rational inference and critical thinking. This course offers you the opportunity to develop your analytical and technical knowledge alongside rhetorical and literary skills. The course begins with core modules from both disciplines and a bridging course studying Turing's pioneering work on computability and artificial intelligence. As you progress, the course provides a wide variety of options with an emphasis on courses near the interface between the two subjects, and you may take more papers in one discipline. Mathematics at A Level is required and Further Mathematics is highly recommended. You will be required to take the MAT.

**INTERESTED? WHY DON'T YOU EXPLORE. . .**

The Information: A History, a Theory, a Flood by James Gleick – a fascinating account of how the information age has revolutionized modern human life

The Emperor's New Mind by Roger Penrose – this book uses the physics of computing to explore the concept of artificial intelligence.

Labyrinths of Reason: Paradox, Puzzles and the Fruit of Knowledge by William Poundstone – an intriguing look into the world of paradox

**NOT THE COURSE FOR YOU?** Consider the straight Computer Science or Philosophy courses, or consider combining Philosophy with Mathematics or Physics.

# Earth Sciences (Geology)

**COURSE LENGTH:** Three years, with an optional fourth year

**PAST INTERVIEW QUESTIONS:**

- How would you go about calculating the total amount of energy reaching the Earth's surface?
- How does the age of ice change as you walk up a glacier?
- List a number of different possible methods for dating a rock specimen.

This course offers a multidisciplinary approach to the study of the Earth, embracing an enormous range of topics, including the evolution of life, the nature of planetary interiors, Earth-surface processes, and the origin and behaviour of oceans and atmosphere. The emphasis of the course is on understanding the underlying physical principles of geological processes. Oxford offers two courses: a BA in Geology and an MEarthSc in Earth Sciences, which are exactly the same for the first three years. You can then choose to continue with the four-year Earth Sciences course or leave with a BA in Geology. A Level Mathematics as well as either Physics or Chemistry are essential and Biology, Geology or Further Mathematics can be useful.

"I enjoyed applying the theory to the real environment, and seeing in front of me, either out in the field or in the lab, things that I had learnt in lectures."

Robert, Earth Sciences (Geology) graduate

**INTERESTED? WHY DON'T YOU EXPLORE. . .**

Earth: Evolution of a Habitable World by Jonathan I. Lunine – an outstanding history of the evolution of Earth.

Igneous Petrology by Anthony Hall – comprehensive treatment of all aspects of igneous rocks.

Global Geomorphology by Michael Summerfield – an in-depth study into surface processes and landforms.

**NOT THE COURSE FOR YOU?** Consider Geography, Human Sciences, Materials Science or Physics at Oxford or Natural Sciences (Physical) at Cambridge.

# Economics and Management (E&M)

**COURSE LENGTH:** Three years

**PAST INTERVIEW QUESTIONS:**

- Are large or small companies more successful?
- What are the arguments for and against a minimum wage?
- Should a Walmart store be opened in the middle of Oxford?

The highly competitive E&M course examines issues central to the world we live in – namely, how the economy functions, and, in turn, how organisations function within it. Economics provides the broader understanding of the economic environment within which all organisations operate; management in turn analyses the goals and frameworks of those organisations. The key advantage of studying E&M is that it combines academic rigour with vocational worth. A Mathematics A Level is essential and you will be required to sit the TSA Oxford.

"I enjoyed the fact that as one of Oxford's most modern degrees, it was relevant for the world in which we live."

Jack, Economics and Management graduate

**INTERESTED? WHY DON'T YOU EXPLORE. . .**

Scale and Scope: The Dynamics of Industrial Capitalism by Alfred Chandler – a thorough analysis of the origins of large corporations.

Rise of the Corporate Economy by Leslie Hannah – looks at crucial periods in the formulation of the modern corporate system.

The Ascent of Money by Niall Ferguson – a brilliant history of banking, giving great insights into the birth of globalisation.

**NOT THE COURSE FOR YOU?** Consider Economics at Cambridge, with an option to take Management Studies in your final year. You might also like to consider History and Economics or Philosophy, Politics and Economics (PPE) at Oxford.

# Engineering Science

**COURSE LENGTH:** Four years

**PAST INTERVIEW QUESTIONS:**
- How does a pendulum work, bearing in mind that the amplitude of the oscillations increases over time rather than decreases?
- Draw an acceleration against velocity graph to describe the motion when you are in a lift.
- Why does a bullet spiral?

Engineering Science encompasses a vast range of subjects, from microelectronics to offshore oil platforms, which will give you a solid theoretical foundation. In the third and fourth years, you can specialise in one of six branches of engineering: biomedical, chemical, civil, electrical, information and mechanical. In the fourth year you will undertake a major research project in the field of your choice and at the end of this broad-based four-year course, you will graduate with a Master of Engineering degree (MEng). A Level Mathematics (with Mechanics modules being particularly useful) and Physics are essential, and Further Mathematics can be very helpful. You will be required to sit the PAT.

> "I loved the way lectures complemented the laboratory work. There were plenty of opportunities to apply what you had learned to practical scenarios."
>
> Thakoon, Engineering Science graduate

**INTERESTED? WHY DON'T YOU EXPLORE. . .**

Invention by Design: How Engineers Get from Thought to Thing by Henry Petroski – looks at the engineering design processes behind objects, machines and buildings.

Cats' Paws and Catapults by Steven Vogel – an introduction to biomechanics.

The New Science of Strong Materials: Or Why You Don't Fall Through the Floor by J. E. Gordon – explores the general properties of all materials.

**NOT THE COURSE FOR YOU?** Consider Engineering at Cambridge or Materials Science or Physics at Oxford.

# English Language and Literature

**COURSE LENGTH:** Three years

**PAST INTERVIEW QUESTIONS:**

- How would you judge a work to be canonical?
- Do you think there is any point to reading criticism?
- Is literature useful when studying a specific time in history?

You will study the full breadth of English literature from its Anglo-Saxon origins to the present day, working through seven different historical periods. Alongside this you'll also be introduced to the conceptual and technical approaches you need to study literature. You will have a lot of freedom to choose authors within each paper as there are no set texts, as well as exploring your interests further through three coursework papers. An English A Level is required to study this course. Good writing skills are key, so you'll be required to sit the ELAT and submit written work before coming up to interview.

"It was a good course for me because although it covered the major authors in each time period, esoteric interests were also permitted which made the course more interesting."

George, English Language and Literature graduate

**INTERESTED? WHY DON'T YOU EXPLORE. . .**

The Art of Fiction by David Lodge – a series of critical readings of classic texts, which are easy to dip into and cover complex ideas.

The Short Oxford History of English Literature – this will give you a chronological overview of English literature since the Middle Ages and is a great guide to choosing preparatory reading from each period.

The Genius of Shakespeare by Jonathan Bate – this book will get you thinking more carefully about literary works in context, be it authorial, social or historical.

**NOT THE COURSE FOR YOU?** Consider English and Modern Languages or History and English. You may also like History, Modern Languages, Theology, Classics, History of Art or you could consider English at Cambridge.

# English and Modern Languages

**COURSE LENGTH:** Four years (with the third or fourth year spent abroad)

**PAST INTERVIEW QUESTIONS:**

- What are the differences between English literature and the literature of the language which you want to study?
- Do you think learning a language is obsolete due to English being spoken internationally?
- Should a work in translation stay true to the original text or be altered to represent a different culture?

Alongside tutorial work on a choice of English literary periods from the Anglo-Saxon era to the present day, and selected texts in your foreign language (Czech, French, German, Modern Greek, Italian, Portuguese, Russian or Spanish), you'll work on your practical language skills. The course is very flexible and allows you to pick and choose modules from both degree courses, as well as linking the two through comparative literature papers. English A Level is required and usually an A Level in the language you wish to study. You will need to sit both the MLAT and the ELAT. You'll also be asked to submit one piece of written work for each subject.

"I loved the year abroad, and the two disciplines that gave me two sets of friends, two faculties, two different approaches to books and two cultures to steep myself in."

Maya, English and French graduate

**INTERESTED? WHY DON'T YOU EXPLORE. . .**

Through the Language Glass by Guy Deutscher – an extremely readable study of how language influences the way we view the world.

Foreign newspapers, such as Le Monde, El Pais, Die Welt – reading the headline articles of the major newspapers of that language will be helpful and may provide content for discussion at interview.

**NOT THE COURSE FOR YOU?** Consider studying either subject on its own, or with History, Classics, Linguistics or Philosophy. You might also like the English or Modern and Medieval Languages (MML) courses at Cambridge.

# European and Middle Eastern Languages

**COURSE LENGTH:** Four years

**PAST INTERVIEW QUESTIONS:**

• How relevant is a seventh-century religious text to the modern world?

• How similar are Christianity, Judaism and Islam?

• What were the long-term causes of the Arab Spring?

The European and Middle Eastern Languages course gives you the opportunity to study a language taught by the Modern Language faculty with Arabic, Hebrew, Persian or Turkish, providing the opportunity for you to take advantage of the cultural and historical connections between the countries and languages. Students study the two languages and cultural aspects such as history and literature of both countries. During their year abroad, students must attend an approved course of language instruction in the Middle Eastern language and are encouraged to spend their vacations in a relevant country to their chosen European language. You would usually be expected to have the European language to A Level but no previous knowledge of the Middle Eastern language is required. You will be required to take both the MLAT and the OLAT.

**INTERESTED? WHY DON'T YOU EXPLORE. . .**

Night and Horses and the Desert. An Anthology of Classical Arabic Literature [in translation] by Robert Irwin – an insightful introduction to Arabic literature spanning the fifth to the sixteenth century, from Afghanistan to Spain.

Turkey and the West: Changing Political and Cultural Identities by Heper, Metin et al – a look at Turkey's evolving sense of identity and its relationship to Europe and the Islamic Middle East.

Language in Time of Revolution by Benjamin Harshav – a provocative study of the worldwide transformation of Jews in the modern age, alongside the revival of the ancient Hebrew language.

**NOT THE COURSE FOR YOU?** Consider Modern Languages or Oriental Studies, or think about taking a Middle Eastern language alongside Classics or Theology.

# Experimental Psychology (EP)

**COURSE LENGTH:** Three years

**PAST INTERVIEW QUESTIONS:**

- How do you measure emotions?
- What use is psychological study for society?
- How can genetics be used in determining an individual's intelligence?

The course is scientific and you will learn to test ideas through experiments and observation rather than introspection. You will spend the first two years studying a broad range of core fields, such as neurophysiology or statistics, as well as optional topics, such as social psychology or language and cognition. In your third year, you get the opportunity to complete your own research project and follow your special interests through a choice of more optional courses. Due to the scientific focus of the course you'll normally need one or more science or Mathematics A Levels, and you'll be required to sit the TSA Oxford.

"The structure meant that you had a thorough understanding of everything that you could possibly need within the first two years, and then you are let loose to do whatever you want with your final year."

Caroline, Experimental Psychology graduate

**INTERESTED? WHY DON'T YOU EXPLORE. . .**

Statistics Without Tears by Derek Rowntree – this book explains statistics using words instead of numbers and is excellent for building your confidence in working with them.

Mindwatching by H J and M W Eysenck – a good introduction to a number of areas in psychology, including experiments.

The Man Who Mistook His Wife for a Hat by Oliver Sacks – interesting short stories about strange neurological conditions.

**NOT THE COURSE FOR YOU?** Consider Human Sciences, Psychology, Philosophy and Linguistics (PPL), Biological Sciences or Medicine at Oxford. You might also be interested in Psychological and Behavioural Sciences (PBS) at Cambridge.

# Fine Art

**COURSE LENGTH:** Three years

**PAST INTERVIEW QUESTIONS:**

- Discuss restoration and conservation. Are they good or bad?
- If you had to save one piece of art in the world, what would it be and why?
- What is the definition of prehistory?

The course combines practical studio work and art history with theory and criticism, and is designed to prepare students to become artists. You will participate in regular workshops to learn techniques and approaches and you'll be assessed through a mixture of studio projects, submitted essays and written exams. In your third year you will also work towards a final exhibition with a portfolio of work made over the final two years of your studies, alongside writing a linked extended essay. You're strongly encouraged to take Art A Level and an Art Foundation Course, and you'll be asked to submit a portfolio to demonstrate your ability and interests, and take a practical test at interview.

"The course is a perfect combination of theory and practice, which is quite unusual for a BA course in Fine Art in the UK. The staff are very interesting and inspiring and the opportunity to be in an art school and at the same time part of a large university is very unique."

Anja, Fine Art graduate

**INTERESTED? WHY DON'T YOU EXPLORE. . .**

Art in Theory 1900-2000: An Anthology of Changing Ideas ed. by Charles Harrison and Paul Wood – a good way to get to grips with both new research and different critical frameworks over the 20th Century.

Keep up to date with contemporary trends by going to current art exhibitions.

Broaden your interests by having a look at Art House cinema, including films by directors such as Chris Marker and Werner Herzog.

**NOT THE COURSE FOR YOU?** Consider History of Art at either Oxford or Cambridge, or consider the Cambridge Architecture course.

# Geography

**COURSE LENGTH:** Three years

**PAST INTERVIEW QUESTIONS:**

- What is the relevance of physical geography to human geography?
- Why should we conserve?
- If you were the policy makers of your home town, what would you do to improve the area?

The course focuses on the relevance and diversity of geography and you will approach it from a range of directions – as a social science, a natural science and an arts discipline. You'll also have opportunities to study how geography relates to other disciplines, such as biology or anthropology. The first year papers cover the full range of geographical topics, preparing you to follow up your interests in optional papers and research over the course of the second and third years. Fieldwork is a key element of the course and trips are part of core study. Good knowledge, analytical skills and the ability to argue coherently are key. Geography A Level is highly recommended and applicants will have to sit the TSA Oxford before interview.

"I most enjoyed my special options in second and third year. The field trip to Tunisia was a highlight – the best part about Geography is seeing it in action, after all."

Max, Geography graduate

**INTERESTED? WHY DON'T YOU EXPLORE. . .**

The Great Divergence by Kenneth Pomeranz – this book will help you to get to grips with the making of the modern world economy.

The Geographical Tradition by David Livingstone – a great introduction to the development of geographical thought.

Earth's Climate: Past and Future by William Ruddiman – detailed projections and insight into the causes of long term climate change.

**NOT THE COURSE FOR YOU?** Consider Earth Sciences (Geology) or Human Sciences at Oxford, or have a look at Geography and Natural Sciences at Cambridge.

# History

**COURSE LENGTH:** Three years

**PAST INTERVIEW QUESTIONS:**

- Do you think History is an art?
- Do you think the concept of nationalism is useful when considering European history before the 18th Century?
- How do we know anything in the past happened at all?

From the outset of the course you will pick and choose options ranging chronologically from the end of the Roman Empire to the present day, and geographically from the British Isles to Africa. You will focus on honing your skills in using source materials and develop sensitivity to the issues that affect your interpretation of history. Independent research is an important focus for second- and third-year students, and you'll produce two extended pieces of written work. History A Level or equivalent is highly recommended. Strong analytical and written skills are essential, so you will be asked to sit the HAT and submit one piece of written work when applying.

"I loved that I didn't have to just study the normal political and economic history we had done at school; I got to delve into the lives of peasants, gender history, cultural history – a whole spectrum that I had never really known to exist."

Louise, History graduate

**INTERESTED? WHY DON'T YOU EXPLORE. . .**

The Penguin History of Britain series – an excellent way to get an overview of any given period and to help you identify what to read to find out more.

What is History Now? ed. by David Cannadine – a response to E H Carr's What is History? which will give you an overview of developments of historical thinking over the past few decades.

Developments in Modern Historiography ed. by Henry Kozicki – a good overview of 20th Century historical approaches.

**NOT THE COURSE FOR YOU?** Consider History (Ancient and Modern), or History combined with Politics, English or Economics. You could also try English, Classics or Philosophy, Politics and Economics (PPE).

# History (Ancient and Modern)

**COURSE LENGTH:** Three years

**PAST INTERVIEW QUESTIONS:**

- How does a historian gather information?
- What is the difference between prehistory and history?
- Why do you prefer older history to more modern history or vice versa?

The Ancient and Modern History course gives you the chance to study the Bronze Age to the present day, from Ancient Greece to Latin America. You can choose modules from both the History and Classics faculties, and in your second and third year it will be up to you to decide whether you want to spend more time on Ancient or Modern History. There is also the chance to carry out independent research for two pieces of extended written work. History A Level is highly recommended and a classical language, Classical Civilization and Ancient History are also useful choices. Written skills and analytical ability are important, so you'll be asked to sit the HAT and submit one piece of written work when you apply.

**"I loved being able to combine my study of the Ancient World with more recent history."**

David, History (Ancient and Modern) graduate

**INTERESTED? WHY DON'T YOU EXPLORE. . .**

A Little History of the World by E.H. Gombrich – a classic piece of historical writing, chronicling human development through the ages.

The Penguin History of Britain series – an excellent way to get an overview of any given period and to help you identify what to read to find out more.

The History of the Ancient World: From the Earliest Accounts to the Fall of Rome by Susan Wise Bauer – traces the chronological rise and demise of ancient civilisations.

**NOT THE COURSE FOR YOU?** Consider History or History with Politics, English or Economics at Oxford. Alternatively, try a Modern Language, Theology, English or Classics at Oxford or Cambridge.

# History and Economics

**COURSE LENGTH:** Three years

**PAST INTERVIEW QUESTIONS:**

• Would it be feasible to have an economy entirely based on the service sector?
• Why does labour move to towns rather than capital to the country?
• How can you define a revolution?

The range of module options will equip you to view real-world issues from the contrasting angles of both historian and economist, and you will learn to apply the methods and analysis of both disciplines to areas of study. Though students continue to study core papers from History and Economics throughout the degree, in your second and third year you will also have some freedom to decide to weight your studies more heavily towards one subject if you wish. History and Mathematics A Levels are highly recommended. You will be required to sit the HAT, which includes a question specifically for candidates applying for History and Economics, and applicants are asked to submit one piece of History and one piece of Economics written work.

**"I loved learning about British economic history. It's given me a much fuller understanding of current economic issues."**

Natalie, History and Economics graduate

**INTERESTED? WHY DON'T YOU EXPLORE. . .**

The Ascent of Money by Niall Ferguson – an engaging history of banking which explains how globalisation happened.

Marx: A Very Short Introduction by Peter Singer – this will help you get to grips with how History and Economics overlap.

Black Swan by Nassim Nicholas Taleb – a pertinent book on the failure of economic science to predict the most recent financial collapse.

**NOT THE COURSE FOR YOU?** Consider History on its own, or have a look at History combined with Politics or a Modern Language at Oxford. Alternatively, try Philosophy, Politics and Economics (PPE) at Oxford.

# History and English

**COURSE LENGTH:** Three years

**PAST INTERVIEW QUESTIONS:**
- Why did imperialism happen?
- What are the connections between language and culture?
- Is literature useful when studying a specific time in history?

History and English is designed to equip you with the skills to study literature and history as interrelated disciplines through the exploration of historical periods and authors. However, the course also gives you the freedom to pick and choose unrelated options from both courses should you prefer variety. Study of the relationship between History and English is built into each year of the course, but you will also have the scope to weight your modules towards either subject. An English A Level is required, and History is highly recommended. You will be required to sit the HAT (but not the ELAT) and you will be asked to submit three pieces of written work, one piece for History and two for English.

"The subjects complement each other perfectly. I loved being able to combine the study of literary texts with the in-depth study of their historical context."

Lewis, History and English graduate

**INTERESTED? WHY DON'T YOU EXPLORE. . .**

Witnesses of War by Nicholas Stargardt – this book uses a range of surprising sources to document the effect of WWII on European children.

The Short Oxford History of English Literature by Andrew Sanders – an excellent way to get an overview of the literature of any given period.

Literary Theory: An Introduction by Terry Eagleton – if you are new to reading criticism and literary theory this is an excellent place to start as it introduces you to many different critical frameworks and their application.

**NOT THE COURSE FOR YOU?** Consider the individual History and English courses, or try Classics, Modern Languages, Philosophy and Theology at Oxford or Cambridge.

# History and Modern Languages

**COURSE LENGTH:** Four years

**PAST INTERVIEW QUESTIONS:**

- Do you think works of literature can be used as sources of historical evidence?
- What are the connections between language and culture?
- How corrupt is Europe? Is the UK less corrupt?

This course allows you to combine the study of history with the study of a European language (Czech, French, German, Modern Greek, Italian, Portuguese, Russian or Spanish) and its literature. You are encouraged to pair papers from the two disciplines in stimulating ways to enrich your study of each. You will undertake a year abroad in third year with the aim of gaining fluency in your chosen language. History A Level or equivalent is highly recommended and you may be expected to have your chosen language to A Level. You will be required to sit both the HAT and the MLAT. You will be required to submit written work for both History and Modern languages, the latter of which may include a piece of work written in the target language.

**INTERESTED? WHY DON'T YOU EXPLORE. . .**

The Cambridge History of Italian Literature – a comprehensive look at the history of Italian literature, set alongside valuable chronological insights.

The German Language in a Changing Europe by Michael Clyne – an interesting analysis of how sociopolitical events have affected the German language and ideas of nationhood

Press, Revolution, and Social Identities in France, 1830-1835 by Jeremy Popkin – an innovative study of the role of the press during the Revolutionary crisis.

**NOT THE COURSE FOR YOU?** Consider the straight course for either discipline, or consider combining History with English, or Modern Languages with English, Classics or Philosophy at Oxford.

# History and Politics

**COURSE LENGTH:** Three years

**PAST INTERVIEW QUESTIONS:**
- Why do we need government?
- How do you organise a successful revolution?
- Differentiate between power and authority.

The History and Politics course will teach you to understand the historical context of modern-day political problems, and equip you with an understanding of political science that will enlighten your study of historical events. The course is unusual in allowing students to choose very varied modules across both subjects, so you might find yourself studying history from 300AD alongside contemporary American politics. In your third year you'll have the choice of researching and writing a thesis on either an historical or a political topic. History A Level is highly recommended. Good analytical thinking skills are important, so you will be required to sit the HAT and to submit one piece of written work.

"I enjoyed the freedom we were given to study subjects of our choice in depth, and the intellectual challenge of tutorials. I met some great tutors who were very giving with their time and expertise."

Luke, History and Politics graduate

**INTERESTED? WHY DON'T YOU EXPLORE. . .**

A History of Political Thought by Bruce Haddock – a lively history of Western political ideas.

The State We're In by Will Hutton – an intriguing analysis of how Britain has become socially, economically and politically out of date.

Iron Curtain: The Crushing of Eastern Europe 1944-56 by Anne Applebaum – a look at how Communism was imposed on previously free societies.

The Economist – keep yourself up to date on current affairs in major world powers in particular and most importantly, work out what you think.

**NOT THE COURSE FOR YOU?** Consider History and Economics, Philosophy, Politics and Economics (PPE) or Law at Oxford. You might also like to consider Human, Social, and Political Sciences (HSPS) at Cambridge.

# History of Art

**COURSE LENGTH:** Three years

**PAST INTERVIEW QUESTIONS:**

- Do you think the written word is more valuable than visual images?
- What is style?
- What do you think are the main factors in dividing different art movements?

History of Art at Oxford offers you the chance to study a broader range of global art than most UK courses. You'll get a strong grounding in more traditional 'fine art' and 'western art' history, but you'll also learn to interpret the making, function, cultural reception and history of almost anything designed by human beings. The Oxford course tends to focus less on architecture than the Cambridge course. You should have taken an essay-based subject at A Level; Fine Art, History of Art, a language or English may be useful. You will need to submit a piece of written work and to demonstrate your artistic engagement and sensitivity by writing a 750-word response to a piece of art, architecture or design.

"The extended reading and the influx of images in the course has immensely changed the way I look at and appraise art. History of Art is so interdisciplinary that it has been a joy to examine historical, social, political and anthropological aspects of contextual evidence."

Rosy, History of Art graduate

**INTERESTED? WHY DON'T YOU EXPLORE. . .**

Art in Theory, 1900-2000 by Charles Harrison – a good place to start getting to grips with conceptual approaches to art through the 20th Century.

Ways of Seeing by John Berger – this very influential book will get you thinking critically about how we see the world around us.

The Penguin Dictionary of Art and Artists by Peter and Linda Murray – this will help you get a good overview and identify areas of particular interest.

**NOT THE COURSE FOR YOU?** Consider Fine Art, History or Archaeology and Anthropology at Oxford, or History of Art at Cambridge.

# Human Sciences

**COURSE LENGTH:** Three years

**PAST INTERVIEW QUESTIONS:**

- Design an experiment to show whether monkeys' behaviour is innate or learnt.
- What is the greatest threat to humankind?
- What use can scientists make of a 19th Century skeleton?

The core of this course is the study of human life, but throughout your studies you'll approach it from biological, social and cultural perspectives. Human Sciences is designed to equip students to understand and go on to address contemporary issues facing humans, from disease to population growth to conservation. You'll study a broad range of modules over the course of your first and second years before following your interests by choosing two optional modules and writing a dissertation. There are no required A Levels, but Biology and Mathematics are useful. You will be required to sit the TSA before interview.

"I now have a broad approach to everything and can look at things from other points of view, generally with an evolutionary underpinning to why people act the way they do."

Mary, Human Sciences graduate

**INTERESTED? WHY DON'T YOU EXPLORE. . .**

Journal of Human Evolution –useful to you keep up-to-date with new theories and discoveries in biological anthropology.

Collapse: How Societies Choose to Fail or Succeed by Jared Diamond – an interesting look at why past civilizations have failed or flourished.

Genes, Peoples and Languages by L. Cavalli-Sforza – an excellent introduction to how genetics, languages and archaeology can be used to study human evolution before written records.

**NOT THE COURSE FOR YOU?** Consider Biological Sciences, Archaeology and Anthropology, or Experimental Psychology (EP) at Oxford. Alternatively, try Human, Social, and Political Sciences (HSPS) at Cambridge.

# Law (Jurisprudence)

**COURSE LENGTH:** Three years

**PAST INTERVIEW QUESTIONS:**

- If a man is stuck in a burning building and he shouts that he will give you all his money if you put a ladder by the window for him to climb to safety, is he obliged to keep his promise?
- What is the difference between intention and foresight?
- What do you think is more important, actions or motives?

The course is designed to give students a firm foundation for further legal training. You'll get this grounding by studying Jurisprudence, the branch of philosophy concerned with the law and the principles behind it. You will develop your skills of analysis, comprehension and presentation to a high level. Over three years of study you cover all the major branches of Law as well as choosing two further optional modules, and you'll normally be assessed only by exam. There are no required A Level subjects for Law, but you do need at least a C grade in GCSE Mathematics. Tutors are looking for students with good communication and reasoning skills, so to help them decide who to invite for interviews you'll be asked to sit the LNAT.

"Law offers the chance to combine practical and academic elements – I developed my argumentation skills and analytical and academic abilities in a very practical context."

Darren, Law graduate

**INTERESTED? WHY DON'T YOU EXPLORE. . .**

Learning the Law by Glanville Williams – an accessible introduction.

The Times Law Supplement – read this regularly to keep up to up-to-date on current legal issues.

Eve Was Framed by Helena Kennedy – this is an interesting and unusual critique of the legal system from new perspectives.

**NOT THE COURSE FOR YOU?** Consider Philosophy, Politics and Economics (PPE) or History and Politics at Oxford, or Law at Cambridge.

# Law with Law Studies in Europe

**COURSE LENGTH:** Four years (with the third year spent abroad)

**PAST INTERVIEW QUESTIONS:**

- A man is lost in the desert and falls asleep. A second man comes along and empties the water from his bottle. A third man comes along and fills it with poison. Who killed the first man?
- Would it be possible to have one legal system for the whole world?
- What is the difference between fault, responsibility and cause?

Three years of this course have exactly the same structure and content as the Oxford Law degree, but students spend their third year abroad studying the law of another European country, in France, Germany, Italy or Spain. Alternatively, you can choose to study European and international law in the Netherlands. The latter is a course taught in English, but for all other countries you'll need to have studied the relevant foreign language A Level (there is an exception for Italian). As with straight Law, you need at least a C grade in GCSE Mathematics. Tutors are looking for students with good communication and reasoning skills, so to help them decide who to invite for interviews you'll be asked to sit the LNAT.

**"Essentially, it is a course that demands hard thinking and problem solving, which I have always enjoyed."**

Helen, Law with Law Studies in Europe graduate

**INTERESTED? WHY DON'T YOU EXPLORE. . .**

What About Law by Catherine Barnard – this will give you an accessible introduction to legal reasoning and the legal system.

Just Law by Helena Kennedy – a good discussion of current legal issues surrounding civil liberties and especially relevant if you are interested in human rights.

The Times Law Supplement – read this regularly to keep up to date on current legal issues.

**NOT THE COURSE FOR YOU?** Consider Law on its own at either Oxford or Cambridge, or Modern Languages.

# Materials Science

**COURSE LENGTH:** Four years

**PAST INTERVIEW QUESTIONS:**
- If I place a cube in water, what shape does it make on the surface?
- Can you think of a logical reason why stress concentrates on the bottom of a crack when you stretch a material?
- If a human being was doubled in size, would he jump higher or not as high?

Materials Science is the study of modern advanced materials, from silicon microchips to bone replacement materials. This makes it an extremely varied course which encompasses elements of physics, chemistry, engineering and industrial manufacturing. Over your first two years of study, you'll focus on understanding the properties, structure and application of materials before undertaking a group design project in your third year and an independent research project in your fourth year. To show tutors that you can cope with the scope of Materials Science you'll need strong logical reasoning skills and be able to apply them to a range of physical science problems. A Level Mathematics and Physics are essential for this course and Chemistry is highly recommended (and essential to GCSE). You will be required to sit the PAT before interview.

"The most enjoyable year is almost certainly the fourth year, with flexibility to research nearly anything."

Ben, Materials Science graduate

**INTERESTED? WHY DON'T YOU EXPLORE...**

The New Science of Strong Materials: or Why You Don't Fall Through the Floor by J.E. Gordon – a great introduction to modern materials science.

An Introduction to Metallurgy by A. Cottrell – this will give you a taster of first-year study.

Structures: or Why Things Don't Fall Down by J.E. Gordon – an excellent place to start getting to grips with engineering.

**NOT THE COURSE FOR YOU?** Consideer Engineering Science or Physics at Oxford. Alternatively, have a look at Natural Sciences (Physical) or Engineering at Cambridge.

# Mathematics

**COURSE LENGTH:** Three years, with an optional fourth year

**PAST INTERVIEW QUESTIONS:**
- Which is bigger: `e to the power of pi' or `pi to the power of e'?
- Describe a complex number to a non-mathematician.
- How do you predict a Pythagorean triple?

The first year consists of core courses in pure and applied mathematics and includes an introduction to statistics. You will complete the core part of the degree in the first term of the second year, introducing complex analysis and ideas from topology and number theory. You will be taught to think mathematically, in order to approach problems like the intricacies of quantum theory and relativity, or study the mathematics of financial derivatives. A Level Mathematics is essential, and Further Mathematics or a science is strongly recommended. AEA or STEP is encouraged, although will not form part of the entry requirement. You will also be required to sit the MAT.

> "I enjoyed the third and fourth years the best as we had free reign over what options we could choose."
>
> Laura, Mathematics graduate

**INTERESTED? WHY DON'T YOU EXPLORE. . .**

A Mathematician's Apology by G. H. Hardy – an engaging memoir written in 1940, extolling the pleasures of mathematical invention.

The Mathematical Tourist by Ivars Peterson – a journey through important mathematical concepts, told in accessible language.

Fermat's Last Theorem by Simon Singh – an interesting read on one of the most notorious mathematical problems.

**NOT THE COURSE FOR YOU?** Consider Mathematics with Computer Science, Philosophy or Statistics. You might also like to consider Physics or Engineering at Oxford, or the Mathematics course at Cambridge.

# Mathematics and Computer Science

**COURSE LENGTH:** Three years, with an optional fourth year

**PAST INTERVIEW QUESTIONS:**

- Why is the number 2.7182818... used in mathematics?
- Tell me about the efficiency of binary searches.
- Explain briefly the difference between science and technology.

The course focuses on the areas where mathematics and computing are most relevant to each other, emphasising the bridges between theory and practice. Combining the study of both subjects will enable you to develop a deeper understanding of the mathematical foundations of Computer Science, whilst the Computer Science element will give you the chance to apply your mathematical knowledge practically. In the second year you will get the chance to take part in an industry-sponsored group practical. A Level Mathematics is essential, and Further Mathematics or a science is strongly recommended. You will also be required to sit the MAT.

"My tutors were wonderful. They were experts in their fields, had written the textbooks, and yet still had time to answer my questions."

Ben, Mathematics and Computer Science graduate

**INTERESTED? WHY DON'T YOU EXPLORE. . .**

In Code: A Mathematical Journey by Sarah Flannery – an account of the way in which Flannery improved public-key encryption.

An Introduction to Algorithms by Thomas H. Cormen et al. – this is quite tricky, but getting your head around the content is likely to impress.

The Emperor's New Mind by Roger Penrose – this book uses the physics of computing to explore the concept of artificial intelligence.

**NOT THE COURSE FOR YOU?** Consider Mathematics with Philosophy or Statistics. You might also like to consider Computer Science or Engineering at either Oxford or Cambridge.

# Mathematics and Philosophy

**COURSE LENGTH:** Three years, with an optional fourth year

**PAST INTERVIEW QUESTIONS:**

- Is mathematics a language?
- Each room in a house has an even number of doors leading out of it. Prove that the exterior of the house has an even number of doors.
- Can faith in quantum physics and invisible forces tie in with faith in an invisible God?

Historically, there have been strong links between mathematics and philosophy; logic, an important branch of both subjects, provides a natural bridge between the two. The study of mathematics raises very interesting philosophical questions about the nature of the subject and the reasoning which forms its basis. This course was constructed with the belief that the parallel study of these two related disciplines will significantly enhance your understanding of each. A Level Mathematics is essential, and Further Mathematics is strongly recommended. You will also be required to sit the MAT.

**"The unique and varied nature of the course means that I found it constantly fascinating."**

Seb, Mathematics and Philosophy graduate

**INTERESTED? WHY DON'T YOU EXPLORE. . .**

The Mathematical Tourist by Ivars Peterson – a journey through important mathematical concepts, told in accessible language.

Think by Simon Blackburn – an engaging overview of the study of philosophy.

Thinking about Mathematics by Simon Shapiro – an excellent introduction to the philosophy of mathematics.

**NOT THE COURSE FOR YOU?** Consider Mathematics with Statistics or Computer Science at Oxford. You might also like to consider the Philosophy course at Cambridge.

# Mathematics and Statistics

**COURSE LENGTH:** Three years, with an optional fourth year

**PAST INTERVIEW QUESTIONS:**

- Prove 'e' is irrational.
- Why do you think people buy lottery tickets when the chances of winning are extremely small?
- Differentiate x to the power of x.

Statistics is primarily the analysis of data, involving advanced mathematical ideas and modern computational techniques. If you are interested in this combination of mathematically grounded method-building, and wide-ranging applied work with data, this could be the course for you. For the first four terms, the Mathematics and Statistics course is identical to straight Mathematics, and then you will follow core second-year courses in probability and statistics. A Level Mathematics is essential, and Further Mathematics is strongly recommended. You will also be required to sit the MAT.

> "I enjoyed the time spent getting to grips with the mathematics software – I found my computational skills developed dramatically."
>
> Amy, Mathematics and Statistics graduate

**INTERESTED? WHY DON'T YOU EXPLORE. . .**

From Here to Infinity by Ian Stewart – a brilliant introduction to modern mathematics.

The Man Who Loved Only Numbers by Paul Hoffman – a biography of the mathematical genius, Paul Erdos.

Mathematics: From the Birth of Numbers by Jan Gullberg – a huge historical overview of the subject.

**NOT THE COURSE FOR YOU?** Consider Mathematics on its own at Oxford or Cambridge.

# Medicine

**COURSE LENGTH:** Three years pre-clinical, followed by a three-year clinical degree

**PAST INTERVIEW QUESTIONS:**

- Why is high blood sugar a problem in diabetes?
- How do bacteria develop antibacterial resistance?
- If you had to choose between being a nurse or a scientist, which would you be?

Medicine is an applied science, but it is equally about human interaction and dealing sympathetically with individuals. The aim of the course is to produce doctors with exceptional scientific knowledge, who have had the necessary training to pursue a career either in hospitals or in general practice. There is a clear distinction between the pre-clinical and clinical years, with the option to move to another hospital for the clinical years. A Level Chemistry and a further two of the following subjects are required: Biology, Physics, and Mathematics. Applicants will also need to sit the BMAT. How well applicants perform in this is an important factor in the selection process.

"Now when I read about a new drug development I critically appraise it before considering prescribing it. Oxford taught me to challenge all of the information that is put in front of me."

Robert, Medicine graduate

**INTERESTED? WHY DON'T YOU EXPLORE. . .**

Human Physiology by Gillian Pocock and Christopher Richards – covers most of the major physiological systems in a clinically relevant way.

Principles of Evolutionary Medicine by Peter Gluckman, Alan Beedle and Mark Hanson – a good review of advances in the field of evolutionary biology.

The Rise and Fall of Modern Medicine by James Le Fanu – a lively account of medical history.

**NOT THE COURSE FOR YOU?** Consider Biomedical Sciences at Oxford, or Medicine or Natural Sciences (Biological) at Cambridge.

# Modern Languages

**COURSE LENGTH:** Four years (with the third year spent abroad)

**PAST INTERVIEW QUESTIONS:**

- Why do some languages have genders when others don't?
- Can you think of examples in poetry or in literature where tone or meaning have been lost in translation?
- What is the difference between poetry and prose?

Languages available to study at Oxford include Czech, French, German, Modern Greek, Italian, Portuguese, Polish, Russian, and Spanish, most of which can be taken singularly or in combination with another language. The course is structured to allow you to attain spoken fluency, as well as develop the ability to write essays and produce translations both into and out of your chosen language(s). The course has a clear focus on literature, and over the four years you will study a wide range of literary texts. The skills required for translation are very different from those needed for writing literary essays, and this dual focus makes studying Modern Languages at Oxford stimulating and rewarding. An A Level in at least one of your chosen languages is usually required. You will be required to sit the MLAT and you will be asked to submit written work in both English and the post-A Level language(s) that will be studied.

"I loved the variety. The course combines the study of the language itself with literature, culture and philosophy – understanding what makes a country tick."

Suzy, Modern Languages graduate

**INTERESTED? WHY DON'T YOU EXPLORE. . .**

Through the Language Glass by Guy Deutscher – an extremely readable study of how language influences the way we view the world.

Foreign newspapers, such as Le Monde, El Pais, Die Welt – reading the headline articles of the major newspapers of that language will be helpful and may provide content for discussion at interview.

**NOT THE COURSE FOR YOU?** Consider Modern Languages, which can also be studied jointly with Linguistics, English, Classics or History. You might also like to consider Modern and Medieval Languages (MML) at Cambridge.

# Modern Languages and Linguistics

**COURSE LENGTH:** Four years (with the third year spent abroad)

**PAST INTERVIEW QUESTIONS:**

- Do you think teaching a child their first language is the same as teaching someone a second language?
- How can language be scientific?
- How does grammar govern tone and style in literature?

One half of your course will be half of the Modern Languages course, whilst the other will focus on linguistics. For this, you will be analysing the nature and structure of human language across a range of topics, from how words are formed to how language is organised in the brain. The two subjects enable you to apply your linguistics knowledge to the study of your modern language. You will need an A Level in your chosen language, unless you are applying for Italian or Portuguese. You will be required to sit the MLAT and to submit written work.

"I loved the combination of rigorous, technical analysis of language with the more conceptual study of literature and culture."

Claire, Modern Languages and Linguistics graduate

**INTERESTED? WHY DON'T YOU EXPLORE. . .**

Through the Language Glass by Guy Deutscher – an extremely readable study of how language influences the way we view the world.

The Language Instinct by Steven Pinker – lucidly explains everything you need to know about language.

Limits of Language by Mikael Parkvall – an enjoyable exploration of linguistics, filled with interesting facts.

**NOT THE COURSE FOR YOU?** Consider Modern Languages as a sole course or jointly with English, Classics, History or Philosophy. You might also like to consider Modern and Medieval Languages (MML) or Linguistics at Cambridge.

# Music

**COURSE LENGTH:** Three years

**PAST INTERVIEW QUESTIONS:**

- What periods are you interested in and why?
- Can the listener and their attitude change the music they hear?
- Is music a language?

The compulsory papers in your first year will allow you to cover the key areas in music including its history, analysis, techniques of composition and keyboard skills. You can then opt to do a performance, extended essay or composition portfolio. Although broad in its base, there is plenty of opportunity to specialise as you progress through the course, and performance options become more prominent in your finals. A Level Music is required, and keyboard ability to ABRSM Grade V or above is highly recommended. You will be asked to submit two pieces of written work along with examples of harmony and counterpoint and/or some examples of original composition. You will also be asked to perform a prepared piece on your chosen instrument/voice at interview. Candidates who do not have keyboard fluency to ABRSM Grade V or above may be required to sit a keyboard sight-reading test at interview.

**"I left Oxford with a better understanding of world politics, culture and history as a result of this course."**

Chloe, Music graduate

**INTERESTED? WHY DON'T YOU EXPLORE. . .**

The Oxford History of Western Music by Richard Taruskin – a several-volume history by a revered musicologist.

Nineteenth-Century Music by Karl Dahlhaus – an important figure in musical history writing, his book gives a fantastic overview of the 19th Century.

A Guide to Musical Analysis by Nicholas Cook – an important introduction to analytical processes and terminology.

**NOT THE COURSE FOR YOU?** Consider Music at Cambridge.

# Oriental Studies

**COURSE LENGTH:** Four years (three for Egyptology)

**PAST INTERVIEW QUESTIONS:**

- What is the difference between a language and a dialect?
- How does culture influence our lives today?
- How filial is Western society?

Oriental Studies is an umbrella term that encompasses courses in Egyptology and Ancient Near Eastern Studies, Arabic, Chinese, Hebrew and Jewish Studies, Japanese, Persian, Sanskrit and Turkish. The course is broadly divided into two parts: the study of the language of your chosen area, and the study of its history and culture. The course draws upon many disciplines, including art, archaeology, history, literature, philosophy, religion, and modern social studies, in order to introduce you to civilisations that are radically different from the Western world. A language A Level can be helpful, but there are no specific requirements. If you are applying for Arabic, Turkish, Hebrew and Persian you will need to sit the OLAT and all students will be required to submit written work.

**"The four years fully immersed me in the study of a completely different culture."**

Nick, Oriental Studies graduate

**INTERESTED? WHY DON'T YOU EXPLORE. . .**

Islam in the World by Malise Ruthven – an introduction to the Islamic world and the challenges it presents to western society.

The Search for Modern China by Jonathan Spence – covers more than four centuries of Chinese history.

The Japanese Today: Change and Continuity by Edwin O. Reischauer – explores politics, history, religion and education.

**NOT THE COURSE FOR YOU?** Consider the combination of Oriental Studies with Theology. Alternatively, explore Asian and Middle Eastern Studies (AMES) or Modern and Medieval Languages (MML) at Cambridge.

# Philosophy and Modern Languages

**COURSE LENGTH:** Four years

**PAST INTERVIEW QUESTIONS:**

- How does the literature you have read affect your opinion of that society?
- What are the similarities between ancient playwrights and ancient philosophers?
- `This bench is long.' What does this mean?

Philosophy and Modern Languages brings together some of the most important approaches to understanding language, literature, and ideas. You can choose whether you want to weight your final degree towards either Philosophy or the Modern Language you have chosen, or split the papers evenly. There is also the option to study papers that overlap across the two disciplines. Depending on your chosen language, you may need a language A Level, and you will be required to sit the MLAT, including the philosophy section. You will have to submit written work.

"The academic independence of my thesis was the best part of the degree, I loved the freedom I had to explore the areas I found most interesting."

Sarah, Philosophy and Modern Languages graduate

**INTERESTED? WHY DON'T YOU EXPLORE. . .**

Through the Language Glass by Guy Deutscher – an extremely readable study of how language influences the way we view the world.

Meditations by Descartes – Descartes is a hugely influential philosopher, and easy to read.

Whatever Happened to Good and Evil? by Russ Shafer-Landau – an excellent introduction to meta-ethics.

**NOT THE COURSE FOR YOU?** Consider Modern Languages, Psychology, Philosophy and Linguistics (PPL), or Philosophy, Politics and Economics (PPE) at Oxford. You might also like to explore Modern and Medieval Languages (MML) or Philosophy at Cambridge.

# Philosophy, Politics and Economics (PPE)

**COURSE LENGTH:** Three years

**PAST INTERVIEW QUESTIONS:**

- Is society greater than the individual?
- Differentiate between power and authority.
- What is the point of privatisation?

The combination of Philosophy, Politics and Economics (known as PPE) forms a very popular and extremely diverse degree, which probes why people think the way they do, and explains how systems relate to theoretical principles. You are allowed to drop one of the subjects after your first year, and most students do. The course comprises a great mix of timeless human debates and modern-day economic and political problems and combines these analytical tools with real-world evidence and case studies. Although not formally required, the vast majority of successful applicants have Mathematics to at least AS level. You will be required to sit the TSA.

"The people I studied with were sharp, fun and interesting – I think that PPE attracts individuals with a lot of verve."

Mark, PPE graduate

**INTERESTED? WHY DON'T YOU EXPLORE. . .**

Political Philosophy: A Guide for Politicians and Students by Adam Swift – a good thematic overview of the key areas in modern political thought.

Anarchy, State and Utopia by Robert Nozick – a key text in political philosophy, which argues in favour of a minimal state.

Keynes: The Return of the Master by Robert Skidelsky – a recently published biography which reopens relevant economic discussions.

**NOT THE COURSE FOR YOU?** Consider Economics or Human, Social, and Political Sciences (HSPS) at Cambridge, or Economics and Management (E&M) or History and Politics at Oxford.

# Philosophy and Theology

**COURSE LENGTH:** Three years

**PAST INTERVIEW QUESTIONS:**
- What is the difference between Theology and Philosophy?
- Is atheism a religion?
- What did Kant say about proving God's existence?

Philosophy and Theology brings together some of the most important approaches to understanding and assessing the intellectual claims of religion, and in particular of Christianity. You will look at theology from a philosophical perspective, bringing critical thinking to the study of God and religion, while you approach philosophy from a theological angle, debating arguments for and against God's existence. Throughout the course, you will touch upon many key thinkers in both spheres, and develop a solid critical appreciation of the debates surrounding religion and philosophy. There are no A Level requirements, although Religious Studies or an essay based subject can be helpful. You will be required to submit written work and sit the Philosophy Test.

"There are some quite arcane options in the further reaches of the Philosophy and Theology prospectus, which turned out to be fascinating."

Lucy, Philosophy and Theology graduate

**INTERESTED? WHY DON'T YOU EXPLORE. . .**

Nicomachean Ethics by Aristotle – one of the most influential philosophical texts, it is also a great basis for Christian theology.

Principles of Christian Theology by John Macquarrie – a very systematic outline of basic, and more complex, Christian doctrine.

Science and Wonders by Russell Stannard – an examination of science, theology and philosophy of religion.

**NOT THE COURSE FOR YOU?** Consider Theology on its own at either university. Cambridge also offers straight Philosophy.

# Physics

**COURSE LENGTH:** Three years, with an optional fourth year

**PAST INTERVIEW QUESTIONS:**

- What is the equation for the motion of a pendulum?
- Explain how a hot air balloon works.
- How would the ratio of elements change in a radioactive substance over time?

Although physics is a fundamental science it is also a very practical subject. The first year will provide you with a solid foundation in mathematics, before progressing on to papers including electromagnetism and quantum physics in your second year. A Level Physics and Mathematics (Mechanics modules highly recommended) are essential and you will be asked to sit the PAT.

"**Physics applies mathematics, logic and experience to help understand the Universe and all its machinations. Why wouldn't you want to study it?**"

Tom, Physics graduate

**INTERESTED? WHY DON'T YOU EXPLORE. . .**

In Search of Schrödinger's Cat by John Gribbin – an enjoyable read explaining quantum physics.

E=mc2 by David Bodanis – a 'biography' of Albert Einstein's famous formula.

The End of Time by Julian Barbour – an important contribution to the theory of time.

**NOT THE COURSE FOR YOU?** Consider Physics and Philosophy, Mathematics or Engineering Science at Oxford. You might also like to consider Natural Sciences (Physical) or Engineering at Cambridge.

# Physics and Philosophy

**COURSE LENGTH:** Four years

**PAST INTERVIEW QUESTIONS:**

- How would you define infinity?
- Explain Newton's three laws of motion.
- Is it a matter of fact or knowledge that time travels in only one direction?

This is a course for you if you have an inquisitive and deeply analytical mind. You will learn the theories of physics – and the mathematics on which they are based – to an advanced technical level, whilst also developing your abstract analytical skills through the study of modern philosophy. The bridging subject, Philosophy of Physics, is studied in each of the first three years of the course. There is the option to complete a fourth year, specialising in either Physics or Philosophy, or continuing to study both disciplines and their interrelations. A Level Physics and Mathematics (mechanics modules highly recommended) are essential and you will be asked to sit the PAT.

> **"I loved thinking philosophically about theories in physics and trying to understand what they could be saying about the world."**
>
> Nia, Physics and Philosophy graduate

**INTERESTED? WHY DON'T YOU EXPLORE. . .**

An Invitation to Philosophy by Martin Hollis – a wonderful introductory text on the subject of philosophy.

The Philosophy of Time ed. by Robin Le Poidevin and Murray MacBeath – a collection of important essays on the philosophy of time.

Warped Passages: Unravelling the Universe's Hidden Dimensions by Lisa Randall – an accessible read on theoretical physics.

**NOT THE COURSE FOR YOU?** Consider studying Physics on its own, or Mathematics and Philosophy at Oxford. You might also like to consider the straight Philosophy course at Cambridge.

# Psychology, Philosophy and Linguistics (PPL)

**COURSE LENGTH:** Three years

**PAST INTERVIEW QUESTIONS:**

- How do we solve the nature vs. nurture debate?
- Does a snail have consciousness?
- What is the relevance of philosophy in science?

Introduced in 2013, PPL is slightly updated from the former Psychology and Philosophy course. You must apply for one of three combinations: Psychology and Philosophy, Psychology and Linguistics or Philosophy and Linguistics. After your second term, you'll have the option to study all three subjects as a tripartite degree, subject to your college's approval. Psychology at Oxford is essentially a scientific discipline, which works through experiments and systematic observation, therefore a science or Mathematics A Level is expected for Psychology courses. If you are applying for a Linguistics course, English Language, another language or Mathematics are helpful. All three courses options will require you to sit the TSA Oxford. If you're applying for a Linguistics course, you will also need to take the MLAT.

"I enjoyed the diversity of the course. Managing my time to cope with both a science and humanities subject was challenging and rewarding,"

Sam, Psychology and Philosophy graduate

**INTERESTED? WHY DON'T YOU EXPLORE. . .**

Psychology: The Science of Mind and Behaviour by Richard Gross – a key reference book which covers all the main areas of psychology.

What Does it all Mean? by Thomas Nagel – this short book gives an excellent summary of basic philosophical themes.

The Problems of Philosophy by Bertrand Russell – a more challenging read by a highly influential philosopher.

**NOT THE COURSE FOR YOU?** Consider Experimental Psychology (EP) at Oxford. You might also be interested in Philosophy or Psychological and Behavioural Sciences (PBS) at Cambridge.

# Theology and Religion

**COURSE LENGTH:** Three years

**PAST INTERVIEW QUESTIONS:**
- How should a modern theologian use the Bible?
- How large a role do you think church history has in Theology?
- Is the relationship between religion and science fragile?

Theology was one of the first subjects offered at Oxford University, and remains relevant to the modern student. Although the first year of the course concentrates mainly on the origins and development of Christian theology, each year of the course gives scope to study the major world religions. In engaging with the many different aspects of the course, you will develop your analytical, literary-critical and language skills. A Religious Studies or essay based A Level is considered helpful, and you will be required to submit two pieces of written work.

"Studying Theology made me question notions I had taken for granted all my life, and helped me to understand my own beliefs better."

Sophie, Theology graduate

**INTERESTED? WHY DON'T YOU EXPLORE. . .**

The Early Church by Henry Chadwick – a great summary of the earliest Christian history.

The Shadow of the Galilean by Gerd Theissen – a novelistic look at Christ's own time.

Science and Wonders by Russell Stannard – an examination of science, theology and philosophy of religion.

**NOT THE COURSE FOR YOU?** Consider Philosophy and Theology or Oriental Studies at Oxford, or Theology at Cambridge.

# Theology and Oriental Studies

**COURSE LENGTH:** Three years

**PAST INTERVIEW QUESTIONS:**

* What is meant by 'self' in Buddhism?
* Do you think religion has a place in today's modern world?
* What is Fundamentalism?

Oriental Studies complements the study of Theology by combining an in-depth look at a number of the world's religions, including Buddhism, Hinduism, Islam, and Judaism, with the study of Christianity (mainly undertaken in the Theology Faculty). Over the course of three years, you will develop a much broader understanding of the history and nature of religions that in some cases are radically different from those in Western societies. You will need to demonstrate the ability to analyse historical and literary texts critically and show an understanding of the histories and cultures of the different religions. An essay-based A Level or experience studying a language can be helpful. You may also be required to take the OLAT if you are applying for Hebrew/Judaism or Arabic/Islam and you will be required to submit two pieces of written work.

**INTERESTED? WHY DON'T YOU EXPLORE. . .**

The BBC Radio 4 archives of the 'In Our Time' program, especially the Religion and Philosophy archives.

Christian Theology: An Introduction by Alister McGrath – an introduction to important theological concepts.

Eastern Religions and Western Thought by S. Radhakrishnan – traces the influence of Indian philosophy and religion upon Western thought from classical times.

**NOT THE COURSE FOR YOU?** Consider Philosophy and Theology at Oxford or Theology at Cambridge.

# 2 CHOOSING A COLLEGE

**DISCOVER THE DIFFERENCES BETWEEN THE CAMBRIDGE AND OXFORD COLLEGES**

# Discover the differences between the Cambridge and Oxford colleges

The collegiate system of Oxford and Cambridge sets the universities apart from most others. This system means that not only do applicants have to consider which of the two universities they wish to apply to, but which of the dozens of colleges they choose – if any. With over sixty colleges in Oxford and Cambridge, it can be difficult to know the best way to make a college selection.

When you submit your UCAS form, you apply to a college within a university directly, unless you choose to make an open application. While there are undoubtedly differences between colleges, each with their own character, traditions, and attractions, being a member of a college means you are a member of the university. In practice, the collegiate system does not place significant restrictions on your university experience. This means that no matter your college, you will receive the benefits of having studied at Oxbridge. College choice is important in making sure your university experience, however, is as suited to you as possible.

When deciding which college to apply to, there are important differences you should factor into your consideration. Many students apply to Oxbridge wanting the 'Oxbridge experience' – so an application to a more modern college might not fulfill this criterion. Conversely, another applicant may simply wish to be close to their faculty and live away from the city centre, making some colleges more appropriate than others. This chapter will explore the differences between the Oxbridge colleges and help you to decide which colleges most suits you.

## THE IMPORTANCE OF COLLEGE CHOICE

When deciding which college you wish to apply to, take some time to consider the following questions which outline how college choice impacts your application and university experience:

WHY IS COLLEGE CHOICE IMPORTANT?

The majority of your teaching at Oxford (tutorials) and Cambridge (supervisions) takes place in your college and your college has a big impact on your social environment and as a result is a key element of the application. You are likely to live in the college grounds for at least one year, and possibly for your entire degree, sharing living space with other members of college. Whilst living in college accommodation, you will be looked after by the college staff: the porters, hall staff and `Scouts' or `Bedders' (see our glossary for more on these terms). Much of your university experience will be local to your college, as many societies and social events are college-specific.

As such, colleges are communities which shape your time at university, and for many graduates, they hold a special place in their heart long after leaving. Alumni return each year for dinners organised by the clubs and societies they belonged to during their time at their college and some even return to get married in the college chapel. Each college has its own reputation and its own prestige – picking the right one for you is an important part of ensuring you have the best possible university experience.

HOW DO I CHOOSE A COLLEGE?

There is no universal way for an applicant to choose a college. For every current student or graduate you speak to, it is apparent that each has their own particular reasons for having chosen their college. Emma, who graduated from Trinity College, Oxford, came to the conclusion that its location between the lecture hall and the centre of town made it the perfect college for her. Nick chose Corpus Christi at Cambridge because he felt the small, close-knit community would make a refreshing change after years at a rather large northern state school. Kate picked Wadham because, after meeting her tutor at an Open Day, she knew she would enjoy exploring her subject under his guidance in her weekly tutorials. As for John, who graduated from Oxford, he didn't choose his college – he was pooled by the university following interview and as a result, spent four happy years at Lady Margaret Hall studying Classics.

It's a good idea to attend an Open Day at Oxford and/or Cambridge, or, if you cannot make those dates, to arrange a separate visit. During your time there you should try and visit as many of the colleges as possible in order to see the main differences between them and determine which would best suit you. On Open Days, students will be around to chat to you about their experience, and many colleges have an `Alternative Prospectus' made by their students, available on their websites.

If college choice is unimportant to you, you do not have to choose a college and can make an open application. After you make an open application, the university's computing system will randomly allocate you to a college. For UK applicants, this usually means you will be allocated to a college which received fewer applicants for your subject than usual that year, while international applicants are randomly divided up among all colleges regardless of applicant numbers. Importantly, the college you are assigned to will not know whether you chose it originally or not and will consider you equally to an applicant who directly applied to that college.

Later in this chapter, we outline the differences between different colleges at Oxbridge and support you to choose a college based on the criteria that matters to you. Before you begin reading in-depth about individual colleges, however, it is worth understanding some of the basics about the college 'pooling system' at Oxford and Cambridge, the possibility of an open offer, and the difference between colleges and permanent private halls.

WHAT IS THE POOLING SYSTEM?
The college you choose may not necessarily be the college you receive an offer from: both Oxford and Cambridge will pass on your application to other colleges if they think you are a strong applicant but do not have space for you, or if they think you would be better suited to another college. This act of having your application passed on to another college is known as pooling. Around 27% of successful Oxford candidates for 2016 entry were placed at a college they had not applied to, and this is usually the case for 20-25% of Cambridge applicants. You should never think that you are an inferior applicant if you have been pooled – Oxford and Cambridge tutors are looking for the best applicants and will do their utmost to ensure good candidates get offers from the university, but some colleges are more oversubscribed than others so the best way to retain talented applicants is to share applicants between colleges. While we stress the importance of making your own choice of college, it is important to note that students are very rarely unhappy where they end up – the college choice is important but will not be the only factor of your university experience.

WHAT IS THE CAMBRIDGE POOLING SYSTEM?
The Cambridge Winter Pool doesn't come into effect until the January following your interview. If your chosen college considers you to be a strong applicant but are unable to offer you a place in that particular year, they will

113

contact you in January to notify you that you have been placed in the Winter Pool. Once in the Pool, you face one of three outcomes. Firstly, you could be offered a place outright by another college who likes your application on paper. Secondly, you could be called to interview at another college in mid-January (and subsequently offered a place, or rejected). Thirdly, you could be rejected if no other college has selected your application from the Pool by 31st January. Around 20% of applicants are pooled each year and of these, 25% are offered a place from a college they did not originally apply to. However, being placed in the Winter Pool does not mean your original college will not offer you a place – in 2015 15% of successful pooled applicants received an offer from the college that pooled them.

## WHAT IS THE OXFORD POOLING SYSTEM?

The Oxford Pooling System is an ongoing process which operates during interviews in December. Oxford colleges will be in constant communication with each other throughout the interview period, distributing applicants amongst them. Those invited to interview at Oxford will usually be required to stay more than one day and during that time may be interviewed at more than one college. Certain subjects, such as Medicine, and certain colleges operate a policy whereby every applicant will interview at a second college to help create a fair and consistent interview process. 45% of Oxford applicants we surveyed in 2016 were interviewed at a college other than the college they applied to. As with Cambridge, being interviewed by another college does not mean you will not be given an offer by your original college – 51% of these students were offered a place at their first choice college.

## WHAT IS AN OPEN OFFER?

Oxford, and occasionally Cambridge, may give what is known as an 'open offer'. This is another way of pooling students following A Level results when a small number of applicants fail to meet the conditions of their offer and in doing so, make room for new applicants in their respective colleges. If you are given an open offer, you are guaranteed a place at the university providing you meet the conditions of your offer, but the college you will attend is yet to be decided. A college will 'underwrite' your offer, which means that in the unlikely event that no vacancies arise at any college, they guarantee that you will be able to attend that college. Receiving an open offer is not a reflection of you as a candidate, it is just another way to ensure strong students are distributed across the colleges.

WHAT ARE PERMANENT PRIVATE HALLS (PPHs)?

If you are applying to Oxford you can either apply to a college or to a Permanent Private Hall (PPH).

PPHs are smaller than Oxford colleges and offer a limited number of courses. Students at PPHs are still full members of the University, but studying at one of the Permanent Private Halls offers a unique Oxford experience. They were originally founded by different Christian denominations but, in most cases, students are not required to be of that denomination to apply (only sympathetic).

In many ways, students at PPHs have a very similar experience to those at colleges. They have the same access to university and faculty libraries, they often share tutorials with students at other colleges, they sit the same exams, and have the same degrees awarded by the university. You should consider PPHs if you like the idea of having a small close-knit community, but also want to make friends university-wide. The size of PPHs means that students often get involved in university activities, or in other college teams, meeting lots of other students from outside of the immediate college community. However, please be aware that they generally offer a more limited selection of courses, so ensure your course is an option at whichever PPH you are considering.

**IMPORTANT FACTORS IN CHOOSING A COLLEGE**

When deciding which college suits you, or whether you will make an open application, the following questions are important to consider:

DOES THE COLLEGE OFFER MY COURSE?

This is most important question to ask when choosing a college. There are a number of colleges that do not have supervision/tutorial provision for every course. You may have fallen in love with Emmanuel College's outdoor pool or King's College's proximity to the city centre, but if you want to study Land Economy then unfortunately you cannot apply to these colleges. It's worth starting your college search by finding the list of colleges that offer your course on the university websites and narrowing down your options from there.

WHAT ARE THE TUTORS LIKE?

If you do visit colleges on the Open Day, speak to tutors from your subject area if possible. Although you are likely to be taught by a variety of tutors

115

from different colleges, the tutors at your college will be a significant part of your university experience. It is important that you feel comfortable with them and that you think you will enjoy the tutor-student relationship. However, remember that there is no guarantee that the same tutor will be there when you arrive at university. Whichever college you go to, you will be in contact with experts in your subject to help you have an enriching academic experience.

WILL I NEED TO SIT AN ADMISSIONS TEST OR SUBMIT WRITTEN WORK?
For certain subjects at Oxford, and for most subjects at Cambridge from 2016, you will be required to sit an Admissions Test whichever college you choose to apply to. However, if you are applying to Cambridge, whether or not you have to submit written work will depend on which college you choose, rather than just the course you are applying for. For example, if you apply for Economics at Queens' College, Cambridge you will be asked to submit one or two essays as part of your application. In contrast, if you apply to Gonville and Caius, there is no written work required. If your writing ability is your strong point, then you might want to consider applying to a college where they give you an opportunity to demonstrate this strength before interview. See Chapter 4 for more information on the Admissions Tests, and Chapter 5 for more information on written work.

WOULD I LIKE TO SPEND THE NEXT FEW YEARS OF MY LIFE HERE?
A significant factor in choosing a college is whether you like it, both on an academic and personal level. Some colleges have more students than others: are you someone who likes to be surrounded by large numbers of people, or would you prefer a smaller, tight-knit community? Would you rather be located in the city centre, or further away from the city centre but closer to the river? Do you want to go to a college with great sporting prowess, or would you rather attend a college that puts academic achievement as its priority? Do you want to eat in a grand, traditional dining hall, or are you happier surrounded by modern buildings?

When considering these questions, bear in mind that your choice of college does not limit your social experience at Oxford or Cambridge. If you are skilled at hockey but your college does not have their own team, there are opportunities to play university-wide. Similarly, most of the drama societies are open to any interested students from the university. There is a wide range of university societies available so students can branch out from their college environment if they so wish.

# College Selection Quiz

This quiz is designed to help you determine which of the colleges might best suit your personality and preferences. Note down the answers to your questions and sum up the frequency of each letter to see which colleges we recommend.

**1) Where would you most like to be based during your time at Oxford or Cambridge?**
   a. Not quite in the busiest part of the city, but close enough to be anywhere in 10 to 15 minutes
   b. Right in the city centre
   c. Close to everything but in a slightly quieter area of the city
   d. Further out of the city with its own community
   e. I don't mind where I'm based – I love the whole city!

**2) What kind of atmosphere would you most like in your college?**
   a. Somewhere small and close-knit where everyone knows each other
   b. Somewhere with a lot of space and a lot of people
   c. Somewhere with lots of activities taking place, but with a relaxed atmosphere
   d. Somewhere with lots of people, but everyone has their own niche
   e. Somewhere relaxed and a bit different to the usual Oxbridge college

**3) How do you feel about the Oxbridge traditions (e.g. formal hall, gowns)?**
   a. I would like my college to have them, but it doesn't need to embrace all traditions
   b. I love the idea, that's part of the reason I want to go to Oxbridge
   c. I like a few traditions but I don't want to be too stuck in the past
   d. I would rather avoid Oxbridge traditions
   e. I would welcome some traditions, especially the more unusual ones

**4) What is your favourite London building?**

   a. St Paul's Cathedral

   b. Houses of Parliament

   c. 10 Downing Street

   d. Southbank Centre

   e. British Museum

**5) What is the least important factor you would consider when choosing your college?**

   a. The extra-curricular activities and facilities

   b. The competition for places

   c. The location

   d. The traditional Oxford experience

   e. Academic excellence

**6) You have finished all your work for the week and you have some free time. What are you doing?**

   a. Spending time with friends from college

   b. Attending formal hall

   c. Playing college sport

   d. Getting involved in drama and music societies or politics groups

   e. Drama, music, sport, student union – I enjoy a range of activities

**7) Which of these notable Oxbridge alumni do you like the most?**

   a. CS Lewis

   b. David Cameron

   c. Hugh Laurie

   d. Emma Watson

   e. Sue Perkins

**MOSTLY A** – You like the idea of going to an old, renowned college where you can have the traditional Oxbridge experience, but you would prefer somewhere small with a close-knit community. You would like the peace and quiet of being somewhere tucked away but still want to have easy access to the centre of the city and university.

CONSIDERING CAMBRIDGE? Explore these colleges: Corpus Christi, Peterhouse, Sidney Sussex.

CONSIDERING OXFORD? Explore these colleges: Brasenose, Blackfriars, Corpus Christi, Lincoln, Mansfield, Queen's, Regent's Park, St Edmund Hall, St Benet's, St Stephen's House, Wycliffe Hall.

**MOSTLY Bs** – You want the traditional Oxbridge experience – the gowns, formal dinners, playing croquet on the college lawn – and for the opportunity to discuss your favourite topics with likeminded people. You want to be in the centre of everything and have the opportunity to make your mark during your time at university.

CONSIDERING CAMBRIDGE? Explore these colleges: Christ's, Downing, Gonville and Caius, Jesus, Magdalene, Queens', St John's.

CONSIDERING OXFORD? Explore these colleges: Balliol, Christ Church, Exeter, Magdalen, Merton, New, Oriel, St John's, Trinity, Worcester.

**MOSTLY Cs** – You love the old buildings in Oxford and Cambridge, but you don't want to study somewhere that is too archaic. As much as you like some traditions, you would like somewhere with a more liberal outlook where the traditions are just a small, fun element of day-to-day life.

CONSIDERING CAMBRIDGE? Explore these colleges: Clare, Emmanuel, Girton, King's, Newnham, Pembroke, Selwyn, Sidney Sussex, St Catharine's, Trinity Hall, Wolfson.

CONSIDERING OXFORD? Explore these colleges: Hertford, Jesus, Keble, Lady Margaret Hall, Keble, Pembroke, St Hilda's, St Hugh's, St Peter's, University, Wadham.

**MOSTLY Ds** – The traditional Oxbridge experience is not that important to you – you would much rather have a modern college with state-of-the-art facilities, even if it is a bit further out of town. You would like everything to be laid-back, relaxed and forward-thinking. You are looking forward to getting involved in university-wide activities and meeting interesting people, and you want the college you attend to reflect that.

CONSIDERING CAMBRIDGE? Explore these colleges: Churchill, Fitzwilliam, Homerton, Lucy Cavendish, Murray Edwards, Robinson, St Edmund's

CONSIDERING OXFORD? Explore these colleges: Harris Manchester, St Anne's, St Catherine's, Somerville.

**MOSTLY Es** – You don't mind if your college is old or new, big or small – you just want somewhere that has a bit of individuality. You are not worried about going to an academically rigorous college, you just want to embrace all that university has to offer and to go somewhere where you can be yourself. To you, going to Oxbridge is an opportunity to throw yourself into something new, meet interesting people and experience new things, both academically and socially.

CONSIDERING CAMBRIDGE? Explore these colleges: Fitzwilliam, Girton, Gonville and Caius, Pembroke, Queens', Robinson, Sidney Sussex.

CONSIDERING OXFORD? Explore these colleges: Mansfield, Pembroke, Regent's Park, St Hilda's, Wadham.

## SPECIALIST INTERESTS OF DIFFERENT COLLEGES

Finally, when thinking about your college choice, it is important to consider which colleges cater to your specialist interests. Below is an overview of which colleges are renowned for their rowing, sport, drama or politics societies to help you to narrow down your college choices:

ROWING:
Downing, Gonville and Caius, Jesus (Cambridge), Magdalene (Cambridge), Magdalen (Oxford), Oriel, Pembroke (Oxford and Cambridge), St John's (Cambridge), Wolfson (Oxford).

SPORT:
Keble, Oriel, Pembroke (Oxford), St Catharine's (Cambridge), St Edmund Hall, St John's (Cambridge), Worcester.

DRAMA:
Corpus Christi (Cambridge), Homerton, Pembroke (Cambridge), St John's (Oxford), Trinity (Oxford), Worcester.

POLITICS:
Balliol, Emmanuel, Kings, Murray Edwards, Peterhouse, St Catherine's, Trinity (Cambridge), Wadham.

MUSIC:
Clare, Emmanuel, Exeter, Fitzwilliam, King's, Lincoln, New, Queens' (Cambridge), Selwyn, St Hilda's. St John's (Cambridge), Trinity (Cambridge), Wadham.

# Christ's College

**Founded:** 1505

**Size:** Medium (420 undergraduates, 200 graduates)

**Academic ranking:** 2015 Tompkins Table = 14/29

**Words that best describe the college:** Friendly, supportive, central, welcoming, green, academic

**This college is for you if:** You want a central college with good facilities

**The college's best features are:**

Its central location

The extensive gardens

The good clubs and societies

**It might not be for you if:** You want to be in a peaceful area of the city – Christ's is right next to a taxi rank and one of the most popular nightclubs

# Churchill College

**Founded:** 1960

**Size:** Large (475 undergraduates, 310 graduates)

**Academic ranking:** 2015 Tompkins Table = 3/29

**Words that best describe the college:** Friendly, informal, recreational, open, sporty

**This college is for you if:** You're looking for an escape from Cambridge's formalities

**The college's best features are:**

Everyone living on site

The dedicated theatre/cinema

The on-site playing fields

**It might not be for you if:** You're looking for ancient splendour – the sixties architecture is not in the traditional style of Cambridge

# Clare College

**Founded:** 1326

**Size:** Large (496 undergraduates, 297 graduates)

**Academic ranking:** 2015 Tompkins Table = 15/29

**Words that best describe the college:** Musical, informal, welcoming, popular, fun

**This college is for you if:** You want a beautiful college that doesn't take itself too seriously

**The college's best features are:**

The great underground music venue beneath Chapel

The beautiful Fellows' Gardens

Ancient architecture

The excellent college choir and orchestra

**It might not be for you if:** You want to live in college – you are more likely to be based in Memorial Court or Clare Colony which are off-site

# Corpus Christi College

**Founded:** 1352

**Size:** Small (280 undergraduates, 220 graduates)

**Academic ranking:** 2015 Tompkins Table = 22/29

**Words that best describe the college:** Friendly, small, historic, convivial

**This college is for you if:** You are looking for a small community

**The college's best features are:**

The Corpus Christi Playroom

The Parker Library

The outdoor swimming pool

The location

**It might not be for you if:** You want to escape the crowds – the college is on one of the busiest streets in Cambridge

# Downing College

**Founded:** 1800

**Size:** Medium (425 undergraduates, 258 graduates)

**Academic ranking:** 2015 Tompkins Table = 9/29

**Words that best describe the college:** Spacious, convenient, friendly, beautiful, supportive, sporty

**This college is for you if:** You're a sports player or fan

**The college's best features are:**
The many sporting victories
Huge, rolling lawns
The sheer amount of space

**It might not be for you if:** You've got lots of friends at other colleges – you have to sign guests into the bar

# Emmanuel College

**Founded:** 1584

**Size:** Large (460 undergraduates, 220 graduates)

**Academic ranking:** 2015 Tompkins Table = 4/29

**Words that best describe the college:** Fun, beautiful, central, open-minded, academic

**This college is for you if:** You want to work hard and play hard

**The college's best features are:**
The famous duck pond
The outdoor swimming pool
Active music and drama societies
The cheap, atmospheric college bar

**It might not be for you if:** You like cooking – there are limited facilities in college

# Fitzwilliam College

**Founded:** 1869 (full college status granted in 1966)

**Size:** Large (440 undergraduates, 335 graduates)

**Academic ranking:** 2015 Tompkins Table = 20/29

**Words that best describe the college:** Relaxed, unpretentious, friendly, fun

**This college is for you if:** You hope to be involved in lots of extra-curricular activities

**The college's best features are:**

The lovely grounds

The brand new library and computer centre

The 250 seat auditorium

The radio studio

**It might not be for you if:** You want to be central – Fitz is a little out of the way (and up the only hill in Cambridge)

# Girton College

**Founded:** 1869

**Size:** Large (500 undergraduates, 280 graduates)

**Academic ranking:** 2015 Tompkins Table = 24/29

**Words that best describe the college:** Distant, sprawling, pleasant, close-knit, unpretentious, easy-going

**This college is for you if:** You enjoy cycling and would like to be separated from the hustle and bustle

**The college's best features are:**

The huge grounds

The on-site sports facilities

The heated indoor swimming pool

The tasty food

**It might not be for you if:** You're not into travelling – Girton is a far away fom the centre of Cambridge

# Gonville & Caius College

**Founded:** 1348

**Size:** Large (560 undergraduates, 250 graduates)

**Academic ranking:** 2015 Tompkins Table = 19/29

**Words that best describe the college:** Traditional, supportive, academic, energetic, sporty, vibrant, sociable

**This college is for you if:** You are an energetic type who wants to work and play

**The college's best features are:**
Stephen Hawking coming to formal dinners
The central location
The strong boat club
The unique blue and black gowns

**It might not be for you if:** You want flexibility at meal times – there is compulsory Hall most nights

# Homerton College

**Founded:** 1895 (full college status granted in 1976)

**Size:** Large (580 undergraduates, 500 graduates)

**Academic ranking:** 2015 Tompkins Table = 27/29

**Words that best describe the college:** Friendly, open, modern, unpretentious, warm, communal

**This college is for you if:** You are slightly more relaxed

**The college's best features are:**
The space
The on-site sports facilities
The beautiful gardens
The lack of academic pressure

**It might not be for you if:** You want to be centrally located

# Hughes Hall

**Founded:** 1885

**Size:** Large (100 mature (21+) undergraduates and 450 graduates)

**Academic ranking:** 2015 Tompkins Table = 25/29

**Words that best describe the college:** liberal, intellectual, cosmopolitan, lively

**This college is for you if:** You like sports – the college is right next to both the university cricket ground and Parkers Piece

**The college's best features are:**

The terrace overlooking the cricket ground

Eating dinner with the fellows

The international community spirit

The delicious restaurants to be found along nearby Mill Road

**It might not be for you if:** You want to live in the historic centre of Cambridge and the university – Hughes Hall is located further away from the other colleges

# Jesus College

**Founded:** 1496

**Size:** Large (510 undergraduates, 380 graduates)

**Academic ranking:** 2015 Tompkins Table = 11/29

**Words that best describe the college:** Friendly, historic, beautiful, secluded

**This college is for you if:** You are a fan of sculpture and like old buildings (without too many tourists)

**The college's best features are:**

The architecture

Being five minutes from the centre of town

The on-site sports facilities

The statues

**It might not be for you if:** You want to live cheaply – the college bar is more expensive than some

# King's College

**Founded:** 1441

**Size:** Medium (430 undergraduates, 280 graduates)

**Academic ranking:** 2015 Tompkins Table = 18/29

**Words that best describe the college:** Open, different, fun, impressive, accessible, liberal

**This college is for you if:** You are looking for an alternative experience

**The college's best features are:**
The architecture
The King's Affair (King's May Ball alternative)
The famous Evensong in the beautiful chapel
The Mingles (large parties held at the end of the autumn and spring terms)

**It might not be for you if:** You don't like tourists – Kings is a very popular college with visitors to Cambridge

# Lucy Cavendish

**Founded:** 1965

**Size:** Large (150 mature (21+) undergraduates, 220 post graduates, female only)

**Academic ranking:** 2015 Tompkins Table = 29/29

**Words that best describe the college:** serene, tranquil, open-minded, informal, supportive

**This college is for you if:** You are a female looking for a modern, relaxed college

**The college's best features are:**
The grounds, including a wild flower meadow, pond and Anglo-Saxon herb garden
The Music and Meditation Pavilion
The themed Formal Halls and al fresco dining area

**It might not be for you if:** You want an academic powerhouse

# Magdalene College

**Founded:** 1428 or 1542, depending on who you ask

**Size:** Small (347 undergraduates, 202 graduates)

**Academic ranking:** 2015 Tompkins Table = 2/29

**Words that best describe the college:** Small, old, welcoming, close-knit, supportive

**This college is for you if:** You are a traditionalist who wants the Oxbridge experience with all the trimmings

**The college's best features are:**
The river bank
The Cambridge-style traditions
The Pepys Library
Its super-central location

**It might not be for you if:** You like your privacy – the small community means that everyone knows everyone

# Murray Edwards College

**Founded:** 1954

**Size:** Medium (360 undergraduates, 170 graduates)

**Academic ranking:** 2015 Tompkins Table = 23/29

**Words that best describe the college:** Modern, dynamic, inspiring, diverse, relaxed, supportive

**This college is for you if:** You're a female who wants a quieter, cleaner place to study

**The college's best features are:**
The luxurious second and third year accommodation
Beautiful lawns you can sit on
Free parking for students
The peace and quiet due to the non-central location

**It might not be for you if:** You don't like cycling – the college is best reached by cycling up the only hill in Cambridge

# Newnham College

**Founded:** 1871

**Size:** Medium (360 undergraduates, 290 graduates)

**Academic ranking:** 2015 Tompkins Table = 21/29

**Words that best describe the college:** Sociable, safe, pretty, comfortable, peaceful, convenient

**This college is for you if:** You'd like beautiful architecture in a more peaceful part of the city

**The college's best features are:**
The gardens (which you are allowed to sit in)
The proximity to many humanities departments
The on-site sports and drama
The food, including a weekly buffet

**It might not be for you if:** You would like a Bedder – there is no one to clean your room for you

# Pembroke College

**Founded: 7**

**Size:** Medium (430 undergraduates, 275 graduates)

**Academic ranking:** 2015 Tompkins Table = 5/29

**Words that best describe the college:** Friendly, relaxed, central, inclusive, beautiful

**This college is for you if:** You are an aspiring thesp or aesthete

**The college's best features are:**
The famous Pembroke brunch
The drama scene
The opportunities to go abroad with the college in the holidays
The lovely gardens

**It might not be for you if:** You'd like a peaceful walk to lectures- the college is right next to the tourist havens of King's Parade and Silver Street Bridge

# Peterhouse

**Founded:** 1284

**Size:** Small (241 undergraduates, 163 graduates)

**Academic ranking:** 2015 Tompkins Table = 6/29

**Words that best describe the college:** Intimate, close-knit, relaxed, supportive, old, quaint, central

**This college is for you if:** You are looking for a small community

**The college's best features are:**

Candlelit dining

The Deer Park

The accommodation

**It might not be for you if:** You get claustrophobic – the small community can get very insular

# Queens' College

**Founded:** 1448

**Size:** Large (490 undergraduates, 450 graduates)

**Academic ranking:** 2015 Tompkins Table = 7/29

**Words that best describe the college:** Large, friendly, relaxed, sociable, extracurricular

**This college is for you if:** You are outgoing and looking for a community feel

**The college's best features are:**

The famous Mathematical Bridge

Entertaining rumours about the history of said bridge

The sports facilities and societies

The Fitzpatrick Theatre

**It might not be for you if:** You like your privacy – some of the rooms are shared sets

# Robinson College

**Founded:** 1979

**Size:** Medium (386 undergraduates, 172 graduates)

**Academic ranking:** 2015 Tompkins Table = 16/29

**Words that best describe the college:** Unpretentious, open, diverse, supportive, modern, social

**This college is for you if:** You are looking for a less traditional experience

**The college's best features are:**
The modern accommodation
The great food
The beautiful gardens and lake

**It might not be for you if:** You want to be surrounded by classical buildings – the modern architecture is not to everyone's liking

# St. Catharine's College

**Founded:** 1473

**Size:** Medium (436 undergraduates, 220 graduates)

**Academic ranking:** 2015 Tompkins Table = 13/29

**Words that best describe the college:** Open, social, inclusive, supportive, engaging, central

**This college is for you if:** You are in search of a friendly, central experience

**The college's best features are:**
The central location
The great accommodation (especially in second year)
The McGrath centre, which houses the college bar, JCR and auditorium

**It might not be for you if:** You like good food – the college food isn't known for being exceptional

# St Edmund's

**Founded:** 1871

**Size:** Large (122 mature (21+) undergraduates, 419 graduates)

**Academic ranking:** 2015 Tompkins Table = 28/29

**Words that best describe the college:** social, spacious, diverse, integrated

**This college is for you if:** You like your space – the college sits on six acres of parkland

**The college's best features are:**

The cheap, student run bar

The social events – including Oktoberfest

The Fitness Room in the basement of the Library

**It might not be for you if:** You want to be surrounded by other undergraduates – the undergraduate to graduate ratio is very low

# St. John's College

**Founded:** 1511

**Size:** Large (569 undergraduates, 351 graduates)

**Academic ranking:** 2015 Tompkins Table = 10/29

**Words that best describe the college:** Big, beautiful, fun, grand, sporty, cosmopolitan, rich

**This college is for you if:** You want a large, prestigious college with lots of opportunities

**The college's best features are:**

The very large college grounds and gardens

The funding

The Michelin star formal food

The May Ball

**It might not be for you if:** You're nervous about 'the Oxbridge thing' – it can get slightly overwhelming at times

# Selwyn College

**Founded:** 1882

**Size:** Medium (400 undergraduates, 200 graduates)

**Academic ranking:** 2015 Tompkins Table = 12/29

**Words that best describe the college:** Sociable, close-knit, academic, supportive

**This college is for you if:** You are looking for a close-knit community, or you're a humanities student who likes to lie in (the college is next door to the main humanities faculties)

**The college's best features are:**
Its proximity to many humanities departments
The friendly atmosphere
The space

**It might not be for you if:** You want to be in the centre of town – it's a short walk away

# Sidney Sussex College

**Founded:** 1596

**Size:** Small (350 undergraduates, 275 graduates)

**Academic ranking:** 2015 Tompkins Table = 17/29

**Words that best describe the college:** Central, friendly, cosy, close-knit

**This college is for you if:** You hope to be involved in university-level activities

**The college's best features are:**
The student-run bar
The beautiful gardens
The very central location
Being housed with all the other first years

**It might not be for you if:** You want a bit of space – Sidney is a small college located right in the centre of town

# Trinity College

**Founded:** 1546

**Size:** Gigantic (695 undergraduates, 350 graduates)

**Academic ranking:** 2015 Tompkins Table = 1/29

**Words that best describe the college:** Grand, traditional, sociable, rich, impressive

**This college is for you if:** You're after the traditional Cambridge experience from both an academic and social perspective

**The college's best features are:**

The excellent academic reputation

The huge library

Living in college for the duration of your course

**It might not be for you if:** You want a small, friendly college – it can be a little too imposing for some

# Trinity Hall

**Founded:** 1350

**Size:** Medium (374 undergraduates, 243 graduates)

**Academic ranking:** 2015 Tompkins Table = 8/29

**Words that best describe the college:** Idyllic, small, central, sociable, sporty

**This college is for you if:** You are a laid back person looking for riverside calm

**The college's best features are:**

Being so central

The beautiful architecture and grounds

The lovely Jerwood Library on the river

The opportunities for musicians

**It might not be for you if:** Want a peaceful library – being on the river means loud groups of tourists punting close by

# Wolfson

**Founded:** 1965

**Size:** Medium (168 mature (21+) undergraduates, 300 graduates)

**Academic ranking:** 2015 Tompkins Table = 26/29

**Words that best describe the college:** lively, friendly, international, informal, pioneering

**This college is for you if:** you want to be well positioned between the town centre, the sports grounds and the University Library

**The college's best features are:**

Dining with the fellows – there is no High Table at formal hall

The Chinese-style Lee Hall

The university renowned entertainment events, including dancing nights and concerts

**It might not be for you if:** Want the classic Oxbridge traditions and architecture

# Balliol College

**Founded:** 1263

**Size:** Large (375 undergraduates, 297 graduates)

**Academic ranking:** 2015 Norrington Table = 4/30

**Words that best describe the college:** Unpretentious, liberal, energetic, high-achieving

**This college is for you if:** You want to be involved in lots of social activities

**The college's best features are:**
The incredible selection of food available from the pantry
The grass you can sit on
The sports societies
The largest (and one of the last) student-run bars in Oxford

**It might not be for you if:** You take a more relaxed attitude to your learning – Balliol sets high academic standards

# Blackfriars (PPH)

**Founded:** 1876

**Size:** Small (4 mature (21+) undergraduates, 39 graduates)

**Academic ranking:** 2015 PPH Norrington Table = 5/6

**Words that best describe the college:** central, diverse, close-knit, social, international

**This college is for you if:** You want a small community where you can get to know both undergraduate and graduate students

**The college's best features are:**
The supportive community
The specialist Philosophy and Theology library

**It might not be for you if:** You want everything to be on-site – Blackfriars doesn't provide food so students eat at nearby Regent's Park or St Benet's.

# Brasenose College

**Founded:** 1509

**Size:** Medium (367 undergraduates, 209 graduates)

**Academic ranking:** 2015 Norrington Table = 24/30

**Words that best describe the college:** Old, stately, warm, easy-going

**This college is for you if:** You'd like a pretty college with a good community

**The college's best features are:**

Living in a castle

The extracurricular societies

The central location

**It might not be for you if:** You like your own space – students live in the small grounds for all three years

# Christ Church College

**Founded:** 1524

**Size:** Medium (429 undergraduates, 174 graduates)

**Academic ranking:** 2015 Norrington Table = 15/30

**Words that best describe the college:** Prestigious, grand, proud, beautiful, traditional

**This college is for you if:** You are looking for the archetypal Oxbridge experience

**The college's best features are:**

The accommodation

The funding and grants

Christ Church Meadows

**It might not be for you if:** You don't like tourists – scenes from Harry Potter were shot here which entices many tourists to the grounds

# Corpus Christi College

**Founded:** 1517

**Size:** Small (249 undergraduates, 95 graduates)

**Academic ranking:** 2015 Norrington Table = 10/30

**Words that best describe the college:** Friendly, supportive, intellectual, quaint, compact

**This college is for you if:** You want to win University Challenge

**The college's best features are:**

The strong academic performance

The accommodation

The wonderful library – one of the wonders of the world according to Erasmus

The central location

**It might not be for you if:** You want lots of space – the small size can get a bit claustrophobic

# Exeter College

**Founded:** 1314

**Size:** Small to medium (319 undergraduates, 185 graduates)

**Academic ranking:** 2015 Norrington Table = 22/30

**Words that best describe the college:** Central, open-minded, beautiful, close-knit, relaxed

**This college is for you if:** You are looking for an idyllic central college

**The college's best features are:**

The central location

The strong musical tradition

WiFi in the college gardens

The beautiful college chapel

**It might not be for you if:** You want to live cheaply – both the accommodation and the food are more expensive than at some colleges

# Harris Manchester

**Founded:** 1786

**Size:** Small (82 mature (21+) undergraduates, 123 post graduates)

**Academic ranking:** 2015 Norrington Table = 16/30

**Words that best describe the college:** international, friendly, central, liberal, pioneering

**This college is for you if:** You want a diverse college with a tight-knit community

**The college's best features are:**

The highly rated formal hall

The spacious library

The beautiful Pre-Raphaelite college chapel

The fishing fountain

**It might not be for you if:** You like sport – the college has no real sports facilities

# Hertford College

**Founded:** 1282 (achieving full college status in 1874)

**Size:** Medium (394 undergraduates, 189 graduates)

**Academic ranking:** 2015 Norrington Table = 14/30

**Words that best describe the college:** Democratic, unpretentious, central, social, relaxed, friendly

**This college is for you if:** You are a progressive type

**The college's best features are:**

The relaxed environment

The Hertford Bridge (popularly known as the Bridge of Sighs)

The bar, which has five separate rooms

The college cat

**It might not be for you if:** You want good food – the college meals are not known for being exceptional

# Jesus College

**Founded:** 1571

**Size:** Medium (331 undergraduates, 190 graduates)

**Academic ranking:** 2015 Norrington Table = 13/30

**Words that best describe the college:** Small, close-knit, welcoming, central

**This college is for you if:** You're a sports fan

**The college's best features are:**
The central location
The gentle atmosphere
The lovely buildings

**It might not be for you if:** You want to live in college for the duration of your course – the external accommodation is quite far from the main site

# Keble College

**Founded:** 1870

**Size:** Large (417 undergraduates, 232 graduates)

**Academic ranking:** 2015 Norrington Table = 9/30

**Words that best describe the college:** Friendly, buzzing, gothic, fun, traditional

**This college is for you if:** You are looking for extracurricular experience

**The college's best features are:**
The proximity to the Science Area
The lack of tourists
The O'Reilly Theatre
The variety of activities on offer

**It might not be for you if:** You want the traditional Oxbridge architecture – Keble has unique red-brick buildings which not everyone finds appealing

# Lady Margaret Hall

**Founded:** 1878

**Size:** Large (395 undergraduates, 205 graduates)

**Academic ranking:** 2015 Norrington Table = 26/30

**Words that best describe the college:** Pretty, friendly, scenic, relaxed, lively, dynamic

**This college is for you if:** You are looking to get away from it all

**The college's best features are:**
The spacious accommodation
The gardens
The atmosphere

**It might not be for you if:** You don't like cycling – the college is a 15-20 minute walk from the centre

# Lincoln College

**Founded:** 1427

**Size:** Small (301 undergraduates, 289 graduates)

**Academic ranking:** 2015 Norrington Table = 5/30

**Words that best describe the college:** Friendly, small, busy, close-knit, high-achieving, lively

**This college is for you if:** You are looking for a sociable community

**The college's best features are:**
The accommodation
The food
The cheap, attractive bar
The location

**It might not be for you if:** You're looking for a big college – Lincoln is one of the smaller Oxford colleges

# Magdalen College

**Founded:** 1458

**Size:** Big (396 undergraduates, 179 graduates)

**Academic ranking:** 2015 Norrington Table = 1/30

**Words that best describe the college:** Big, inspiring, beautiful, surprising, challenging

**This college is for you if:** You want the traditional Oxbridge experience

**The college's best features are:**

Living in all three years

The space

The great music and drama scene

Having your own Deer Park

**It might not be for you if:** You want a relaxed, laid back environment – Magdalen can be somewhat intense

# Mansfield College

**Founded:** 1886 (full college status granted in 1995)

**Size:** Small (222 undergraduates, 122 graduates)

**Academic ranking:** 2015 Norrington Table = 18/30

**Words that best describe the college:** Unpretentious, small, friendly, accommodating, relaxed, liberal

**This college is for you if:** You'd like a smaller, laid back college

**The college's best features are:**

The friendly community

The access-orientated approach to admissions

Being close to the Science Area and University Parks

**It might not be for you if:** You want access to funds and bursaries – Mansfield is not the richest of colleges

# Merton College

---

**Founded:** 1264

**Size:** Small (291 undergraduates, 279 graduates)

**Academic ranking:** 2015 Norrington Table = 27/30

**Words that best describe the college:** Small, central, academic, pretty, friendly

**This college is for you if:** You are academically focused and an extremely high-achiever

**The college's best features are:**
The great teaching and tutorial support
The cheap food and rent
The central location

**It might not be for you if:** You take a more relaxed attitude to your work – the college expect students to perform well

# New College

---

**Founded:** 1379

**Size:** Large (430 undergraduates, 279 graduates)

**Academic ranking:** 2015 Norrington Table = 2/30

**Words that best describe the college:** Social, big, active, academic, competitive, fun

**This college is for you if:** You're out-going and like to socialise

**The college's best features are:**
The Chalet in France, shared with Balliol and University College
The beautiful and spacious surroundings
The celebrated musical tradition

**It might not be for you if:** You're after a small, friendly college – New can be intimidating

# Oriel College

**Founded:** 1326

**Size:** Small (325 undergraduates, 186 graduates)

**Academic ranking:** 2015 Norrington Table = 12/30

**Words that best describe the college:** Sporty, small, old, traditional, central, warm-hearted

**This college is for you if:** You are a rower or sports enthusiast

**The college's best features are:**

The excellent facilities for sports

The central location

The well-stocked library

**It might not be for you if:** You want to cook for yourself – the catering facilities are limited

# Pembroke College

**Founded:** 1624

**Size:** Medium (367 undergraduates, 216 graduates)

**Academic ranking:** 2015 Norrington Table = 30/30

**Words that best describe the college:** Inclusive, busy, sporty, friendly

**This college is for you if:** A sporty type (especially if you're interested in rowing)

**The college's best features are:**

The location

The relaxed atmosphere

The unbeatable boat club

**It might not be for you if:** You want to be at a high-achieving, very academic college

# The Queen's College

**Founded:** 1341

**Size:** Medium (342 undergraduates, 122 graduates)

**Academic ranking:** 2015 Norrington Table = 25/30

**Words that best describe the college:** Cosy, friendly, down-to-earth, old-fashioned, relaxed

**This college is for you if:** You are looking for a close-knit, community-feel in a college

**The college's best features are:**
The beautiful architecture
The relaxed student body
The central location, on the High Street

**It might not be for you if:** You want to get involved in politics – Queen's has a reputation for being apathetic

# Regent's Park College (PPH)

**Founded:** 1752

**Size:** Small (115 undergraduates, 70 graduates)

**Academic ranking:** 2015 PPH Norrington Table = 3/6

**Words that best describe the college:** friendly, familial, down-to-earth, busy, homely

**This college is for you if:** You want to get involved in wider university life

**The college's best features are:**
Formal hall
The college tortoise, Emmanuelle
The JCR – one of the best in Oxford

**It might not be for you if:** You want lots of space – the college grounds are quite small

# Somerville College

**Founded:** 1879

**Size:** Medium (388 undergraduates, 145 graduates)

**Academic ranking:** 2015 Norrington Table = 28/30

**Words that best describe the college:** Friendly, open-minded, homely, supportive, untraditional

**This college is for you if:** You're looking to avoid Oxford clichés

**The college's best features are:**

The library

The community spirit

Living in Jericho – a very trendy area

**It might not be for you if:** You want the traditional Oxford experience

# St. Anne's College

**Founded:** 1879 (full college status granted in 1952)

**Size:** Large (422 undergraduates, 308 graduates)

**Academic ranking:** 2015 Norrington Table = 8/30

**Words that best describe the college:** Sociable, relaxed, down to earth, spacious, unpretentious

**This college is for you if:** You are relaxed and not looking for tradition

**The college's best features are:**

The large site

Good food

The lack of regimented traditions

**It might not be for you if:** You want a picture-perfect college – it's not the prettiest

# St Benet's Hall (PPH)

**Founded:** 1897

**Size:** Small (48 undergraduates, 4 graduates)

**Words that best describe it:** familial, traditional, collegiate, pastoral

**Academic ranking:** 2015 PPH Norrington Table = 5/6

**This college is for you if:** You want a friendly, traditional and unstuffy college but want to throw yourself into the wider university

**The college's best features are:**
The monks
The social events
The camaraderie

**It might not be for you if:** You like to be private – the small community can be very intense

# St. Catherine's College

**Founded:** 1963

**Size:** Large (476 undergraduates, 322 graduates)

**Academic ranking:** 2015 Norrington Table = 6/30

**Words that best describe the college:** Social, friendly, sporty, vibrant, modern, laid back

**This college is for you if:** You are looking for a college with a modern touch

**The college's best features are:**
The excellent facilities for sports and the arts
Good food
The biggest college bar in Oxford

**It might not be for you if:** You take an instant dislike to the architecture – it can be very polarizing

# St. Edmund Hall

**Founded:** c. 1371 (full college status granted in 1957)

**Size:** Large (405 undergraduates, 257 graduates)

**Academic ranking:** 2015 Norrington Table = 29/30

**Words that best describe the college:** Sociable, small, sporty, intimate, relaxed, central,

**This college is for you if:** You are into sport

**The college's best features are:**
The sports prowess
The good location
The social life and college spirit

**It might not be for you if:** You want somewhere with good, cheap food. 'Teddy Hall' has some of the highest food prices

# St. Hilda's College

**Founded:** 1893

**Size:** Medium (412 undergraduates, 162 graduates)

**Academic ranking:** 2015 Norrington Table = 17/30

**Words that best describe the college:** Relaxed, friendly, spacious, inviting, fun, supportive

**This college is for you if:** You would love a bit of riverside charm

**The college's best features are:**
The excellent music facilities
The spacious gardens right on the river
The college allotment
Being very close to the University sports complex

**It might not be for you if:** You want the traditional experience – it lacks the classic Oxford trimmings (cloisters, quads, etc.)

# St. Hugh's College

**Founded:** 1886

**Size:** Large (435 undergraduates, 296 graduates)

**Academic ranking:** 2015 Norrington Table = 21/30

**Words that best describe the college:** Spacious, unpretentious, relaxed, friendly, calm

**This college is for you if:** You are looking for a bit of tranquillity

**The college's best features are:**
The large grounds
The well-stocked Art Deco library
The tranquil setting
The cheap bar

**It might not be for you if:** You want to live in the city centre – it's quite far out

# St. John's College

**Founded:** 1555

**Size:** Large (386 undergraduates, 225 graduates)

**Academic ranking:** 2015 Norrington Table = 7/30

**Words that best describe the college:** Friendly, rich, big, academic, diverse, high-achieving

**This college is for you if:** You're an academic high achiever

**The college's best features are:**
The central location, including on-site accommodation in all three years
The resources and facilities
The reputation

**It might not be for you if:** You want to meet people outside college – living on-site for three years can make it a bit insular

# St. Peter's College

**Founded:** 1929 (full college status granted in 1961)

**Size:** Medium (341 undergraduates, 166 graduates)

**Academic ranking:** 2015 Norrington Table = 23/30

**Words that best describe the college:** Open, friendly, grounded, central, caring, cosy

**This college is for you if:** You are looking for a modern, relaxed Oxford experience

**The college's best features are:**
The very central location
The good food, especially on special occasions
The friendly, unpretentious student body
The laid back, student-run college bar

**It might not be for you if:** You plan on doing lots of sports – it is quite far from the Iffley Road sports complex

# St. Stephen's House (PPH)

**Founded:** 1876

**Size:** Small (24 mature (21+) undergraduates, 48 graduates)

**Academic ranking:** 2015 PPH Norrington Table = 1/6

**Words that best describe the college:** vibrant, friendly, relaxed, sociable

**This college is for you if:** you are looking for a laid-back and welcoming community

**The college's best features are:**
The brilliant musical events and trips
The Christmas formal fall
The barbeque in the communal gardens

**It might not be for you if:** You want to be in the centre of Oxford – St Stephen's is a bit further out of town

# Trinity College

**Founded:** 1554

**Size:** Small (305 undergraduates, 136 graduates)

**Academic ranking:** 2015 Norrington Table = 19/30

**Words that best describe the college:** Spacious, inclusive, friendly, warm, beautiful, open

**This college is for you if:** You would like to have beautiful surroundings and a good community feel

**The college's best features are:**
The exquisite gardens
The central location
The high-quality food

**It might not be for you if:** You want to cook for yourself – there are limited self-catering options on the main college site

# University College

**Founded:** 1249

**Size:** Medium (372 undergraduates, 193 graduates)

**Academic ranking:** 2015 Norrington Table = 20/30

**Words that best describe the college:** Relaxed, fun, diverse, welcoming, cosy

**This college is for you if:** You are looking for a close-knit community

**The college's best features are:**
The relaxed atmosphere
The central location
The distinguished history

**It might not be for you if:** You want space – it's not got as much physical space as some of the other colleges

# Wadham College

**Founded:** 1610

**Size:** Large (453 undergraduates, 136 graduates)

**Academic ranking:** 2015 Norrington Table = 3/30

**Words that best describe the college:** Alternative, open, political, sociable, friendly, unpretentious, inclusive

**This college is for you if:** You are looking for a diverse and progressive community

**The college's best features are:**

The relaxed atmosphere

The fantastic annual college events

The politically involved student body

**It might not be for you if:** You've been dreaming of the Oxbridge traditions – there is no official formal hall

# Worcester College

**Founded:** 1714

**Size:** Large (429 undergraduates, 157 graduates)

**Academic ranking:** 2015 Norrington Table = 11/30

**Words that best describe the college:** Beautiful, friendly, relaxed, sociable, welcoming, sporty

**This college is for you if:** You are looking for a sociable community

**The college's best features are:**

The accommodation

The good quality food

The enormous, beautiful grounds, which include a lake

The sports and music facilities

**It might not be for you if:** You want to be next door to your lectures – the college is a bit away from both the humanities and science schools

# Wycliffe Hall (PPH)

**Founded:** 1877

**Size:** Small (77 undergraduates, 28 graduates)

**Academic ranking:** 2015 PPH Norrington Table = 1/6

**Words that best describe the college:** supportive, diverse, communal, welcoming

**This college is for you if:** You are interested in going into ministry

**The college's best features are:**

The impressive library

The proximity to the city centre and to the beautiful University Parks

The vibrant community

**It might not be for you if:** You're not very religious – Wycliffe Hall has a Christian focus

# OXFORD & CAMBRIDGE

## in numbers...

**200+**
OXFORD
**STUDENT
SOCIETIES**

**400+**
CAMBRIDGE
**STUDENT
SOCIETIES**

**79**
OXFORD
**BOAT RACE
WINS**

**82**
CAMBRIDGE
**BOAT RACE
WINS**

**6**
OXFORD
**APPLICANTS
PER PLACE
AVAILABLE**

**5**
CAMBRIDGE
**APPLICANTS
PER PLACE
AVAILABLE**

# 3 PERSONAL STATEMENT

A PRACTICAL GUIDE TO WRITING YOUR
PERSONAL STATEMENT

# A practical guide to writing your personal statement

The personal statement is a requirement of the application process. This document allows you to convey your interest in the courses you are applying for, as well as why you are a suitable applicant to study those same courses. For Oxbridge, the personal statement is used to demonstrate your academic capabilities and subject interests – extra-curricular activities are less relevant to Oxbridge Admissions Tutors. Those applying to Oxbridge are strong academically, and the personal statement is an opportunity to convey why you are uniquely suited to study the course.

In this chapter, we explain the purpose of the personal statement and how it influences your application. Following this, we provide a guide to planning, writing, and proofing your personal statement to help you begin the writing process.

When beginning to write your personal statement, you should consider the following questions:

### How important is the personal statement?

A strong application to Oxford or Cambridge, or indeed any top UK university, requires you to excel at every stage of the process – including your personal statement. However, when applying to Oxbridge, there are many points of contact between you and the university Admissions Tutors, meaning that a strong personal statement is not enough to secure you an offer. The statement can help you at interview as it demonstrates your interests to Admissions Tutors, which in many cases will form part of the interview discussion.

## How is the statement used at interview?

You should view everything you say in your personal statement as a potential springboard for discussion at interview: you may be asked to elaborate on something you have written about, be it a book, work experience, particular areas of academic interest, or an extended project.

We surveyed thousands of students who applied to Oxbridge in 2015 to understand the topics they discussed at interview. 64% were asked about their personal statement. Below they describe some questions they were faced with:

- ENGINEERING – "I was only asked one question relating to my personal statement about some work experience I had done"

- PHILOSOPHY, POLITICS AND ECONOMICS – "I was asked about an idea on my personal statement. What ideas would you use as a basis for your moral theory? (I said equality) Where do you derive the idea of equality from? Moral? Theological? Is equality an intrinsic or extrinsic good? (I answered, with reference to Plato's Republic, both)"

- MODERN & MEDIEVAL LANGUAGES – "A lot of discussion on cultural things I had mentioned in my statement"

- HISTORY – "Some broad and some specific questions about my personal statement... I wrote about gender history for example, and was asked very broadly, 'tell me about gender history'."

- ENGLISH – "The tutor primarily asked questions relating to my personal statement... for example, as I had noted that I had set various Blake poems to music, she asked how I thought poetry and song lyrics were similar or different from each other"

- GEOGRAPHY – "I see you've written that you enjoy plate tectonics in your personal statement... talk to me about it"

- HISTORY AND MODERN LANGUAGES – "You mentioned British Imperialism in your personal statement; do you think Spanish Imperialism differed?"

- ECONOMICS AND MANAGEMENT – "Why do you question the basis of economics – rationality and the behaviour of firms – in your personal statement?"

- MEDICINE – "We discussed action potentials, haemoglobin, cardiac output, respiratory systems, hormones, the liver, mental health...bear in mind nothing was asked out of the blue – it all led on from what I had said in my personal statement or stemmed from a graph"

Even if you're not asked about your personal statement at interview, the preparation that goes into researching and writing it will give you the knowledge and confidence to talk about and explore new ideas within your subject, which will only help to make your application stronger.

### How can I write my personal statement when I am applying for different subjects?

You can only submit one personal statement through UCAS, so it will be read by Admissions Tutors at all of the universities you apply to, even though you may be applying to slightly different courses at each. This can be a particular problem if you are applying for one of Oxbridge's unique courses – such as Human Sciences (Oxford) or Land Economy (Cambridge) – and yet still trying to make your personal statement fit with the courses you are applying for elsewhere.

The best advice here is to take a thematic approach. It is unlikely that the courses you are applying for have no similarities, so find a connection between them that interests you. Focus on a topic or theme that is relevant to all of your courses. If you are in this position, ensure that you include an interest area that demonstrates your knowledge and attraction to the unique course, supported by your independent research or reading. For example, if you are applying to Land Economy at Cambridge but Economics elsewhere, you should focus on an area of economics you are interested in, but consider making a connection to law or the environment to reflect your understanding of the Land Economy course. If you don't mention law, you should definitely be prepared to show your willingness to study the law modules when you go for your interview, and be prepared to answer law-style questions.

### Should I include extra-curricular activities in my personal statement?

Besides course differentiation, it is important to consider how much you include content which does not relate directly to the course you are applying for. Oxford and Cambridge are not particularly interested in whether you are a gifted athlete or play instruments to Grade 8 standard. They do, of course, recognise the scale of these accomplishments and they can indicate characteristics that will boost academic success. Ultimately, however, the Admissions Tutors reading your statement care about one thing: how much potential do you have as a student in the course you have applied for? Other universities are often more interested in students as 'well-rounded' people, where your extracurricular activities are of value, even if they don't directly relate to the subject. As such, it is a good idea to include these, but if you're applying to Oxbridge, you must strongly weight your statement towards subject-specific content. The guide later in this chapter how you can do this.

**Can I submit more than one personal statement?**

While you can only submit one personal statement through UCAS and the universities you apply to, there is one exception. Applicants to Durham have the option of submitting a 'substitute personal statement', which allows you to submit a separate personal statement to Durham directly following your UCAS application.

The Admissions Tutors at Durham will then disregard the personal statement submitted along with your UCAS application, and only read the submitted substitute statement. The substitute personal statement has exactly the same requirements as the original (i.e. 4000 characters) and must be submitted within 3 days of receiving Durham's email acknowledging your application.

**What is the SAQ?**

For Cambridge applicants, the Supplementary Application Questionnaire (SAQ) provides you with the opportunity to elaborate upon your motivations for applying for your chosen course. As part of the SAQ, you have the opportunity to write an additional statement, which Admissions Tutors consider in addition to your personal statement. This is your chance to mention anything you have not been able to include in your personal statement, including further reading or more detail on your extended essay or EPQ. If you are applying for a course that is unique to Cambridge (e.g. HSPS, Land Economy, Natural Sciences), use this section wisely – here is where you can mention your specific interests relating to the course at Cambridge, rather than to all of the courses you are applying to.

The SAQ must be completed by all UK and EU applicants by the deadline of 22nd October (one week after the 15th October UCAS deadline). The form is designed to gather further information about your application,

163

grades and subject motivation. One part of the SAQ, for example, requires you to submit your individual module marks in AS and/or A Levels. You'll receive an email with the details you need to complete the SAQ form once you have submitted your UCAS form. If you are submitting a COPA (see our International Applicants section) you will not need to fill in the entirety of the SAQ, but will need to complete your UCAS ID number and COPA Reference Number to submit.

## Writing your personal statement: a practical guide to turning a blank page into 4000 characters

This section explains how you can begin the process of writing your personal statement, using advice from the book 60 Successful Personal Statements For UCAS application, co-wrote by Guy Nobes, Head of Guidance for Marlborough College, and Gavin Nobes, Senior Lecturer at the University of East Anglia.

Staring at a blank page and no idea where to begin? Try the steps below...

### Step 1: Structure and planning

1) Take a piece of A4 paper, draw a line across it about 3 inches from the top. Do the same, 3 inches from the bottom.

2) Start with the bottom third. Bullet-point all the extracurricular achievements you can think of. Good at piano? Put it in. Climbed Mount Kilimanjaro? Put it in. Played Polonius in the school play? DofE gold medal? Sure, why not? You don't need to hold back yet – this is just the plan!

3) Now the top third. The opening sentence is often the hardest, but this is a good way to get past that. Take 15-20 minutes to think seriously about the real reason you're choosing your degree. Try not to feel embarrassed about clichés and trite statements yet. This is your plan, so you can make it sound sophisticated later. Really strong personal statements begin with a real sentiment, rather than something you think the Admissions Tutors will want to hear.

The question 'Why do you want to study x?' is almost guaranteed at the beginning of the interview. Don't disregard it, however, as a warm up question. This is probably the single most important element of your application. A good answer demonstrates a real understanding of what the academic discipline of your subject is all about, as well as your motivation for pursuing it.

4) Now the middle. Your middle section is your content. Which novel did you read from your syllabus that really highlighted for you what it is you love about teasing out nuances in literature? Which extra project did you do that best demonstrated what you love about problem solving? Which exhibition did you visit which highlighted to you what is fascinating to you about history? This has to be the academic section, and crucially it has to demonstrate work you've done outside of your A Level (or IB or equivalent) syllabus.

To help focus your thoughts and ideas and get your creative juices flowing, try jotting down some answers to the following questions on a separate sheet.

Remember, this is all about your subject so keep it relevant:

- What have you read and/or done to help further your understanding of this chosen course?

- How do you think your current academic subjects support your chosen course and will help you to excel at university?

- What part of your current studies has most inspired you and why?

- What books or articles have you recently read?

- What did you enjoy about them? What do you feel you learnt from reading them? (Think about what challenged you or whether anything surprised you). Did you agree or disagree with the author/s? Did the particular book/article make you want to learn more about a certain subject? If so, what exactly?

- What work experience have you done that is relevant to your subject?

Once you've got these, select the strongest points and bullet them in your middle section. It's a good idea to start making a list of all of the relevant things you've done or books you've read as soon as you've decided on your course, so that you ensure early on that you will have something interesting to write about.

## Step 2: Refining and writing

1) Bottom third. Reassess your extracurriculars. Could any of them have furthered your understanding in your subject? Select two or three stand-out achievements and find elements of them that would contribute to you being good in your subject. Perhaps you ran a marathon? Tenacity and mental stamina will be invaluable if you plan to pursue a career as a doctor etc.

2) Look at your bulleted content for the middle section again. What was it about these experiences that highlighted to you what is so special about your subject? Once you have considered this for each one, look at how you might draw thematic links between them in order to lead comfortably from one idea to the next.

3) It's a good general rule of thumb to approach your subject and what interests you about it from three different angles across three paragraphs. If you are reading Chemistry, what interests you about organic, inorganic and physical? Can you find an example of organic that links closely with inorganic? This would be a great transitional hinge to move from one point to the next.

## Step 3: Checking your tone

When you are planning and eventually writing this, it is vital to be aware of the following distinction: bad personal statements try to make a mini essay out of each subject brought up in order to try to demonstrate knowledge of the text or idea. There is not enough space to develop a complex idea – save that for your interview! When you write your personal statement, isolate a particular reason as to why you personally have engaged with your course, and then use specific examples to back this general idea up.

When writing, you can assume a certain level of knowledge in the reader: you wouldn't have to explain what the Duke of Edinburgh Award Scheme is, for example. This applies, more importantly, to books you are writing about. You don't need to describe what the books are about – rather what you think of them and what the argument means to you. Be specific and give examples to show that you have actually read the book and have formulated an opinion.

## How to use your personal statement

Your personal statement should mention texts that you feel comfortable with. Everyone will tell you to be sure to read those texts – you've seen in the examples above, where many students were asked to expand on themes and ideas in their statement – but also it's vital to think of those texts or areas of study as doorways to a network of further wider reading that you've looked into.

"I was not asked about any of the books on my personal statement. However, I was asked if I'd read any books other than the books on my personal statement which related to its theme (i.e. what other books have you read that could relate to the slums of Mumbai?)"

Sara, Geography applicant

This is why it is so key to have more material ready than is in your 4000 characters.

Check out the bibliographies or the journals and articles referenced in the book on your personal statement, and read some of those. This way, when you go into your interview, you have a wealth of material to draw from as a foundation so that you are not caught short when trying to answer a question using an example.

## Some inspiration

OPENER: ENGINEERING AT CAMBRIDGE

I find the built environment fascinating and perplexing, marvelling how engineers build such towering skyscrapers with complex designs that appear surprisingly simple. In reality it takes a vast amount of effort and skill to achieve the end result. This focused my desire to study engineering. I began to understand that it embraces not just bridges and buildings but water systems, nanotechnology and robotics. I like the idea of being involved in large-scale projects with tangible results and that each project could be different, each with a different set of problems to solve and requiring flexibility. Engineering is innovative and I am fascinated by the idea of developing new mechanisms that have never been attempted before and I am excited by the opportunity to apply the theory of physics and mathematics in a practical way.

## MAIN CONTENT PARAGRAPH 1: GEOGRAPHY AT CAMBRIDGE

I enjoyed the opportunity to pass on my knowledge of the formation of fold Mountains, U-shaped valleys and how the mountain has been shaped by human influences, such as tourism when I went walking with my brother in Wales. I read 'New Internationalist' and 'Geography Review', whose articles on climate change, multiculturalism, and globalisation have since complemented and expanded my academic studies of human geography. I enjoyed 'Development, Bottom Up or Top Down?', as this explored the nature and limitations of different development schemes, and 'Climate Change and Crops', which advanced my knowledge of the impact of climate change, and how new crops could lead to further environmental damage.

## MAIN CONTENT PARAGRAPH 2: CLASSICS AT OXFORD

The critical examination of sources within History has augmented my analytical and evaluation skills, whilst the study of English has enhanced my ability to express ideas in a clear, coherent way. My initial love for language was triggered by French lessons and through this, I have observed the value of reading literature in its original language and learnt to appreciate the subtleties which can so often be lost in translation. As my school does not offer Classical languages, I decided to pursue them myself by attending JACT summer schools with the aim that I would be able to one day read the original works in Latin and Greek.

## MAIN CONTENT PARAGRAPH 3: LAW AT OXFORD

Undertaking work experience at Lincoln House Chambers allowed me to engage with a case and witness criminal proceedings at Manchester Magistrates' Court. A placement at the South Manchester Law Centre, where I actively assisted with an immigration case and attended tribunals, raised my awareness of the necessity of legal funding and pro bono work to attempt to make the law accessible for everyone. My appreciation for politics and international relations can also be seen through my involvement with Model United Nations, where I consistently received awards for debating and practised forming and justifying arguments – a skill which I believe stems from a history of dramatic arts with my local theatre company and LAMDA examinations.

## THE ENDING: MEDICINE AT CAMBRIDGE

Although aware of its negative aspects and limitations, I still believe medicine is the ideal career for me. Becoming a doctor would allow me to help others in a job combining my strong interest in science, enjoyment of communicating with others, and working within a team as well as diverse future opportunities such as teaching and research. As a keen, diligent, and determined individual capable of working well under pressure, I feel I will be prepared for the demands of the course and the career.

## Ten golden rules for writing your personal statement

1. Research the courses you are applying for thoroughly, to show enthusiasm for and understanding of the subject
2. Be specific and display precise knowledge – never be vague
3. Be honest – only include what you know and are confident about discussing
4. Try to sound interesting and interested, but don't overdo it, gush or come across as arrogant
5. Express your information and ideas clearly
6. Don't be negative – try to see any failures as 'learning experiences'
7. Organise your material clearly and logically
8. Don't state the obvious or repeat yourself
9. Consider spelling, apostrophes, and grammar (mistakes are irritating and don't reflect well on you!)
10. Don't misuse words in an attempt to look clever – your personal statement needs to be clear as well as reflecting the way you communicate

## The platinum rule: show, don't tell

Rather than just claiming to be enthusiastic or informed about your subject, demonstrate your interest and understanding by describing:

- The background to your interest in the subject
- Ways in which you are currently following up this enthusiasm
- What exactly you know about the subject

Remember, while the personal statement can take a good deal of your time, do keep reminding yourself that this is the chance to write about a very interesting subject that no one else will be writing about: you!

# 4 ADMISSIONS TESTS

HOW TO PREPARE FOR YOUR ADMISSIONS TEST
WITH EXAMPLE QUESTIONS FOR YOU TO TRY

# How to prepare for your Admissions Test with example questions for you to try

Admissions Tests are required for many Oxbridge applicants as part of the admissions process. In this chapter, we outline which courses require which tests, the type of format each test takes, and sample questions.

The Admissions Tests are intentionally different from exams students encounter in their school career. By having a format which will be unfamiliar to all applicants, the universities can use this as a more objective measure of an applicant's aptitude for further study. The tests are there to see if students can think critically, creatively, and logically outside of what they are taught at school.

The most important part of preparing for Admissions Tests is firstly knowing that preparation really is possible and to be encouraged. You are highly likely to perform better if you understand what the test requires of you before you sit it. Although most Admissions Tests do not require any subject-specific knowledge outside of your A Levels, that is not to say that extra preparation can't be done.

Rather than developing subject-specific knowledge, you can develop skills which will aid you in the test by practising past papers. By practising past papers, you improve your ability to apply your knowledge and skills within the time limit. 44% of students we surveyed in 2016 found that the hardest thing about the test was the time pressure, so familiarising yourself with the test format can help you avoid this issue.

Through practising questions, you will also identify which skills you need to work on. Should you practise problem solving or analysing language? Identifying arguments in the newspaper or mental mathematics?

In this chapter, we detail a number of the Admissions Tests, including advice from our Oxbridge-graduate tutors on the preparation that can really make a difference when approaching Admissions Tests. Always check the individual test and university websites for all the latest updates, including dates, timings, deadlines, marking, and structure of the tests. More resources can also be found on the Admissions Testing Service website or through Oxbridge Applications.

## Types of Admissions Tests

To see which Admissions Test your course requires (if any), check the table below:

| | |
|---|---|
| **BioMedical Admissions Test (BMAT)** | Oxford Medicine and Biomedical Sciences, Cambridge Medicine and Veterinary Medicine (also used by Imperial, Royal Veterinary College, UCL, LKC, Brighton and Sussex and Leeds) |
| **Cambridge at–interview assessments** | Archaeology, Architecture, Classics, Computer Science, Education, History of Art, Law, Linguistics, Modern and Medieval Languages and joint schools, Philosophy |
| **Cambridge pre–interview assessments** | Anglo Saxon Norse & Celtic (ASNAC), Asian and Middle Eastern Studies (AMES), Economics, Engineering, English, Geography, History and joint schools, Human, Social, and Political Sciences (HSPS), Natural Sciences, Psychological and Behavioural Sciences (PBS), Theology |
| **Classics Admissions Test (CAT)** | Oxford Classics and joint schools |
| **Cambridge Law Test (CLT)** | Cambridge Law |
| **English Literature Admissions Test (ELAT)** | Cambridge English, Oxford English and joint schools |
| **History Aptitude Test (HAT)** | Oxford History and joint schools |

| National Admissions Test for Law (LNAT) | Oxford Law (also used by Birmingham, Bristol, Durham, Glasgow, King's, Nottingham, SOAS and UCL) |
|---|---|
| Mathematics Admissions Test (MAT) | Oxford Mathematics, Computer Science and joint schools (also used by Imperial) |
| Modern Languages Admissions Test (MLAT) | Oxford Modern Languages, Linguistics and joint schools |
| Oriental Languages Aptitude Test (OLAT) | Oxford certain Oriental languages |
| Physics Aptitude Test (PAT) | Oxford Engineering, Materials Science and Physics |
| Philosophy Test | Oxford Philosophy and Theology joint course |
| Sixth Term Examination Paper (STEP) | Cambridge Mathematics. Some colleges may use STEP for Computer Sciences, Economics, Engineering and Natural Sciences (also used by Warwick) |
| Thinking Skills Assessment Cambridge (TSA) | Cambridge Land Economy |
| Thinking Skills Assessment Oxford (TSA) | Oxford Economics and Management (E&M), Chemistry*, Experimental Psychology, Geography, Philosophy, Politics and Economics (PPE), Philosophy, Psychology and Linguistics (PPL) |

* Chemistry applicants take the TSA Chemistry, which is Section 1 of the TSA Oxford only

In the following sections, we will examine each test in more detail. Firstly, we will discuss the tests used by both universities.

# Tests used by both universities (BMAT, ELAT, TSA)

## The Biomedical Admissions Test (BMAT)

The BMAT is a compulsory test for Medicine at Oxford and Cambridge, Biomedical Sciences at Oxford, and Veterinary Sciences at Cambridge. It is also used for admissions for Medicine, Biomedical Sciences, Veterinary Sciences and Dentistry courses at Brighton and Sussex, Imperial, Lancaster, Leeds, Lee Kong Chian School of Medicine (Singapore), and UCL.

To be successful in all three sections of the test, you need to understand both the skills examined and the type of question you can expect to encounter. Test yourself with the examples below:

SECTION 1: APTITUDE AND SKILLS (marked out of 9) – 35 multiple choice questions with four possible answers testing numeracy, verbal reasoning, problem-solving, and data analysis. You'll need to be able to do quick mental mathematics, interpret graphs and diagrams, and think through a spatial, numerical or verbal reasoning problem logically. It's vital that you are able to work quickly and accurately, and that you have a speedy way of checking your answers as you go along. Bear in mind that there is no negative marking (you won't be marked down for getting a question wrong) so if you're really stuck, it's worth making an educated guess – you have a 25% chance of getting it right after all.

EXAMPLE QUESTION 1

'Increases in blood pressure associated with old age are common in developed countries, but are rare in underdeveloped countries where people of all ages remain physically active even into the later stages of life. In younger generations, obesity and diabetes are more common in developed countries, where physical activity is limited due to a largely sedentary lifestyle.'

Which one of the following can be drawn as a conclusion from the passage above?

**a.** Further gains in longevity in developed countries require a change in lifestyle.

**b.** People who are not physically active will suffer from obesity and diabetes.

**c.** Lifelong exercise is associated with maintaining good health.

**d.** A lack of exercise affects young people more than old people.

SECTION 2: SCIENTIFIC KNOWLEDGE AND APPLICATION (marked out of 9) – 27 multiple choice questions with five possible answers testing applied science and mathematics knowledge. This section will ask you to use the skills that have been tested in Section 1, and a level of scientific knowledge is required as well – from knowing how dominant and recessive genes work, to how the pH of blood changes according to whether it's arterial or venous. The BMAT isn't testing sophisticated knowledge, rather your ability to apply what you've learnt to work your way through a problem logically.

EXAMPLE QUESTION 2

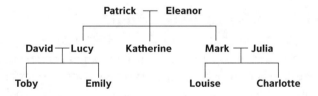

Patrick carries a recessive allele on his X chromosome. Which other members of his family could have inherited this allele?

**a.** David, Lucy, Katherine, Mark

**b.** David, Lucy, Katherine, Julia

**c.** Lucy, Katherine, Mark, Toby

**d.** Katherine, Lucy, Toby, Emily

**e.** Katherine, Toby, Emily, Louise

SECTION 3: WRITING TASK (marked on content, 1-5, and quality of written English, A-E) – a choice of four questions testing your ability to structure a logical argument and support your arguments with evidence. The essay questions are broad and do not require specific factual information. However, your answers should demonstrate your scientific knowledge: an average answer to an ethical question might address the moral and economic issues at stake, whereas a good answer would discuss specific medical cases and show a detailed scientific knowledge and understanding, supported by clear and pertinent examples. Our Medicine graduates would also advise that you refer back to the question to ensure you don't stray from the topic. Furthermore, focus on the quality, not quantity of your writing: you will only be marked up to a certain word count – so make sure that you don't lose marks by bringing your conclusion in too late!

EXAMPLE QUESTION 3

`Our genes evolved for a Stone Age lifestyle. Therefore, in order to be healthy, we should adopt Stone Age habits.´ Discuss.

For the answers to all the above questions, as well as advice on how to approach them, visit www.oxbridgeapplications.com.

## English Literature Aptitude Test (ELAT)

You'll need to sit the ELAT if you are applying for English Language and Literature and English and Joint Schools at Oxford or English Literature at Cambridge. You will be given six unseen literary texts – prose, drama and poetry, either full texts or extracts – of which you must choose two or three to compare and contrast in any way you find interesting.

CHOOSING YOUR TEXTS

It's wise to dedicate some time to choosing which texts you want to compare and contrast – this will after all dictate your essay content and the direction you take. Don't be afraid to choose two texts to compare rather than three. You won't lose marks for looking at fewer texts, the examiners are more concerned with the development and quality of your argument. Usually you will be told a common theme between the different texts (e.g. death, or nature), but when you are choosing which ones to write about, try and identify something interesting about the ways in which the different texts approach or portray this theme, and the different (or similar) effects this has. Think about different forms, periods and styles; consider how you could marry this with your analysis of the themes within your essay.

PLANNING YOUR ESSAY

You have 90 minutes in total and it's worth using 15-20 minutes to plan your essay. Consider how you are going to structure the essay, what each paragraph will address, and which aspects of the text you are going to emphasie. You should also consider how you're going to carry out your comparison. Will you compare the two texts alongside each other, or focus on one text and draw your comparisons from a second (and possibly third) text? Make sure your essay isn't just pointing out literary techniques – you should always be explaining and relating how particular sounds and structures contribute to the text's overall treatment of the theme. Finally, be sure to plan a strong conclusion – the Admissions Tutors are looking to see how you structure arguments when writing a critical analysis.

WRITING YOUR ESSAY

Once you've chosen your texts and planned your essay structure, you will begin writing your essay in earnest. Try to keep your writing clear and focused – don't be tempted to pepper your essay with long words for the sake of it. Clarity of communication is vital; it's what the Admissions Tutors are looking for. You should quote from the texts that you are examining. Keep the quotations short and quote the line number as a reference. Never leave a quote standing on its own: quotations should build your argument, not just illustrate it, so you should always comment on what you have quoted. Finally, make sure you give yourself 5-10 minutes at the end of the test to read over your essay and check for any spelling, grammar or punctuation mistakes.

To excel in the ELAT you need to focus on close critical analysis, while keeping a firm hand on the argument you decide to explore. Ensure you understand the purpose of the test and then try our example question below.

## EXAMPLE QUESTION 1

### Compare and contrast these two extracts

'Tell me more about Mr Dorian Gray. How often do you see him?'

'Every day. I couldn't be happy if I didn't see him every day. He is absolutely necessary to me.'

'How extraordinary! I thought you would never care for anything but your art.'

'He is all my art to me now,' said the painter gravely. 'I sometimes think, Harry, that there are only two eras of any importance in the world's history. The first is the appearance of a new medium for art, and the second is the appearance of a new personality for art also. What the invention of oil-painting was to the Venetians, the face of Antinous was to late Greek sculpture, and the face of Dorian Gray will someday be to me.'

Extract from The Picture of Dorian Gray, Oscar Wilde (1891)

My mistress' eyes are nothing like the sun;
Coral is far more red than her lips' red;
If snow be white, why then her breasts are dun;
If hairs be wires, black wires grow on her head.
I have seen roses damask, red and white,
But no such roses see I in her cheeks;
And in some perfumes is there more delight
Than in the breath that from my mistress reeks.
I love to hear her speak, yet well I know
That music hath a far more pleasing sound;
I grant I never saw a goddess go;
My mistress, when she walks, treads on the ground:
And yet, by heaven, I think my love as rare
As any she belied with false compare.

'Sonnet 130', William Shakespeare (1609)

For our English graduate's approach to the above texts, visit www.oxbridgeapplications.com. We've also got up-to-date information on test dates and deadlines and information on how your ELAT score will be used in your application.

# Thinking Skills Assessment (TSA)

Both Cambridge and Oxford use versions of the Thinking Skills Assessment (TSA) as part of their admissions process.

The TSA Cambridge consists of 50 multiple choice questions which must be completed in 90 minutes – 25 problem solving questions and 25 critical thinking questions. The test is taken at interview if you are applying for Land Economy. There are also smaller thinking skills sections in the pre-interview assessments for Geography and Psychological and Behavioural Sciences (PBS).

The TSA Oxford consists of 50 multiple choice questions, 25 problem solving questions and 25 critical thinking questions, which must be completed in 90 minutes. You then have 30 minutes to answer one essay question from a choice of four. You will be required to sit the TSA Oxford if you are applying for Economics and Management, Experimental Psychology, Geography, Human Sciences, PPL (any combination) or PPE. If you are applying for Chemistry, you will need to sit the multiple choice section only, known as the TSA Chemistry.

## PROBLEM SOLVING QUESTIONS

These multiple choice questions often boil down to a mathematical equation, either presented in a simple or more complex format. You need to be able to identify the key elements of the equation in order to attempt the answer and have the mental mathematics knowledge and speed to be able to work quickly through the problem. Make sure you have revised percentages, fractions, and key formulae (e.g. speed) before you take the test.

## EXAMPLE QUESTION 1

Lauren has gone to the sweet shop to buy sour fizzballs for her friends. She knows that yesterday they were 5p each and has brought enough money to buy a certain number to share amongst her friends. When she arrives at the sweet shop there is a special offer on sour fizzballs: if you buy 10 or more the price of all fizzballs is reduced by 1p each. She finds that she can now buy 3 more than she had initially planned to, spending the exact amount she brought.

How many can she buy today?

**a.** 12

**b.** 15

**c.** 10

**d.** 17

**e.** 20

## EXAMPLE QUESTION 2

It is currently 10:00 in Existan and 14:00 in Fediland. James posted a parcel to Sam from Existan at 16:00 yesterday and it arrived with Sam in Fediland at 07:30 today. How long did the parcel take to be delivered from the moment James posted it to the moment it arrived with Sam?

**a.** 9 hours 30 minutes

**b.** 11 hours

**c.** 11 hours 30 minutes

**d.** 10 hours 30 minutes

**e.** 12 hours 30 minutes

## EXAMPLE QUESTION 3

Lucy is an author. She receives a royalty fee of 40% of profits from each of her books that is sold by Aquarocks. In 2011, Aquarocks sold 1,400 of her books, with a total revenue of £56,000 and a profit of half this sum. In 2012, it is expected that 20% more books will be sold and Lucy has negotiated a new royalty fee of 50% of the profit, plus £5 for each extra book sold compared to 2011.

If the expectations turn out to be true, and, as in 2011, profit is half of revenue, how much money will Lucy receive in 2011 if the price of the books stays the same?

**a.** £16,800

**b.** £25,200

**c.** £35, 000

**d.** £68,600

**e.** £18,200

CRITICAL THINKING QUESTIONS

In these multiple choice questions, you may be asked to identify or draw a conclusion from a passage, identify an assumption, identify an argument with the same structure or principle as the passage or identify one key piece of information that will weaken or strengthen the argument in the passage. You should try to break down the passage so that you can identify what the argument is and an example that could strengthen the argument. Think carefully about the wording being used – it can be very easy to skim over a word (especially when you're under time pressure) and miss a fundamental flaw in the argument.

EXAMPLE QUESTION 4

Person A: 'I would never go white water rafting since it essentially involves being carried along a dangerous current in a rubber dinghy.'

Person B: 'But the guides are well trained and there is very little risk of getting hurt.'

Person A: 'But it could still go wrong and the consequences could be disastrous.'

Person B: 'Lots of people go white water rafting when they are on holiday and there are very few accidents in spite of this.'

Which of the following conclusions can be reliably drawn from the above argument?

**a.** The white water rafting guides prevent any accidents from occurring.

**b.** White water rafting accidents are always fatal when they happen.

**c.** It is safer to white water raft in the UK than elsewhere in the world.

**d.** Many white water rafting accidents are not reported in the press.

**e.** White water rafting seems to be a safe hobby.

## ESSAY QUESTIONS

Only the TSA Oxford contains essay questions. These questions are usually quite broad, so think carefully about what the most important points are, which you would like to include in your answer, and how they link together. If you're making an argument for one point of view, ensure you give a reasoned explanation and consider alternative arguments. Ensure this plan is clear in your introduction; it shows that you're developing an essay structure, rather than simply racing through the arguments. If the question asks you to form an opinion, you should always come to a conclusion in order to show your thoughts are fully developed.

## EXAMPLE QUESTION 5

Should fines be based on the individual's income?

For the answers to all the above questions visit www.oxbridgeapplications.com. We've also got up-to-date information on test dates and deadlines and information on how your TSA Oxford score will be used in your application. You can also try your hand at the questions in the LNAT and TSA Cambridge section for further practice.

# Cambridge Admissions Tests

Unlike Oxford, Cambridge also have at-interview assessments in addition to the more standard pre-interview assessments. In this section, we will discuss which tests are sat when, and what each test involves.

## Cambridge at-interview assessments (introduced 2016)

These assessments are new tests introduced by Cambridge in 2016 to standardise the admissions process. They will be sat at the interview. The subjects requiring the at-interview tests (not including the Thinking Skills Assessment, discussed earlier in the chapter) are:

| Subject | Test Format |
| --- | --- |
| Archaeology | 1 hour critical response to text(s) |
| Architecture | 30 minutes short essay response to a question, 30 minutes graphical and spatial ability test |
| Classics (3 year) | 1 hour translation (see page 196 for Oxford Classics Admissions Test for preparation ideas) |
| Classics (4 year) | 1 hour oral language aptitude assessment (see page 196 for Oxford Classics Language Aptitude Test for preparation ideas) |
| Computer Science | 100 minutes maths assessment, divided into two sections (second section worth more marks) |
| Education | 15 minutes reading/listening/watching stimulus, 45 minutes critical response |
| History of Art | 1 hour written response to two pairs of images of works of art |
| Law* | 1 hour written response to a problem, comprehension or essay question |
| Linguistics | 20 minutes structured analysis of language data, 20 minutes quantitative data analysis, 20 minutes short essay |
| Modern and Medieval Languages/History and Modern Languages | 40 minutes response to text in chosen modern language, 20 minutes response to same text in English |
| Philosophy | 20 minutes logic problems multiple choice, 40 minutes essay |

* The Cambridge Law test existed pre-2016 which means there is a greater understanding of how the test works. This test is described in full in this section.

## Cambridge pre-interview assessments (introduced 2016)

The Cambridge pre-interview assessments are all 2 hours long, and split into two main parts, one of which is multiple choice, and one of which involves more complex problem solving or a written response. Use the table below to see which type of question you can expect to see in your Admissions Test (with the exception of the ELAT and BMAT, discussed earlier in the chapter). In this section, we will also discuss how you can approach each type of question.

| Subject | Comprehension multiple choice | Critical Response | Essay | Maths/ Science multiple questions | Maths/ Science open questions | Thinking Skills multiple choice |
|---|---|---|---|---|---|---|
| Anglo-Saxon, Norse and Celtic | ✓ | ✓ | | | | |
| Asian and Middle Eastern Studies | ✓ | ✓ | | | | |
| Economics | | ✓ | | ✓ | | |
| Engineering* | | | | ✓ | | |
| Geography | ✓ | ✓ | | | | ✓ |
| History/History and Modern Languages/ History and Politics | ✓ | ✓ | | | | |
| HSPS | ✓ | | ✓ | | | |
| Natural Sciences | | | | ✓ | ✓ | |
| PBS | ✓ | ✓ | | ✓ | | ✓ |

* The Engineering test includes maths/science structured multiple choice questions, in addition to the normal maths/science multiple choice questions.

# How to approach the different questions in the Cambridge Admissions Tests

## The Cambridge Law Test (CLT)

### Law

The Cambridge Law Test is a one-hour Admissions Test required by most colleges at the University of Cambridge for the undergraduate Law course. It is an essay-based exam consisting of three questions, of which you will have to answer one.

It was introduced by Cambridge to replace the LNAT (National Admissions Test for Law), which you are required to sit when applying for many other undergraduate Law courses. It is a paper-based test and you will answer one question within the hour. The questions are selected by the individual colleges from a question bank and come in three types: problem, comprehension or essay. Most colleges will use only one of the three types, so it is wise to check the individual college website in case this information is shared prior to the interview period.

There is no factual preparation necessary for the CLT since no legal knowledge is required. The test is designed to test your logic, reason, and ability to transfer this into writing. That being said, an awareness of current events is likely to be an asset, as these can be used as examples in answers. This is also true for your interview. Make sure that you keep up-to-date with newspapers and endeavour to read more in-depth legal analysis where possible.

Additionally, learning to identify exactly what each question is asking (i.e. determining what the implications of each question are) is crucial; it will help demonstrate that you have considered each possible argument or viewpoint.

Although you only have one hour, it is important that you plan your essay first and we advise splitting your time between planning for 15 minutes and writing for 45 minutes. You can prepare by writing essay plans to time to ensure you are adept at this process. In the test, also make sure you also give yourself time to check through your answer so you can correct any spelling or grammar mistakes and bridge any logical gaps.

## QUESTION TYPE 1: PROBLEM

- You will be given a statement of law which you will have to apply to different situations
- This question assesses your ability to understand and apply the statement and explain your reasoning

## EXAMPLE QUESTION 1

'Frustration occurs whenever the law recognises that without default of either party a contractual obligation has become incapable of being performed because the circumstances in which performance is called for would render it radically different from that which was undertaken by the contract'. – Davis Contractors v Fareham

When a contract is frustrated, it is brought to an end with neither party being held blameworthy for not performing their side of the contract.

A is a jockey and B is the owner of 'Flash', a prizewinning racehorse. B has contracted A to ride Flash in an upcoming race. Has frustration occurred in any of the following situations?

**a.** The day before the race, A is involved in a car crash and breaks both his legs, leaving him unable to race.

**b.** The race rules are changed the week before the race to say that only novice racehorses may run.

**c.** A gets a phone call that a friend has been taken into hospital while on holiday in France, and flies out to see them. A's flight back that night is cancelled and he is unable to get back in time for the race.

## QUESTION TYPE 2: COMPREHENSION

- You will be given a passage of text which you will have to summarise and on which you will answer a series of questions
- This question assesses your ability to understand the text and present balanced, structured arguments

Visit www.oxbridgeapplications.com for a practice comprehension question and advice on approaching a question like this.

## QUESTION TYPE 3: ESSAY

- You will be given a statement of opinion which you will have to discuss
- This question assesses your ability to give opinions in a coherent, structured and balanced way

## EXAMPLE QUESTION 3

"To question the validity of the trial process is to weaken the one protective safeguard that stands between us and arbitrary state power".

How far do you agree with the statement? Give reasons for your answer.

For the answers to all the above questions, as well as advice on how to approach them, visit www.oxbridgeapplications.com

## Comprehension Multiple Choice

**Anglo-Saxon, Norse and Celtic, Asian and Middle Eastern Studies, History and joint schools, and Human, Social, and Political Sciences.**

This section is split into four tasks, each of which consists of one or more text excerpts and a set of four-option multiple choice questions. This section is not subject-specific; texts included will be on a variety of topics and from a range of sources. Tasks 1, 2 and 3 of this section are also used for Geography and Psychological and Behavioural Sciences Admissions Tests.

## TASK 1: UNDERSTANDING SHORT TEXTS

Two short (max 200 words) abstracts or reviews on a common topic. This task is assessing your ability to identify features of a text, and compare and contrast them with features of another. The questions have an emphasis on identification of opinion, attitude, purpose, and inferred meaning, rather than the retrieval of facts given to you directly in the text.

## TASK 2: MULTIPLE MATCHING

Four short (max 200 words) extracts, either from the same source, or on the same theme by four different writers. In this task you need to be able to distinguish similar ideas from one another, identifying where a particular idea is expressed. To do well in this task, you will need to have the ability to scan texts to locate arguments, but also to be able to read closely and understand the nuances of these arguments.

## TASK 3: UNDERSTANDING EXTENDED TEXT

One extended text (max 1000 words). You will be assessed on your understanding of the argument and supported claims of a longer academic texts, as well as your ability to recognise references to previous work and ideas of a particular field.

## TASK 4: UNDERSTANDING EXTENDED TEXT

This task is the same as Task 3, except that the text given may be longer (max 1,200 words), testing again your ability to read closely and understand a longer piece of academic writing.

The best way to prepare for this type of test is to spend time reading academic articles and making sure you have fully understood their argument and purpose. Texts could include newspapers, general interest magazines (the Economist, or History Today would be good places to start), book reviews, abstracts for research papers or journal articles, and professional websites. The more you practice close reading, the more efficiently and successfully you will be able to pick out the arguments in the exam.

## Critical Response

**Anglo-Saxon, Norse and Celtic, Archaeology, Asian and Middle Eastern Studies, Education, History, History of Art, Geography, Modern Languages, Psychological and Behavioural Sciences**

There is no specific-subject knowledge required, but the stimulus given will be relevant to the course you are applying for, apart from Asian and Middle Eastern Studies which will provide more general texts. Although this section is subject-specific, and therefore the questions will vary depending on the subject, the skills being assessed in this section are similar across the board.

*To Texts*
**Anglo-Saxon, Norse and Celtic, Archaeology, Asian and Middle Eastern Studies, Economics, History** (Linguistics may also use a text for the final short essay question, but this could also be a study)

For all of these subjects, an ability to write and argue well is an essential skill to be successful. This section is an opportunity to show off your ability to write clearly and precisely, and produce coherent arguments in response to both the text (or two texts for History and possibly Archaeology) and the question. You will need to show that you can think analytically and make connections between sources and ideas. As you are under time pressure, it is important that you address the question you are given directly and include relevant information. For Anglo-Saxon, Norse and Celtic, Economics, and History, you will need to be able to bring in your awareness of the broader context of the field, and for Asian and Middle Eastern Studies they will also be looking for your ability to engage with creative thinking.

For the Modern Languages assessment, you will first be asked to respond to the text in your chosen foreign language. This question will usually expect you to summarise the argument of what you have read, followed by giving your own opinion. The idea of this section is to test how well you can express yourself in the foreign language alongside your comprehension skills, so where possible, use this opportunity to show off your vocabulary. Be wary of just translating the argument from English, as this is not demonstrating your ability to use language creatively. For the second part of the Modern Languages assessment, you will be asked to respond in English, and assessors are looking for good written and communication skills as well as an understanding of the text.

### To a 'Stimulus'
### Education

To study Education, the ability to engage with the arguments of others is essential, and its consistently topical nature means that these arguments may not be presented in a written form. The stimulus given in the assessment could be a text, but could also be a video or audio clip. The approach you take should be the same; whichever stimulus you receive, the test is an opportunity to show your engagement with the source in front of you and your critical discussion of it, understanding the purpose of the source, but also being able to give a personal insight. You need to ensure that your answer presents a coherent argument, and they will also be looking for evidence that you understand the social and political contexts of educational practices. You will be given 15 minutes to read/watch/listen before you respond, and you should be sure to use this time to make notes, especially if the stimulus is not written.

### To Graphical Data
### Geography

Geography students will regularly have to analyse and interpret graphical data, as well as to write succinctly. This section of the Geography Admissions Test gives you the chance to demonstrate both your ability to describe and explain a graphical stimulus (a graph or a map) clearly, but also to critique it and consider the wider implications it presents. The broad nature of this task allows you to include anything that you may find interesting about the stimulus. However, be sure that whatever ideas you present are well reasoned. You will be given specific points for consideration which should help you direct your approach.

### To Images
### History of Art

A crucial skill for History of Art students is the ability to understand images. You will be given 5 pairs of images of works of art, and you will be asked to comment on two pairs. This is a chance to demonstrate your visual acumen. You will be expected to show both general and detailed observation of the works, as well as analytical skills, both internally within the works, and through reference to any external factors that occur to you. Don't worry if you've never studied History of Art before, as they will look at your test in this context, but if you have, and you think of something relevant that you've studied, use it to deepen your analysis. However, be wary of including external references for the sake of it, as this will undermine your answer. Do not underestimate the value of your own ideas – tutors will also be assessing your comparison of the works, and any ideas that the juxtaposition may direct you towards.

### To a Study

**PBS** (Linguistics may also use a study for the final short essay question, but this could also be a text)

A large part of the PBS course will include critiquing and designing psychological studies. This section is a chance for you to demonstrate your understanding of the challenges that psychologists may face when designing studies, and what factors need to be considered at each stage. You will need to show your ability to think analytically and develop a coherent argument, as well as your ability to identify potential problems and suggesting effective research solutions. Please note, you may be asked to design a survey rather than critique an existing one, but the assessors will expect you to demonstrate the same abilities.

## Essay

### Human, Social, and Political Sciences, Philosophy, Architecture, PBS

The ability to argue well is an essential skill for HSPS and Philosophy applicants. The second parts of these assessments are designed to allow you to demonstrate this ability by answering one question from a choice of 12-15 (HSPS) or 2 (Philosophy). For HSPS, all questions will fall broadly within the social sciences subjects that make up the course – Social Anthropology, Sociology, Politics, and International Relations. The questions given may be approached from a number of angles, allowing you to use your background and interests. For Philosophy, the questions will present a problem of philosophical significance and ask you to discuss it. In both, you will need to show your ability to develop a logical, coherent and persuasive argument, using evidence to support your claims. You will also be assessed on your use of English and clarity and quality of expression, so make sure you take the time to read over your essay.

## Approaching written questions

With all written question styles, your essay writing skills are being assessed alongside your analytical skills, so it is important to ensure your answer is well written:

READ THE QUESTION(S) AND THE TEXTS THOROUGHLY
For each of these tests, part of the assessment criteria will be your ability to respond to the question directly and relevantly. It's worth taking 5-10 minutes to read the text/graph/study closely, make sure you understand it, and annotate it with the question in mind. For HSPS, you will need to take some time to read all of the questions and choose the one you think you can answer best.

PLAN YOUR ANSWER
Although it may seem like you are wasting precious time, it will be much easier to produce a well-written and structured essay if you have taken the time to plan before you begin. It's a good idea to spend 5-10 minutes bullet-pointing the ideas you want to use, and working out the order in which your ideas will form the best argument.

CHECK YOUR ANSWER
Remember that your ability to write well is being assessed, and small grammatical or spelling mistakes or awkward expressions can really undermine the reader's impression of your essay. Try and leave 5 minutes spare at the end to read through your answer and rectify any mistakes, or improve wording where necessary.

## Graphical and Spatial Awareness

### Architecture

It is essential for Architecture students to be able to assess their environment and think creatively about it. In this section of the Architecture assessment, you will be asked to observe and interpret an indoor or outdoor setting through drawing. This is a chance to demonstrate your visual and spatial thinking and your ability to record your spatial impressions and interpret your environment. You will need to prove you have an awareness of your environment, so you should spend time leading up to the test practicing drawing from life and interpreting what's around you. You don't need to worry about learning technical skills – it is much more about demonstrating your aptitude at the skills you will need for the course.

## Maths/Science Multiple Choice

### Economics, Engineering, Natural Sciences, PBS

These questions are designed to test your ability to use and apply your mathematical and scientific knowledge. The presumed knowledge for each test and each section can be found on the Cambridge admissions website. It's important to remember that the test is designed to be challenging, in order to help tutors differentiate effectively between applicants who they already know are very able, and may all be achieving the highest possible grades in their exams. You are not allowed a calculator in these sections.

For the multiple choice sections, the main thing to keep in mind is timing. For example, those applying for Natural Sciences will need to respond to 54 questions in 80 minutes, giving you around a minute and a half per question. If you are stuck on a question and it's taking too long, it's best to move on and come back to it at the end. If, at this stage, you've run out of time or you still have no idea, it's worth making an educated guess – there is no negative marking so you can only gain marks by doing this.

The best form of preparation for these questions is to look over your A Level syllabus and practice working out problems, which will help you improve your speed. There are some specimen questions on the Cambridge website to give you an idea of what to expect.

## Maths / Science Open Questions / Structured Multiple Choice

### Engineering, Natural Sciences, Computer Science

These questions aim to test your mathematical and scientific ability in longer, more difficult problems. You may need to apply your knowledge in an unfamiliar context, so it's a good idea to make sure you are really solid on the content (which can be found on the Cambridge website) as this will make you feel more confident when applying it in new situations. You are allowed to have a calculator in these sections.

Showing your workings is essential to be successful in these sections of the assessments. Some departments will not give you the mark if you haven't demonstrated your working on the paper. It's an easy way to lose marks, so be sure to write out every calculation, even if you do it on your calculator.

Although some of the questions may be connected to other questions, you may be able to solve later parts of a question even if you get stuck on the first part. Again, it's important not to waste too much time on a question you can't answer; it is better to pick up as many marks as you can later on in the test.

Specimen questions are available on the website to help you practise, but it is also worth taking a look at our sample MAT and PAT questions as well as past papers for these tests, as the style of question is similar.

## Multiple Choice Logic Problems

### Philosophy

An important element of the Philosophy course is logic, and this part of the assessment is designed to test your ability to think in a logical way. You will have to answer 18 multiple choice logic questions in 20 minutes. The answer options are likely to be very similar, as they are aiming to see if you can understand the nuances of different logical arguments. Ensure you read the questions and the answers quickly but carefully, and give yourself time to check for any mistakes. You don't need to have any technical logical knowledge, but it is worth taking a look at Samuel Guttenplan's The

Languages of Logic or books on informal logic or critical reading to help give yourself a basic understanding of philosophical approaches to arguments.

## Quantitative Language and/or Data Analysis

### Linguistics

There are a variety of skills involved in linguistics, including an understanding of language and written skills, and it is important to be able to interpret quantitative data. This section asks you to demonstrate this ability by answering questions on graphs related to a linguistic study. A good way to practice this is to look at data-driven linguistics research papers and study the data closely, considering what analysis you could draw from it.

## Sixth Term Examination Papers (STEP)

### Mathematics

Sixth Term Examination Papers in Mathematics consist of three papers, which Cambridge consider in addition to A Level grades. The questions test your insight, originality, grasp of broader issues in your subject, and the ability to apply what you know to more complex or unusual situations. STEP is used by colleges as part of a conditional offer and you will sit it in the summer before beginning university. Some colleges may require it for other courses in addition to Mathematics such as Economics, Engineering or Natural Sciences. Your application to take STEP should be organised through your school or college.

# Oxford Admissions Tests

## Oxford Classics Admissions Tests

### Classics

Classics applicants will take one or two sections of the Classics Admissions Test, depending on whether you have studied a classical language to A Level or equivalent before:

- Latin Translation Test

- Greek Translation Test

- The Classics Language Aptitude Test

If you do have Latin or Greek to A Level or equivalent (Course I), you will take a translation test in the language(s) that you are studying. If you do not have Latin or Greek to A Level or equivalent (Course II), you must sit the Classics Language Aptitude Test.

For the Latin and Greek translations, revise the points of grammar you need to construct accurate sentences. The best way to practice for this test is to translate one sentence of Latin and/or Greek a day, using a dictionary if you get stuck, but making sure to make a note of new words as you come across them. It is also worth reading through some of the translations you have done before to refresh your vocabulary, but it is not worth learning pages of new words without using them in context.

The Classics Language Aptitude Test (CLAT) tests your ability to pick up language skills. The best preparation is to think about the languages that you know and how they are constructed. It can also be useful to go over the way that Latin and Greek function so you can practice thinking logically about language.

# History Aptitude Test (HAT)

## History or History and joint schools at Oxford

To write a successful answer paper you need to be confident analysing and constructing arguments, finding nuance in a source, and using logic to summarise your thoughts efficiently. Practice and enthusiasm for historical skills will help you.

QUESTION 1A AND 1B (10 and 20 marks)

You will be asked to read a source and summarise a particular point in one sentence. You will then be asked to explain one of the arguments in the source briefly, from the perspective of the author. Both questions ask you to answer in your own words; you need to be able to show that you have understood what you're reading and can pick out the important points. 1a and 1b both specify that your answers should be short – aim to be clear and concise and get straight to the point.

This passage is from a historical study of English History. Read the extract carefully and think about the issues it raises.

I PURPOSE to write the history of England from the accession of King James the Second down to a time which is within the memory of men still living. I shall recount the errors which, in a few months, alienated a loyal gentry and priesthood from the House of Stuart. I shall trace the course of that revolution which terminated the long struggle between our sovereigns and their parliaments, and bound up together the rights of the people and the title of the reigning dynasty.

EXAMPLE QUESTION 1A AND 1B

**1a.** In the first paragraph, why does the author think the relationship between parliament and the monarch has been so important? Answer in one sentence using your own words.

**1b.** How does the author account for 'the greatness of England'? Answer in not more than 15 lines and use you own words.

To read the full source, visit our free online resources for the HAT at www.oxbridgeapplications.com

QUESTION 1C (40 marks)

This question takes the theme of the source and asks you to apply it to a period of history with which you're familiar. It's quite a different approach to A Level History, and tests whether or not you can think laterally about causes and consequences beyond what you've studied. It also separates those who stick to their syllabus and those who try to explore ideas further – another excellent reason to start reading around your subject early. Your essay should be a clear argument, which you can strengthen with clear and pertinent examples. Try to use your examples to build your argument, rather than just as illustrations. This will give you a much clearer direction and a more sophisticated essay.

EXAMPLE QUESTION 1C

'In history, long-term causes are everything; short-term events only determine when they bear their fruit.'

Discuss the accuracy of this statement with reference to a particular historical period or topic with which you are familiar.

QUESTION 2 (30 marks). (This question is not answered by student applying for History and Economics, who will answer Question 4 instead)
This question will be an essay question that will ask you to apply a particular historical concept, often related to the source from the first question, to a historical situation. This is an opportunity for you to demonstrate your knowledge as you can apply evidence to your argument from any area of history. You will usually be given guidance as to how long your response should be so make sure you stick to the essay limit. You should spend some time planning your essay before you begin writing, as this will help you to develop a clear, strong argument.

EXAMPLE QUESTION 2

In an essay of two or three sides, discuss the difficulties or complications which arise as a result of your knowledge of later events and developments when studying a society or period. You may answer with reference to any society or period with which you are familiar.

QUESTION 3 (40 marks)

You have to analyse an unseen source. Don't worry if it's on a subject you've never studied before and that you're being asked to talk in depth about ideas and ideologies you're unfamiliar with – all the answers are in the source and this is your chance to go right back to the fundamental skills required to be a good historian. You should dedicate some time to planning your answer: how are you going to approach each section? What examples from the text can you use to back up your reasoning and how will you bring your argument together to finish with a strong conclusion?

EXAMPLE QUESTION 3

This is an extract from the first official Life of St. Francis of Assisi, commissioned by the Pope and written two years after Francis's death, in 1228.

*You are not expected to know anything about St. Francis of Assisi or the period. You must read carefully and critically, and use your skills of historical analysis to interpret the extract.*

*The first work that blessed Francis undertook after he had gained his freedom from the hand of his carnally minded father was to build a house of God. He did not try to build one anew, but he repaired an old one, restored an ancient one. He did not tear out the foundation, but he built upon it, ever reserving to Christ his prerogative, though he was not aware of it, for other foundation no one can lay, but that which has been laid, which is Christ Jesus.* (1 Corinthians 3.11)

What can the extract tell us about religious ideas, gender relations and culture in thirteenth-century Europe? (Write about one to two sides)

QUESTION 4 (30 marks) (for History and Economics applicants only, in place of Question 2)

This question was introduced in 2015 and consists of a few parts designed to test your problem solving, writing and comprehension skills. Have a look at our TSA example problem solving questions to help you practice. There are also specimen and past papers available on the Oxford website.

For answers to all the above questions and to read the rest of the extracts, visit www.oxbridgeapplications.com

# The National Admissions Test for Law (LNAT)

## Law (Jurisprudence) and Law with Legal Studies in Europe

You'll need to sit the LNAT if you're applying for Law or courses involving Law at Birmingham, Bristol, Durham, Glasgow, King's College London, Nottingham, Oxford, SOAS, or UCL. The first section is multiple choice, where you'll be asked to analyse 12 passages and answer three or four questions on each (total of 42 questions). You also need to write an analytical essay from a choice of three titles.

Below, we discuss different types of questions that occur in the LNAT and example questions for each.

IDENTIFYING ASSUMPTIONS

An assumption is something which is not stated in the argument, but taken for granted in order to draw the conclusion. The first step is to work out what the conclusion of the argument is. Once you have found the conclusion, you should investigate the reasoning the author gives to support this conclusion, and think about any important point which is not actually stated. You are trying to spot the missing link, the reason that should be stated but has been left out.

EXAMPLE QUESTION

"The symptoms of mental disorders are behavioural, cognitive, or emotional problems. Some patients with mental disorders can be effectively treated with psychotherapy, but it is now known that, in some patients, mental disorders result from chemical imbalances affecting the brain. Thus, these patients can be effectively treated only with medication that will reduce or correct the imbalance."

Which of the following is an underlying assumption of the above argument?

**a.** Treatment by psychotherapy can produce no effective reduction in or correction of chemical imbalances that cause mental disorders.

**b.** Treatment with medication is superior to treatment with psychotherapy.

**c.** Most mental disorders are not the result of chemical imbalances affecting the brain.

**d.** Some patients with mental disorders can be effectively treated with psychotherapy, others need medication.

**e.** Treatment with psychotherapy has no effect on mental disorders other than a reduction of the symptoms.

## TACKLING INFERRING QUESTIONS

An inference is something that the reader can conclude based on the information given in the passage. In order to answer this, you need to evaluate which of the five statements could legitimately be a conclusion following on from the information given. If one of these statements relies on some other information, then it is less likely to be an inference directly from the information given.

## EXAMPLE QUESTION

"Partly because of bad weather, but also partly because some major pepper growers have switched to high-priced cocoa, world production of pepper has been running well below worldwide sales for three years. Pepper is consequently in relatively short supply. The price of pepper has soared in response: it now equals that of cocoa."

Which of the following can be inferred from the above statement?

**a.** Pepper is a profitable crop only if it is grown on a large scale.

**b.** World consumption of pepper has been unusually high for three years.

**c.** World pepper production will return to previous levels once normal weather returns.

**d.** Surplus stocks of pepper have been reduced in the past three years.

**e.** Pepper growing profits over the last 3 years have been unsustainable.

## WRITING YOUR ESSAY

For the second section, you will have 40 minutes to answer one of three essay questions. Structure is very important in the LNAT. Have a clear introduction which tells the reader where you're going, 'set any parameters that you'd like to impose on the essay, and define any ambiguous terms used in the question. The body of the essay should contain your argument and, if possible, you should try to deal with one or two counter arguments. Using a real-world example makes your argument more concrete and shows the reader that you have an awareness of the world around you. It's important to keep up-to-date with current affairs so you have a ready supply of pertinent examples. Make sure your conclusion reiterates the main body of your argument without simply repeating itself.

EXAMPLE QUESTION

"Women now have the chance to achieve anything they want."

How do you respond to this statement?

For the answers to all the above questions visit www.oxbridgeapplications.com

## Mathematics Aptitude Test (MAT)

### Mathematics, Mathematics and joint schools, Computer Science or Computer Science and joint schools at Oxford or Imperial

The test is the same for the different courses, but there are particular sections to answer depending on which subject you're applying for. We recommend checking which questions you need to answer beforehand so that you're clear before you go into the test as the division of questions can be quite complex.

MULTIPLE CHOICE QUESTIONS (40 marks)

The questions are simple and solving the problem will normally only require one stage of mathematics. All the questions draw on the mathematics you've been taught in C1 and C2 modules of A Level Mathematics, but the questions might not be as straightforward – they require you to apply your mathematical knowledge to new problems. You should have enough time to check through your answers when you've finished and you should do so, as no marks are awarded for correct workings but an incorrect answer.

If you're really stuck on a question, make an educated guess – you have a 25% chance of getting it right and you won't be marked down if you're wrong.

EXAMPLE QUESTION 1

Which of the following is a factor of the polynomial
$x^5 + 6x^3 + x^2 + 8x + 4$?

**a.** $x + 4$

**b.** $x^3 + x + 2$

**c.** $x^3 + 2x + 1$

**d.** $x + 4$ & $x^3 + x + 2$

EXAMPLE QUESTION 2

Which of the following is the graph of

$f(x) = \dfrac{x \sin^2 x}{\cos x}$ between $-2\pi$ and $+2\pi$?

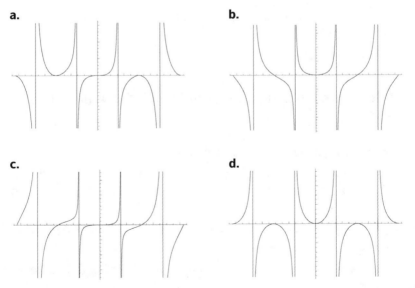

**a.**

**b.**

**c.**

**d.**

## TACKLING LONGER QUESTIONS (60 marks)

In the second section of the test, which you should spend about 90 minutes on, you need to answer longer questions. These questions are dependent on the course that you're applying for. These questions usually require more than one stage, so you might need to take different aspects of your Mathematics course and combine them to reach the right answer. The questions have been designed so that you can still approach them, even if you're not studying the A Level syllabus, but it would be wise to check through what C1 and C2 cover if you haven't done them. There really is no substitute in your preparation for doing practice questions. Even if you don't answer the questions, being able to quickly identify the right method to solve the problem will be very useful when you come to take the test.

## EXAMPLE QUESTION

**a.** A glass has a circular base of radius $r\_1$ and a circular top of radius $r\_2$. If the height of the glass is H, find an expression for the volume.

**b.** If you half fill the glass with juice, up to (H over 2 – use from last year), and put a straw, length l, diameter d to the base of the glass and suck the drink up until it reaches your mouth (i.e. it fills the whole straw), find a polynomial equation for Hn, the new height of juice in the glass.

For the answers to all the above questions visit
www.oxbridgeapplications.com

## Oxford Modern Languages and Linguistics Admissions Tests

### Modern Languages and/or Linguistics

You will take the test at the start of November. This test includes the following papers, of which you shall have to sit one or two, depending on the course for which you're applying:

- Language Test (for Czech, French, German, Modern Greek, Italian, Portuguese, Russian, Spanish, if taken to A Level)

- Language Aptitude Test (for courses involving Celtic, Italian and Russian ab initio)

- Linguistics Test (for all courses involving Linguistics, single language courses (except French and German) and all joint courses with Polish (except French and German))
- Philosophy Test (for Philosophy and Modern Languages)

The Language Test is 30 minutes and tests your vocabulary, writing, comprehension, and translating skills, as well as certain parts of the language's grammar. Brush up on your A Level (or equivalent) grammar and try to go a bit further by asking your teachers what the next stage of grammar learning is. You should be able to recognise new grammatical forms, even if you can't yet use them. Practice manipulating your language so you can deal with any gaps in your vocabulary when you come to translate.

The Language Aptitude test lasts 30 minutes and tests you with grammatical and comprehension questions on a language which has been invented for the test. Revise the terms used to describe parts of language, for example suffix, pronoun, and preposition, so you understand what the question is asking you. Think about how the languages you know are constructed – how do French and English differ in the way they express doubt, for example? Try to spot patterns in different languages and practice applying grammatical rules to explain them.

The Linguistics Test is 30 minutes and tests how you tackle unfamiliar linguistic data and your awareness of subtleties in language and meaning. Tutors will look at your reasoning behind how you solve the questions – not necessarily at whether you got the answer correct or not. It can be helpful to do some research into how different languages are constructed. You should also practice analysing graphs and tables of data as this is something that often comes up in the test.

## The Philosophy Test

### Philosophy and Theology
This is a one-hour test sat by Philosophy and Theology applicants. There is no expectation of any prior philosophical knowledge; the test is instead designed to assess your skills of reasoning. You will usually be

given a comprehension exercise where you will answer questions on a philosophical text, followed by a short essay or structured exercises testing your reasoning and/or skills of argument.

# The Physics Aptitude Test (PAT)

### Physics, Engineering or Materials Science

The Physics Aptitude Test is a two-hour test, sat in November prior to interview. The mathematical and physics knowledge you will need in order to answer the questions corresponds roughly to the GCSE and AS Level Mathematics and Physics syllabus. Therefore, to be successful in both sections of the test you need to revise these. Calculators are not allowed.

SECTION A: MATHEMATICS FOR PHYSICS (50 marks)

This section consists of mathematical problems

EXAMPLE QUESTION 1

Find the set of real numbers $\lambda$ for which the following quadratic equation holds:

$x2 + (\lambda - 5)x + 4\lambda = 0$

SECTION B: PHYSICS (50 marks)

This section consists of questions based around physics

EXAMPLE QUESTION 2

What would the minimum length of a plane mirror need to be in order for you to see a full view of yourself?

**a.** ½ your height

**b.** ¼ your height

**c.** ¾ your height

**d.** Your full height

For the answers to all the above questions visit
www.oxbridgeapplications.com

# 5 WRITTEN WORK

**A GUIDE TO CHOOSING AND PRODUCING YOUR WRITTEN WORK**

# A guide to choosing and producing your written work

For many courses at Oxford and Cambridge, you will have to submit one or two pieces of written work to your college between the UCAS deadline and your interview. This varies by course and you should look at your course requirements to determine whether you need to submit written work. For Cambridge in particular, written work requirements vary by college in addition to course, so you must also be aware of the requirements your college has for written work.

If your course requires you to submit written work, you should ask yourself the following questions:

## HOW IMPORTANT IS WRITTEN WORK?

Written work is another stage at which the aptitude for your chosen course will be assessed, in particular your skills of writing and argument. Although outstanding written work is unlikely to make a significant difference as to whether or not you are interviewed, it can have a bearing on your overall application. It is another way for you to demonstrate your aptitude and suitability for the course, and for the Admissions Tutors to separate you from other applicants.

## HOW IS WRITTEN WORK USED AT INTERVIEW?

As with your personal statement, your written work may form the basis of your interview. Of those applicants who submitted written work, 51% of those we surveyed in 2016 were asked about it during their interview. To prepare you for this possibility, you should ensure that the topic of the work you submit is one you are knowledgeable about and have an interest in. It is advisable to re-read your written work before your interview to ensure you recall the arguments and subject matter in detail.

"The whole first interview was based on my submitted work, and the second interview was based on an unseen source."

Applicant for History, Cambridge

## HOW SHOULD I CHOOSE WHICH WRITTEN WORK PIECES TO SUBMIT?

It's important that your written work is of a high standard and demonstrates your essay writing skills at their best. You should look at work that you have written recently, not as part of your GCSE work, for instance, as this will not reflect your current ability. The work you submit has to be part of your normal school work, but if you do not have anything suitable, you can ask your teacher to set you a relevant essay which they can then mark. Similarly, if you are applying as a post-qualification applicant, you can contact your old teachers and ask them to set and mark work for you, so that you can submit work that shows your current ability. If you are a mature applicant and are unsure whether you will be able to find someone to mark your work, you should ring the college you are applying to to ask how best to proceed.

## HOW LONG SHOULD MY WRITTEN WORK BE?

Oxford specify that all written work should be no more than 2,000 words. Cambridge is not as prescriptive with their word count, and specifications vary from college to college, but it is still a good idea to submit an essay around this length. Any work shorter than 1,500 words is unlikely to show off your written skills sufficiently, but too long and the tutor may not have the time or inclination to read it in full. 2,000 words provides you with the room to put forward a well-developed, while still concise, argument.

## CAN I SUBMIT MY EPQ OR EXTENDED ESSAY?

Due to Oxford's word limit, you cannot submit your whole EPQ or extended essay, and it is unadvisable to do so to Cambridge. You can, however, submit an extract, although you should be wary of this as it restricts how much of your argument you can develop. If you are keen to talk about it in your interview, mention it in your personal statement, or on your Supplementary Application Questionnaire if you are applying to Cambridge.

## WHAT DO I DO IF I'M NOT STUDYING THE COURSE I APPLIED FOR AT SCHOOL?

It may be that you are applying for a subject that you are not taking as an A Level, such as Archaeology & Anthropology, or History of Art. Some courses may ask you for one of your pieces to be a shorter piece more specific to the subject: for example, for the History of Art course at Oxford, you will need to submit a response to a piece of art, architecture or design.

Outside of these specific requirements, you can submit an essay from any of your sixth form subjects. If possible, it is advisable to pick the subject most relevant to what you hope to study. For example, if you are applying for HSPS and you are studying Government & Politics and English at school, your Politics essay is more relevant. If you are applying for Philosophy, Religious Studies is a good crossover, and so on. If you are not studying anything within the same subject area, then submit work of a similar style that demonstrates the right skills (e.g. of argument, analysis) – History and English in particular are useful subjects from which to submit written work. There will be some instances where submitting a science report is appropriate, for example, if you are applying for Economics but studying only science subjects. If you are unsure, you should get in touch with the college to clarify.

## DOES MY WRITTEN WORK HAVE TO BE IN ENGLISH?

If you are applying to read Modern Languages at Oxford or for most colleges at Cambridge, you will be required to submit a piece of work in each of the languages you are applying for and currently studying at A Level, as well as a piece in English in some cases.

Outside of this requirement, all written work must be in English. If you are an international student and the original work is in another language, you will usually have to submit both the original work and a translation in English.

## CAN I BE CREATIVE WITH MY CHOICE OF WRITTEN WORK?

Although you need to submit an essay that falls within the realms of your curriculum, try and pick something that is going to be interesting to the interviewer. Many English students, across multiple exam boards, study *Othello,* and often submit an essay focused on this play. There is nothing wrong with doing this, but if you have an essay on a more unusual text, you will stand out more to the Admissions Tutors and it potentially will lead to a more interesting discussion at interview. Similarly, a lot of History students study Stalin or Hitler. If you do decide to write on a more common topic, ensure you make a sophisticated argument that is going to demonstrate your individuality.

## EXAMPLE OF WRITTEN WORK FROM SUCCESSFUL OXBRIDGE APPLICANTS

To help you understand what real applicants use for their written work, we asked successful Oxbridge applicants to discuss what they submitted for their application.

### HISTORY, CAMBRIDGE

"When I applied, my college asked me to submit two essays, one of which needed to have a comparative element. My teacher advised me to avoid the more generic subjects we'd studied (like Hitler), so for one piece I submitted my extended essay on Richard III and for the second, I sent a timed essay which compared Indian and Algerian independence movements. I was asked about both during my interviews and the interviewers seemed really interested in the topics I'd picked and what I knew about them. For me it was a great chance to discuss areas of history I was excited about and show off my knowledge."

### PHILOSOPHY & THEOLOGY, OXFORD

"I was applying for a joint course, and as such I wanted to make sure that I demonstrated an aptitude for both subjects. I was asked to submit two pieces of written work, with the only specification being that it was marked by a teacher. I ended up sending one from Philosophy that was actually heavily highlighted in different colours by me, something our RS teacher encouraged, and one from History. I was not asked about either during my interview, apart from to note the highlighting, but it was clear that they had read them and I later learned that my writing style was a key reason that I was selected as a candidate."

### MODERN LANGUAGES, OXFORD

"For my application to read Russian & Spanish, I had to submit two short written pieces, one in each language, and a longer essay in English on any topic. Although I studied Russian outside of school, Oxford agreed to take it unmarked, so do get in touch if you have any unusual circumstances like mine. My Spanish teacher told me to make sure to use as many complicated structures as possible and to write about an unusual topic (in my case La Ley de Tallas in Argentina). I followed the language advice

211

in Russian but focussed on literature (Gogol's *Revizor*) and would advise students applying for Modern Languages to include at least one work on literature. For the work in English, I used a Politics essay on Marxism for its relevance to Russian. Although my written work did not come up in my interview, it gave me the chance to show my range of interests within the two subjects and show my strengths as a candidate."

## ENGLISH, OXFORD

"When applying to read English at Oxford, I was asked to submit one piece of critical writing. The choice was entirely mine: it could vary between anything from an in-depth analysis of a single poem to a sustained comparative exploration of several texts. Having spoken to a couple of English tutors at an Oxford open-day, I was advised to submit the latter, since it is more reflective of the kind of work expected of an undergraduate. Throughout the course, I discovered that comparison is the most important (and engaging!) critical instrument of the course, and so I would similarly encourage prospective students to opt for a comparative piece. With regards to the interview, whilst we only spoke briefly about the submitted piece itself, it provided a springboard for subsequent discussions and ultimately steered our entire conversation."

## HUMAN SOCIAL & POLITICAL SCIENCE (HSPS), CAMBRIDGE

"My college requested two pieces of written work as part of my application. As I hadn't formally studied any parts of the course before, I wasn't able to give them a subject-specific piece, so I instead submitted two English essays which demonstrated my essay writing skills. I submitted two timed essays, both on Shakespeare – one discussed the racial politics of Othello, and the other discussed Shakespeare's subversive use of gender and sexuality in Twelfth Night – both had strong ties to anthropology in terms of what you study in the course, which was the basis of my decision to pick these two essays. In my interview, neither were questioned in-depth, but I think it was a useful basis to show the interviewers my writing skills and did begin a discussion about race and gender politics in modern societies."

# 6 THE INTERVIEW

## UNDERSTANDING THE PURPOSE OF THE OXBRIDGE INTERVIEW

# Understanding the purpose of the Oxbridge interview

To excel in the Oxbridge undergraduate teaching system, you must be able to converse confidently, engage academically with and absorb information about your subject, and develop your own informed opinion on the topics you are studying. In essence, the interview acts as a mini tutorial or supervision to assess, along with all the other aspects of the application, whether you will enjoy learning in this environment and whether the tutors will in turn like teaching you.

The majority of Cambridge applicants are invited to attend an interview in December. Cambridge invites a greater percentage of applicants to interview than Oxford, with the latter using Admissions Test scores to inform their decision and filet out candidates. Interviews are the final piece of the application process, and it is from there that the university makes its ultimate decision.

Interviews allow Admissions Tutors to explore exactly how you think, how you adapt to new concepts and ideas, and how you handle the pressure of reaching conclusions aloud. For example, if an admissions tutor gives you a physics formula to solve that you have not previously encountered, how do you react? Do you attempt to work through it or do you freeze with terror at the thought of making a mistake in front of your interviewer? If the first scenario sounds more like you, it is a good indication that you might be an interesting student to teach; you are showing that you are responsive to new ideas and can apply your existing knowledge to problems you have not seen before, a skill you will have to exercise in a real tutorial/supervision.

When preparing for the interview, you should ask yourself the following questions:

## WHAT ARE ADMISSIONS TUTORS LOOKING FOR IN AN INTERVIEW?

They are looking for genuine motivation and enthusiasm for the chosen subject, in addition to logical, critical and lateral-thinking skills, and an ability to think flexibly and independently. This might seem a daunting list but, in reality, many bright applicants will already have these qualities.

Like the personal statement, the interview gives you the chance to demonstrate your interest in your chosen subject. It is easy to say that you have understood a philosophical concept in your personal statement, but can you summarise the point in a sentence and then explore its application to a situation you have not previously considered? Genuinely passionate individuals will tend to be those who have really thought about why they want to read their chosen course at university, and have examples to support their points.

## WHAT IS UNSEEN MATERIAL? WHY IS IT USED IN AN OXBRIDGE INTERVIEW?

Admissions Tutors may also use the interview to discuss how to approach material that has not yet been looked at in the application process. In an interview for Music, you may be given a score and asked to break it down to demonstrate your theoretical and critical appreciation of compositions. In a language interview, you may be asked questions in the language you wish to study, to assess oral ability and, crucially, whether you enjoy speaking, testing new constructions, and learning from your mistakes. In English interviews, you are likely to be given a poem or extract from a play or novel and in Engineering, you may be given a new problem, and so on. You may be able to talk confidently about topics you have covered at school or in your own time, but interviewers are trying to assess if you can you apply the logic and knowledge you have to situations beyond your experience.

## HOW SHOULD I RESPOND IF THE INTERVIEWER QUESTIONS A POINT I MAKE?

One thing you can't control in the interview is how the interviewer reacts to you. You may be faced with a tough interviewer, who engages you in rigorous intellectual discussion that you are unprepared for. The interviewer isn't trying to make you crumble, but to see whether you can stand your ground in a heated academic debate. They want to see whether you can strike a balance between listening to your interviewer and taking their views into account, whilst also defending and maintaining your own viewpoint.

If you find yourself in this situation, a key thing to remember is that you must remain respectful and rational. Be prepared for 'such as?' and 'for example?' type questions, but do not let these guide you to a conclusion you do not support. Every time you make a case, ensure you have an example to hand to support and strengthen your point.

Additionally, whilst you may wish to argue your point to its logical end, do not be afraid to adjust your argument in light of new material or prompts offered to you by your interviewer. This isn't necessarily a sign of weakness, and often your interviewer will want to see how you assimilate new information. The interview isn't the place for stubbornness or pride. Remember that your interviewers have studied the topic under discussion for a lot longer than you and they might decide to play devil's advocate in the interview to see how you react under pressure.

## HOW SHOULD I RESPOND IF THE INTERVIEWER KEEPS PROMPTING ME?

In an Oxbridge interview, it is likely that you will be prompted to develop an answer on singular or multiple occasions. While you may respond to a question and feel as if you have given a thorough answer, your interviewer may question your point and expect you to elaborate.

It is important to know that in this situation, you are being invited to explore your ideas in further detail or from a different angle. There are two good tips when tackling this situation: you could either try to develop your initial answer further or, alternatively, pause and reconsider the implications of the question. Never be afraid to give yourself a couple of seconds to think. It's much better to give a considered answer after a few moments than to plough on without much direction.

If you have tried both these responses and you are still met with 'And...?' it may mean that the interviewer has a specific response in mind that you cannot fathom. If you have explored your answers as far as you can take them, gracefully disengage yourself by asking them either to re-phrase the problem for you, or admit that you don't know the answer that they're looking for and ask them to help you. The humble admission, 'I'm afraid I don't know but I'd like to find out,' turns the problem into a virtue, as you seem willing to learn and engaged.

## HOW CAN I PREPARE FOR MY INTERVIEW?

When it comes to preparing for your interview, the general rule is to be ready for anything. You may be interviewed by one person or two, or even three or four. When there is more than one person in the room, a good tip is to address your answers to the interviewer who asked the question, with regular glances to include the rest of the interview team. It may be the case that one party leads the interview, whilst another observes and takes notes.

You may have one general interview and one subject interview (more likely at Cambridge) or two or more subject interviews. You may be interviewed at a college to which you have not applied (more likely at Oxford) or you might be interviewed at the college to which you applied, as well as one or two others.

You can't know what is going to come up in your interview, but you can ensure that you feel confident approaching questions relating to your subject, discussing your interests, and applying your knowledge to new material and ideas. Many successful applicants are surprised to find the interview an enjoyable experience. Think of the interview as a two-way conversation, not as an interrogation. If you find yourself enjoying the experience, the chances are your tutor will be too.

Over the page we look at past interview questions and in the next chapter we explain how to approach different questions and try applying it to other, similar questions. You can also try looking at extracts, articles, images or scores, and consider how you might go about approaching them in an interview setting. See our list of further resources at the end of this book for some ideas of where to look for this material.

# Interview Questions

50 real-life past interview questions to help you practise ahead of your interview.

## HUMANITIES AND THE ARTS

- What is the architect's role in society? (Architecture)
- What are the benefits and drawbacks of empathy in trying to understand the past? (Classical Archaeology and Ancient History)
- To what extent are the arts a vital component of a comprehensive education? (Education)
- How can you measure the validity of statistics? (History and Modern Languages)
- What is the difference between patriotism and nationalism? (History and Politics)
- Does geography shape history? (History)
- Does art still have the ability to shock? (History of Art)
- How has music evolved over time? (Music)
- What do you think thinking is? (Philosophy)
- Should Britain be a Christian country? (Theology)

## LANGUAGES AND LITERATURE

- Why do you think we see allusions to Homer in Virgil's The Aeneid? (Classics)
- Who is the 'Caesar' mentioned in the 64 AD inscription? (Classics)
- How are music and a language similar? (English and Modern Languages)
- Would you use poetry or prose to drive political change? (English)
- Do you think Hamlet was genuinely mad? (English)

- Would Jane Austen have been better off writing tragedies rather than comedies? (English)
- Why does the English language have a world for 'home' when the French language doesn't? (Linguistics)
- What do you notice about the sentence 'we passed the old port'? (Linguistics)
- What is the role of a translator? (Modern Languages)
- How does speaking a language help you to understand more about a particular culture or society? (Modern Languages)

## SOCIAL AND POLITICAL SCIENCES

- What are the similarities between a product warranty and an educational degree? (Economics and Management)
- What is the difference between the poor cities and the rich cities in China? (Economics)
- Is technology or behaviour more important in tackling climate change? (Geography)
- How big is a cloud? (Geography)
- Is too much information ever negative? (HSPS)
- Describe this teabag. (HSPS)
- What steps would you take to respond to a natural disaster in the UK? (Land Economy)
- Should judges have a legislative role rather than just a judicial one? (Law)
- Why did Communism spread so quickly in Russia? (Law)
- If you had infinitely many single dollar bills, how would you give infinite dollar bills to infinite people? (PPE)

## PHYSICAL, MATHEMATICAL AND CHEMICAL SCIENCES

- If I took the water in this glass and spread it out in a layer one molecule thick, what area would it cover? (Chemistry)

- Explain how the periodic table is arranged. (Chemistry)
- Calculate the mass of nitrogen gas in the interview room. (Engineering)
- Describe the flight of an aeroplane. (Engineering)
- How many zeros are there in 100? (Mathematics)
- Find the mass of sugar in a can of coke. (Nat Sci P)
- How many atoms from Joan of Arc's body are currently in your body? (Physical Natural Sciences)
- Calculate the ratio of the intensity of light on the earth from the sun and the moon. (Physical Natural Sciences)
- Draw $\sin(x)/x$ (Physics)

## MEDICAL AND BIOLOGICAL SCIENCES

- Imagine you have a random bacteria that thrives at room temperature. How could it evolve to live at 120 degrees Celsius instead? (Biological Natural Sciences)
- Describe the differences between these brains. (Biological Natural Sciences)
- Detail the characteristics of the chloroplast that indicates that initially it was an individual organism. (Biological Sciences)
- In what way is communication different from language? (Experimental Psychology)
- What diseases were common in 18th century Britain compared to modern day Britain? (Medicine)
- How would you measure the volume of a lake? (Medicine)
- How would you determine how long it takes for a person to become unconscious in a sealed room? (Medicine)
- Why can't you tickle yourself? (Medicine)
- What is attention? (Psychological and Behavioural Sciences)
- How does a cat judge exact distance? (Veterinary Medicine)

# 7 APPROACHING QUESTIONS

## HOW TO ANSWER OXBRIDGE INTERVIEW QUESTIONS

# How to answer Oxbridge interview questions

Working with a team of Oxbridge graduates from different subject disciplines, we look at how you might approach sample interview questions. Some of the questions discussed here are real and have been put to applicants at their interviews, while others are based on past questions and have been carefully created by Oxbridge graduates to ensure they provide insight into subject-specific interviews.

With any Oxbridge interview question, there is seldom a right answer unless it is a specific mathematical problem you are asked to solve, or a fact-based question. Oxbridge are famous for asking unusual questions which may seem impossible to know the answer to, but if you are asked something like this, you should think about how you can apply what you do know to the question you're being asked. Our graduates have made suggestions as to how you might approach a question, but their answers are by no means to be interpreted as a set 'model answer' or are meant to suggest that there is a standardised approach to both generating and answering such questions.

The points made are to serve as a guide as to how you might go about responding to these questions successfully. Each year, interviewers come up with a host of new and appropriately challenging questions and problems to see how aspiring Oxbridge applicants go about tackling them. Therefore, please do not expect that just because we've concentrated on a question, that you will be asked this in your interview – the chances of this are exceedingly slim. It's much better to get to grips with the logical and creative thinking that these questions require, rather than trying to revise specific answers.

# Humanities & the Arts

## ARCHAEOLOGY & ANTHROPOLOGY (ALSO USEFUL FOR HSPS)

### Questions you should consider:

How would you carry out the ethnography of a curry?

How would you describe the role of the media within American politics?

If you were shown the jawbone of an animal, how would you identify which animal it belongs to?

### Describe your school in anthropological terms (past question)

This question aims to encourage the consideration of the cultural make-up of your school and moves into wider discussion on issues such as multiculturalism, gender and class. It would be easy to meander and go off point. Be conscious of what you are saying and support your points with examples and evidence.

Anthropology is concerned with people and cultures, so the interviewer will be expecting you to be able to analyse your school as an anthropological field site. In anthropology, this kind of focused study (i.e. site-specific) is termed as an ethnographic investigation. The notion of an 'anthropological perspective' is very broad and encompassing, and this can be demonstrated even within the site of the school. For example, within a single site, an anthropologist could examine a number of topics, including cross-cultural, gendered, socio-economic status, and age interactions between people.

You could expand your argument to compare your own schooling system to another cross-culturally. A provocative current example is the expression of religious freedom, as exemplified in how lenient the schooling system should be in permitting religious symbols (such as the headscarf) to be on 'display' in so-called secular sites such as the school. You could link in issues of multiculturalism and secularism, and how this has been tackled in the educational system in different ways in different countries, comparing, for example, Britain's lenient approach to headscarves in schools in contrast to the French government's 2004 ban on headscarves in schools. Other possible issues you might consider: Is your school single-sex or mixed; How does gender impact on education? Is it a state school or private; Should education be free? Are school uniform regulations a breach of human rights?

You may also be asked how you would carry out this investigation. This relates to methodology, and you would be expected to demonstrate a range of approaches in your answer (conducting interviews, questionnaires, doing cross-cultural comparisons, utilising archival resources), including offering a realistic timeframe for such an investigation.

**Would you agree that tourism, if it is led by indigenous people, will lead to a more positive result for the culture of the country?**
(past question)

In answering this question, avoid jumping straight in. Don't go for a wild stab and avoid a dogmatic 'yes/no' response. The interviewer will be looking for how you can engage intuitively and contemplatively with a complex current issue in anthropology.

A good place to start is to identify the key themes in the question. Here, for example, the question relates to cultural representation, identity, multiculturalism, and globalism. You could ask what defines the 'tourist'? Does the fieldwork ethnographer count as a tourist? What about the gap-year student? Note the problems in terminologies: 'tourist', 'indigenous', 'primitive', 'authentic' – such words are inherently ideologically fuelled and there is a risk that we are dividing them into two simplified categories, 'Us/Them'. Is there a need to distinguish between the categories of tourist and indigenous in this way? (especially in this time of so-called global cosmopolitanism).

You could argue that these categories – born specifically from a Western social setting – are ultimately deeply ingrained in a set of persistent and preconceived ideas – West/rest, primitive/modern, old/new. Yet with such cultural multiplicity, and in a time of increasing social change, such static constructions simply cannot hold force. By paying respect to the dynamics and differences of cultural situations, the task of anthropology is to re-contextualise the pervasive us/them polarities in favour of a more processual, scientific approach.

James Clifford argues in his book The Predicament of Culture, that one ought to hold all such dichotomising concepts in suspicion, attempting instead to replace their essentialising modes of thought by thinking of cultures 'not as organically unified or traditionally continuous but rather as negotiated, present processes'.

## Our advice

If you are interested in studying Archaeology & Anthropology and want to find out more about the types of issues raised by these questions, you might want to dip into J. R. Bowen, Why The French Don't Like Headscarves: Islam, The State, and Public Space; Joy Hendry, Reclaiming Culture: Indigenous People and Self-Representation.

# ARCHITECTURE

## Questions you should consider:

Does visiting a historical site give you a better appreciation of the architecture than you can grasp from a picture/photo?

What issues that were important in building Ancient Greek temples are still relevant today?

Why do we need architects?

Do you think architecture changes views of society?

## What is your favourite building and why? (past question)

A handy hint with this sort of question is to try and think about specific details of why you like a building. Is it the building type, location, integration of sustainable/eco-friendly systems, material, shape, façade, interior, exterior that you appreciate? Remember that architecture is more than just 'buildings' as such. It is about design with certain proportional qualities, or design order with a conscious spatial awareness.

One Architecture graduate we spoke to said that her favourite building is the Dutch Embassy in Berlin by OMA. It is a good example of a modern building which uses interesting (and inexpensive) materials. The programme is expressed on the façade through the building's materiality (cantilevered green glass) which gives it a subtly iconic look. When inside the building, the processional circulation allows one to experience the building from the outside in, which makes it an interesting building to visit. The details of the different working areas from an interior perspective make the place feel special and the employees take pride in working there. The building also responds well to its context on the Berlin urban block next to the river.

With a question like this, do try and choose a building you have visited. Remember that it is ok to pick a well-known, iconic building but make sure you are very specific as to why it is your favourite. It may be more interesting to choose something that is perhaps more unusual and less likely to be chosen by another applicant. This is typical of the types of questions that have been asked in previous interviews and therefore it is good to have a few examples of different buildings that you like and that you feel confident to talk about. You should also know which architect (if relevant) designed the building, and a bit about some of their other work, which you might like to refer to.

**Do architects need to consider light within buildings differently in different countries?** (past question)

This question tests how much you have thought about the specifics of design with respect to context and location, as well as testing your environmental knowledge. It is asking you to identify that different countries have different climates and seasons which need to be examined with regards to construction and design in order to help maintain a comfortable microclimate within a building.

You could tackle the question by thinking of examples of why light may be considered differently. What is the building's function? Who are the end users? Where is the building located? Think about what other factors are dependent on light – heat (solar gain) and thus ventilation, and how these might be manipulated for different climates. Diagrams are always a good idea to help illustrate your answer. For example, you might want to show

how light changes seasonally (low light in winter versus a higher sun in summer).

If 'yes' is your answer, you can support your point by stating that tropical countries around the equator have similar daylight hours all year round, compared with more northern and southern countries that have a large seasonal flux of sunlight. In order to prevent too much solar gain from direct sunlight, it would be preferable to use shading devices and materials with a high thermal mass to keep a building cool in hot weather. In countries where solar gain needs to be maximised to help heat a building, lots of glass might be used to let in large amounts of light (like a conservatory).

A poor attempt at the question would avoid the environmental issues related to light (i.e. for aesthetic purposes) and also one where the applicant simply stated a 'yes' or 'no' response, without elaborating further.

### Our advice

Your portfolio is a key part of the application process. Do think really carefully about how to organise this. What is special about your portfolio and what are your individual strengths? Think about the order of your work, how you can explain why you have chosen the pieces that you have and the links between them. What skills can you show? Can you produce work in different media? Does your work illustrate what inspires you and your technique? It is a skill to be able to combine and present a multiple medium portfolio effectively and quickly. It is usually more convenient to have the pages free and not contained within plastic sheets so that interviewers can see the quality of the work better, and where possible original drawings (as opposed to scans/copies/prints) should be used. If models or art works are too big to carry then try and make sure they are well documented with photos.

Before the interview, think about architecture in respect of the profession. As one graduate stated, a great architect is, 'for me, a professional who understands the requirements and aspirations of a client (budget, aesthetics, functionality), with respect to designing a practical and buildable structure, and with the capability to respond sensitively to its context and potential environmental impact.' Take the time to think about what it really means to be an architect.

# FINE ART

## Questions you should consider:

Can you use a variety of media to communicate your ideas?

Would you like to be treated as an artist from the word go?

Do you think artistically and does your work exist in its own right?

Interviews for Fine Art tend to be a mix of testing artistic awareness, perception and skill. Our Fine Artists have offered the advice below, based on their own interview experiences, which they believe would be helpful to any aspiring Fine Art applicant to think about in advance of their interview, with its focus on both the theoretical and the practical. Fine Art at Oxford is an extremely competitive course (with only 25 students each year). The Ruskin School is world renowned, and applicants have usually completed an art foundation course before applying. Our Fine Art graduate explains elements of the application process.

Art tutors tend to be quite different animals from other academics. They can be very inviting and hospitable, incredibly patient, and somewhat laid-back. It is true to say that they are like practicing artists (as most of them are) and that they are intensively interested in what you make or more importantly what are you are going to make in the future, and they are there to help you achieve it. The more personal your artwork, and the greater relevance it has to you and your view of the world, the more likely it is that the tutors will believe your passion and sincerity.

## Portfolio (go for quality not quantity)

Your portfolio should weigh no more than 10 kg, and should be submitted to the Ruskin School. The deadline is in mid-November, but make sure you check the Oxford website for the exact day. You should demonstrate development and diversity in your ongoing approach to art by including:

## Types of art

Drawing should be central to your portfolio

Preliminary studies with final work

(Good quality) photographs of 2D and 3D work

BIG work is beautiful (it tends to hit home!)

Black and white drawings, not only colour

Art in a mixture of media

Work that isn't 'perfect' or 'finished'

## Features of art work

Make it recent and exciting

Produce a spread of ideas and subject matter

Demonstrate your ability and potential

An evident commitment to art and design

Inventiveness and originality

Experimentation with materials and sources

Logical presentation

## Sketchbooks

Sketchbooks and personal notebooks are paramount to your application. They are of great value in recording images and exploring ideas, and should not be too contrived. They should also show your artistic thought processes and on-going development. Limit the number of sketchbooks you submit by providing those that show the greatest variety.

## The Interview

One of our tutors had a panel of five artists (four tutors and a current student) firing questions at them. Their advice is: 'Do not be afraid to argue and create a heated debate. I enjoyed bearing witness to the tutors' passionate and emotional debate about art, and to suddenly realise that I was contributing to it! In interviews, tutors tend to look through and pick out pieces of your art work, complimenting and questioning your work, in an attempt to locate your driving force and reason for creation. They may help you to see the relevance of your work to the greater art world and also suggest peripheral artists who are dealing with similar problems or issues. Taking new work to the interview is crucial. The tutors need to see that you are artistically inquisitive and continually researching and expanding on ideas. This will provide further fuel for the interview, and you must demonstrate a deeply informed awareness of contemporary art.'

**Practical Test**

One full day is spent on a practical test. The aim is to take you out of your comfort zone, but also to allow you to be in your element while at interview. You should remember that they will probably compare your portfolio work with what you produce on the test, so try to approach the topic they give you with fresh ideas, while maintaining your usual thought processes or means of engaging with a topic. The work you produce in the practical test should not seem incongruous. Use the materials provided creatively and you may wish to bring your favourite charcoal or paints.

# HISTORY

**Questions you should consider:**

What is a historical source?

If you are closer to an event, will you record it more accurately?

How do historians obtain evidence?

What is the position of the individual in history?

**Should history aim to please the public?** (past question)

In this question you are being asked to comment on the subject as a concept. Your judgement is also being assessed. What is history? Who does it serve? And what is it for? These are all crucial questions that form the subtext. Your ability to define, conceptualise, and think deeply about your subject is what lies at the heart of this question. You have the opportunity to show that you have thought long and hard about history – what it means to you and what it means to others. Remember that your interviewer will have, in all probability, some very fixed views on what his/ her subject is about. You must, therefore, be prepared to defend anything you say. There is nothing wrong with disagreeing, arguing, or debating with your interviewer – in fact it can be a good thing – but you must have a well-constructed argument to do so. As one Oxford History graduate commented, 'If I were an interviewer, I would expect candidates with views differing from my own to be able to engage in debate and to take the conversation somewhere interesting and new for me.'

There are three elements to tackling this question. Firstly, your definitions, both of history and what it means to 'please the public'. Secondly, your argument based on these definitions. Thirdly, your conclusion, following on from your chosen approach.

A good way to answer this question is to state your conclusion to the question – 'yes' or 'no' – and then go on to explain your answer. If it is 'no,' you might argue 'I do not think that history should aim to please the public. For me, history is about – or is at least aiming to be about – objective truth, and 'pleasing the public' should never be a factor in a historian's judgement.' History that is guided by what the public or certain people want to hear is nothing less than propaganda. It is subjective and therefore, in all likelihood, ignores counter arguments and facts that would lead towards a more accurate understanding. Most historians accept that it is impossible to be entirely objective in their work, but equally most – unless they are postmodernists – recognise objective history as the goal of their research.

### Can you give me an example of where historians may be looking into the past for patterns that are not there? (past question)

In this question your knowledge of historiography, independent reading, and understanding of historical methodology are being assessed. You could perhaps give an example of a historian and then explain the nature of his/her work and the conclusions that he/she has drawn. You could then apply your analytical judgement to assess whether or not the Historian was justified in looking for patterns. The obvious answer/example in my mind is Marxist Historians such as Christopher Hill, E. P. Thompson and Eric Hobsbawm.

Another Oxford Historian we spoke to said, 'As I understand it, Marxist Historians – at least in their pure form (there are very few left) approach History from a unique perspective fostered by the political and economic ideology – Marxism. They believe, following on from Marx, that the "history of all hitherto existing societies" has been the history of "class struggle" [The Communist Manifesto]. In its simplest and crudest form, Marxists believe that the social hierarchy is divided into three – the aristocracy, the bourgeoisie, and the proletariat – and that there is a permanent antagonism between them. Based on their rather more complicated theory of the laws of production, Marxists believe that the history of modern Europe (indeed of all societies) sees, or will see, the overthrow of the aristocracy by the bourgeoisie and then the overthrow of the bourgeoisie by the proletariat. This is not an objective conclusion, (although the Marxists try to prove their theory by facts), but an ideological conviction that has as much significance for contemporary politics as it did for history'. Therefore, Marxists Historians have searched, within their individual areas of research, for social and economic patterns that point towards the proof of this theory.

Such is a bare-bones answer to the question, but a strong candidate would develop his/her answer further to involve a commentary on the pros and cons of Marxist History.

### Our advice

Try and tackle questions head on. Pick a position and argue your case, showing an awareness of the complexities of the question. Definitely try and take a position rather than faffing in the middle, although `not necessarily' is always a valid answer.

Do keep up your source work as this is likely to be tested at interview as well as through the HAT (History Aptitude Test) at Oxford University. You may be presented with a source at interview and asked to talk around it or to answer a specific question. Ensure that you work with what you are given. Do not underestimate the amount of information you can draw from the text. Try to leave your ethical and moral positions aside and look at the piece in the context of its style, its purpose and its meaning.

You should always be prepared to bow to the superior knowledge of your interviewer, if indeed he or she is right. (The likelihood is that they are!) There is no point in maintaining stubbornly that the battle of Trafalgar was fought in 1804 when it clearly wasn't. When you do give ground, however, (accepting a point of view is obviously a key part of education) you should do so in a way that shows your willingness to learn and grasp new ideas. Therefore try and take what you have just learned and run with it.

You may be asked factual questions, although this is not particularly common. Make sure you are hot on the work you have done at school, the arguments you have picked up from your reading outside school and be aware of what is going on in the press, particularly with regard to politics and economics. Try and demonstrate interest in societies and the way in which they interact.

Try and ensure that you show chronological breadth in terms of your reading and understanding of history. Many students come into the interview room with lots of information on modern history: Stalin, Hitler, Weimar Germany and Russia in the 19th century. Can you compare different periods and/ or show understanding of ancient, medieval, early modern and modern history?

Although it is important to have facts at your fingertips in historical research, how you organise and draw conclusions from information is the toughest skill. When you are confronted with difficult questions, on paper or in an interview, remember that focusing on human motivation behind actions can be a good place to start and that, pulling apart a question or logically breaking down your approach to it can take you somewhere exciting.

## HISTORY OF ART

### Questions you should consider:

What is art?

Have you ever thought about why a building was constructed?

Are you interested in art created in a particular medium?

Do you enjoy art galleries and exhibitions?

These are some questions you should think about if you are considering History of Art. With so few places on the courses at both Oxford and Cambridge, our History of Art graduate suggests some ways in which you can successfully prepare for the interview...

### What is the value of art?

What monetary value can art have? You should demonstrate an awareness of the modern art industry and how it works, such as who owns the art, who decides the price (for example, auction houses like Sotheby's), and the process by which it is commissioned, distributed and sold. Be aware, too, that the motivations behind selling art are sometimes different from those behind making art.

Who decided the canon of art and what is it? The responsibility lies with critics and Art Historians (such as E.H. Gombrich). Be aware of prejudices in their selection of artists (for example, Giorgio Vasari's Lives of the Artists, published in 1556, selected the 'best' artists. They were all Italian, and the emphasis was on his great friend, Michelangelo). Why do Western universities still focus on the Western canon when teaching their students? Does this propagate a one-sided approach to art? Have Art Historians attempted to look elsewhere?

What is the emotional value of art? An individual can connect with a visual stimulus in a unique way. Additionally, in the Middle Ages, the majority of people were illiterate and visual images of biblical stories allowed them to connect with their faith. Today, we can still connect with figures in art through powerful facial expressions.

What cultural significance can art have? How does art reflect culture and what role does it play? What can we find out about past cultures through art? To an Art Historian, art is a valuable source with which to research costumes, relationships, the role of women, and the role of foreigners.

### Your response to a piece of art

Oxford requires you to submit a 750-word response to a piece of art or design before you come for interview. Both universities may use images you have never seen before at interview. Here are some points to consider: General, Your initial response, Purpose and provenance, Material, Texture, Colour, Size and scale, Location, Style and period, Subject matter, Sculpture, Production method (carving or lost wax?), Form (open or closed?) and Presentation (is it mounted?).

### Our advice

With your submitted written work, demonstrate that you can describe and analyse an image in words. Avoid simply dropping names of artists in your personal statement. Try to engage with some of their art too!

# MUSIC

**Questions you should consider:**

Is music useful within society?

Why are musical events written about?

Is the study of an instrument a valuable pursuit?

How is music related to free will?

The following questions highlight some of the issues within the study of academic music today. Our Musicians have shed some light on all the components of their interview process, and the differences between Cambridge and Oxford, to help a potential Music applicant jumpstart their interview preparation.

**Is some music more important than others?**

With a question like this, take time to consider the parameters. Are there different ways in which music is important? Is music more important if it is performed and heard, talked and written about, or if we can see its impact on our past, present or future? Has it started a revolution or served as an anthem for an army or a nation?

How do we measure importance? Why are certain composers perceived as geniuses? Why does our regard for Bach, Mozart and Beethoven cause debate today? Should we use the term 'musical canon'? Are certain composers or pieces of music important because of their effect on a genre? Perhaps you could think about Wagner and opera or Beethoven and the string quartet. Is society aware that we marginalise certain musical styles? The study of ethnomusicology (music of non-Western cultures) is a hot topic in the academic study of music.

Use musical examples you feel comfortable with in tackling this question. This approach will allow you to support your arguments and speak with assurance.

**Musical Analysis and 'Preparatory Study'**

You may be asked to look at a score shortly before your interview, or in the interview itself. Without hearing the piece of music, you should be able to identify some of the following features: The form: is it in binary, ternary or sonata form? How do the instrumental or vocal lines interact? Are the cadences perfect, imperfect or interrupted? What do you notice about the phrase lengths, climaxes, keys and modulations?

You can have a go at some musical analysis on our website www.oxbridgeapplications.com

You may be asked to analyse a piece of prose, such as an account of an opera performance. Once again, remember to think critically about what the writer is saying and why they are saying it.

PERFORMANCE: Oxford asks you to perform, on your principle instrument, a piece of music no more than five minutes in length. Choose a piece that suits you and is perhaps by a composer you mentioned in your personal statement. Tutors may enjoy something they do not hear regularly.

HARMONY: Cambridge may ask you to harmonise a soprano line and/or transcribe a phrase of a four-part Bach Chorale (which will test both your harmony and aural skills).

### Our advice

You need to be able to write clearly about music – demonstrate this! Go beyond your school reading and demonstrate mature research skills.


# PHILOSOPHY

Questions to get you thinking:

Discuss Plato's theory of knowledge.

What is a lie?

Is death rational?

What's the difference between intelligent, wise and clever?

Oxford and Cambridge Philosophy interviews test your logical and lateral thought and require a critical and rational response to challenging philosophical questions. Our team of Philosophy graduates have put together some example questions, based on real ones, to help you to explore philosophical ideas and concepts, and give you a taster as to how you might approach potential interview questions such as these.

**If a person is teleported by being destroyed and re-created exactly, is this the same person?**

This question tests your ability to recognise issues of personal identity within this thought experiment.

That the person is destroyed might suggest that they no longer exist, but in their being re-created exactly, we are tempted to say that the re-created being is the same person. The bundle theory claims that if there is psychological continuity, where the re-created being has the same memories and personality as the destroyed being, then the recreated person is the same person. But what if two copies are made of the destroyed being? Surely they cannot both be you?

At this stage you could draw the distinction between numerical and qualitative identity. You are numerically identical to the person you were 15 years ago in that you are still the same person, but you are not qualitatively identical as you do not have the same qualitative properties, for example, you may have a different set of teeth.

For this thought experiment, you therefore might conclude that the person who is re-created could be the same person as the person who was destroyed, in the sense that they are qualitatively identical. This would also be the case if there were two copies of the re-created person. They are not, however, numerically identical.

**If I am young today then I will be young tomorrow; if I am young tomorrow I will be young the day after that... so I will be young in 80 years' time. Discuss.**

This question tests your ability to see past the tricks of language to detect the logic underneath, and your ability to argue rationally in the form of: premise one, premise two, conclusion. We can show that premise one is invalid by comparing, 'if I am young today then I will be young tomorrow' with 'if I am wearing red today then I will be wearing red tomorrow'. The structure 'if x today, then x tomorrow' is not logically sound.

Premise one would be true if it followed that, if you were young on day A, you would be young on day B. If we accept premise one, then premise two, 'if I am young tomorrow I will be young the day after that' logically follows, because what is true on day A would be true on day B (it would be a transitive property). Thus the conclusion 'so I will be young in 80 years' time' holds.

As we have pointed out, premise one is incorrect. The quality of youth is affected by the progress of time. A person becomes progressively older each day. Therefore age, or 'youngness', is not a static quality, it is incremental.

With these types of question, Admissions Tutors are looking for you to demonstrate logical thought and reasoned opinions. Above all, they want to see how you a build and structure a coherent argument. Think aloud and be sure to work steadily through the question so that you come to a sound conclusion. And if you get stuck at any stage, do not be afraid to ask the interviewer. They want to see how you think and if you need to ask a relevant, intelligent question, this shows you are capable of thinking independently and willing to explore the subject.

## Our advice

In Philosophy interviews, students can all too easily rely on their intuition. Avoid this as much as possible. Think through your answers and support your arguments with evidence of logical thinking. Read books to help you to develop a genuine interest and understanding of the subject (not just A Level material) such as Wilfrid Hodges, Logic and Edward Craig, The Shorter Routledge Encyclopedia of Philosophy.

# THEOLOGY

### Questions you should consider:

Are we in a position to judge God?

Is Britain a secular society?

Is it morally wrong to attempt to climb a mountain?

### Can you think of any circumstances in which murder would be justifiable?

A question like this tests your knowledge of applied ethics. It might work well to answer this with reference to Christian philosophers or theologians, such as Kant.

Kant was a deontologist (someone who considers the morality of an action to be intrinsically linked to its adherence to certain rules). It is likely that someone following Kant's ethical approach would take a firm view against murder.

A Kantian position would adopt the categorical imperative, which states that an act should only be pursued if you would want it to become a universal law.

In the case of justifying murder, take a situation where we will gain a huge amount of money if the person is killed. In this instance, we could not reasonably wish this maxim to be universalised and therefore, following Kant's logic, we would judge the murder as unjustifiable.

Another example could be killing one person to save the lives of twenty others, for example, Bernard Williams' 'Jim and the Indians' thought experiment. Kant would respond, given that the other part of his categorical imperative demands that you treat people as ends rather than means, that killing one person as a means to save twenty is never acceptable.

You can conclude that murder, from a deontological Christian standpoint at least, would never be justifiable. From this point, the discussion would develop with your tutor, who may want to examine different sides of the problem.

### Should the church compromise?

This type of question focuses on current and historical issues that face and have faced the church. A good way to approach this question is to start by breaking the question down and analysing the language used: 'Should the church' is a difficult start to the question. A good answer may make the point that there is no discrete entity called 'the church', so remember to make appropriate distinctions where possible between different churches.

### What does the question mean by 'compromise'?

The word compromise suggests forsaking or adjusting one's own position in order to accommodate another view.

Here is one possible approach: there are many different churches, for the purposes of this example, let's take the Church of England. The issue here is whether the C of E should stick resolutely to its position on a particular issue or whether it should be prepared to adapt and change with society. If the Church is not open to compromise or change this would suggest the 'truth' resides solely within the Church. However, from a Christian perspective, the Word has been created by God and the Holy Spirit can operate and inspire individuals, independent of the Church. It is possible, then, for individuals or groups outside the Church to discover truths that the Church should accept. History provides numerous examples of this happening. The Church has compromised in the past and modified its views on a whole range of issues such as slavery, its relationship with other religions, and women priests.

You could then qualify this by saying that the Church should compromise on an issue for the right reasons – that is, because the compromise represents a more authentic witness to the life and vision of Christ than the previous position. For example, you could suggest that the Church should allow certain sexual relationships outside marriage, provided they are a genuine expression of love between two consenting adults. An act of compromise, such as this, does not undermine fundamental Christian values, such as self-sacrificial love (agape). It is possible to justify a compromise theologically, with reference to scripture and other parts of the Christian tradition. Jesus, for example, privileges the commandment to love others, and was himself prepared to break the established laws on occasion e.g. Matthew 5:38.

**Our advice**

At your interview you may be asked a variety of questions. Generally speaking, our graduates said that it is unlikely you will be asked about any specific theologians unless you have mentioned them in your personal statement. Moreover, you are more likely to be asked questions either pertaining to ethical and philosophical issues within theology or a critical evaluation of modern theology.

# Literature & Languages

## CLASSICS

**Questions you should consider:**

What role did the chorus have in Greek plays and how well does it translate into a modern context?

What would happen if the Classics department burnt down?

What parallels can be drawn between East-West cultures today and the gap between classical civilisation and now?

Classics interviews often ask you to analyse a classical text. For the purposes of this exercise, we have chosen a particular poem.

**Comment on this poem by Catullus.**

*odi et amo. quare id faciam, fortasse requiris?*
*nescio, sed fieri sentio et excrucior.*

The interviewer will not expect you to offer a complete translation into English and you do not need to understand every word. An unseen commentary allows you to apply your existing knowledge of vocabulary, grammar and context intelligently and gives you the opportunity to offer insightful and analytical suggestions as to why Catullus chose that word, that image, that syntax etc. in his poem. Be instinctive and concentrate on your impressions of the poem – look, understand, evaluate, and respond.

You might start by commenting on the form of the poem – it is a couplet. You could point out that Catullus expresses paradoxical, conflicting feelings: 'Odi et amo' – 'I hate' and 'I love'. You could then highlight the fact that he exploits this couplet form well by asking a question in the first line and then answering it in the second line. What might strike you next as you look closer at the poem is the use of verbs – 'odi... amo... faciam... nescio... sentio... excrucior' – six verbs all in the first person, which focus the reader's attention on the author's intense feelings and actions, which are contradictory and successfully communicate the push-pull of emotions. He hates, he loves, he does, he does not know, he feels and he is in torment. Look at the first three words and the last three words, which mirror the same construction: verb – conjunction – verb. If you analyse the four verbs used – 'odi...amo...sentio...excrucior', you might notice that the two outer verbs indicate a negative feel and the two inner words are generally positive, producing an ABBA chiasmus in the poem. It can even be said that positioning the first word and the last word – 'I hate' and 'I am in torment' at the very beginning and at the very end of the poem suggests that the overriding feelings are negative, and renders the overall tone of the poem gloomy. You could also suggest that his tight structuring is an attempt to organise and comprehend his conflicting emotions.

You might also know that Catullus was a member of the Neotericoi – the 'new poets', who were experimenting with a shorter form of poem, which they called an epigram and which aimed at brevity, succinct phrasing and intense emotion contained in few words. You might comment on how successful you feel he has been to this end. It is the structure of this poem, the syntax and the word choice which are the most notable features – the analysis of which can lead to the most thorough understanding of the state of mind of the author. Commenting on how and where certain words are used allows you, the reader, to understand the author's intentions and to impress the interviewer with your analytical ability.

For more tips on analysing an unseen extract, see the approaching questions section for English.

**Would ancient history be different if it were written by slaves?** (past question)

A question like this calls on your on-the-spot intuition and it allows you to draw on your knowledge of any texts you have studied. The interviewer is looking for you to demonstrate an ability and a willingness to think for yourself and to develop an argument that cannot have been simply digested and regurgitated from another source. As an interviewer, you are looking for someone who has read enough ancient history to have sufficient knowledge of the subject matter to express an informed opinion, coupled with an ability to analyse the subject matter interestingly and originally enough to come up with a stimulating and persuasive argument.

Firstly, you might like to stress that there were many different types of slave, and many different possible experiences of history in the Ancient World. A Greek private tutor, a paedogogus, might have had very different ideas from a gladiator. Some household slaves, particularly those with an ability to educate Roman youth or with knowledge of medicine, would have had very different ideas from a German slave, prized for his physical strength, used in an auxiliary army role. Secondly, you could mention how slavery in Greece varied from city state to city state: a helot would view things very differently from a slave in Athens (where striking a slave was forbidden and masters apparently tolerated back-chat from slaves). Here you could refer to the comedies of Menander, Plautus and Terence, where the slaves have a relatively jolly time of it. Thirdly, it might be a good idea to comment on how treatment of slaves changed over time and how the law evolved. A slave in the Roman Republic would have had fewer rights than a slave of the Imperial period (when the right to kill a slave at a whim was removed).

You could mention that it helps, when you are writing history, to have taken part in it. The majority of ancient historians were wealthy men with leisure and contacts. Herodotus travelled through many lands at a time when this was unusual. This required a private income (a big one) and free time (lots of it). Livy was a provincial of Plebeian origin, but he was educated in oratory and Greek, indicating rank. The educational level required to write history, the leisure time, the breadth of experience, would have been so far removed from the experience of most slaves that an answer to this question is, at best, highly speculative.

That said, one of Claudius' freedmen (ex-slaves) would have had the ear of the emperor and would have had much to say about foreign policy – and would have been in favour of the Imperial system, as opposed to the romantic Republican (and historian) Claudius, or Livy, who wanted to abolish the system of emperors (where slaves favoured by the emperor could wield real influence) and bring back the old Republic (where masters had the right to maim or kill their slaves). We can speculate that an Athenian slave would have written favourably of the legislator Draco, who made the murder of a slave punishable by death, despite his prevailing reputation for severity. He might have had less rosy an opinion of Aristotle, for whom slaves were 'living tools' fit only for physical labour, or Homer, who wrote that 'Jove takes half the goodness out of a man when he makes a slave of him'.

**Our advice**

In Classics interviews, you might be asked about overarching topics of classical literature and your interviewer might touch on philosophy, history, archaeology, art, philology or linguistics. It is highly beneficial to develop in-depth knowledge of at least one of these topics, in order to enter into a discussion with your interviewer.

Developing a special interest can help. Soak up a particular author (e.g. one of the great Greek Tragedians Aeschylus, Sophocles or Euripides or study Ovid's use of myth), a genre (e.g. Latin love elegy, Ancient Greek political comedy etc.), a historical period (e.g. Peloponnesian War or the final days of the Roman Republic) architectural style or period of art. Do not be afraid to have strong or even controversial opinions and reactions to ancient authors or historical events. The interviewer is looking for someone who has passionate reactions to the Ancient World; just ensure you use examples to support your argument. Show initiative and be proactive in your search for new knowledge. Visiting museums (for example, the Parthenon friezes at the British Museum), Ancient Roman and Greek archaeological sites, going to the theatre to watch an Ancient Greek play, or simply watching a suitable documentary on the BBC or History Channel can show you are a motivated student, capable of going one step further to research your subject away from the classroom.

It's always good to brush up on grammar and your vocabulary to prepare for unseen passages you might be presented with in the interview, but do not spend hours revising. You may be asked about the essays or commentaries you have submitted as well as what you are studying at A Level, what you enjoy about Classics and what you look forward to studying on the course. Re-read any submitted essays/commentaries and develop new arguments and points in case you are questioned on them in the interview.

It's good to develop your critical thinking skills. Train your analytical responses to the literature you have already studied by reading scholars' critical responses (secondary literature) and deciding whether you agree with their views. You are entitled to have an opinion, you just need to have evidence to support your case.

**Our advice**

The interviewer may want to test your ability to react critically and analytically to a literary text, as this exercise makes up a large part of the course. Delve into a literary genre or start reading a particular author in any language and assess your reactions to the text in terms of style, language, context, themes, imagery, tone, register etc. Why did you like/not like it? Read a selection of plays/prose/poetry in translation to help you develop an understanding of the genres and periods and to get you excited about them. One possibility is to choose an author, for example Ovid or Aristophanes, who has left us a large legacy of work and track their literary development to gain a better understanding of the historical context.

It can be helpful to familiarise yourself with terminology used in literary criticism such as anaphora, pathetic fallacy, soliloquy, oxymoron and onomatopoeia, but do not get too caught up revising every single critical word and its meaning. Start familiarising yourself with the epic poets Homer and Virgil. Begin to learn the Greek alphabet and try translating some passages of Greek and Latin into English with the help of a dictionary and grammar guide to get to grips with basic language structures.

# ENGLISH

### Questions to consider:

Do you think that the director of a play should have absolute power, or should he/she be flexible?

Why study English at university rather than read in your spare time?

How is poetry linked to music and the other arts?

Is a protagonist's gender important?

English interviews usually consist of a mixture of broad questions about literature, more in-depth questions about specific works of literature that you've read, and analysing an unseen poem or passage.

### Analyse this poem by Philip Sydney

Having to analyse a poem on the spot might sound terrifying, and many Oxbridge applicants consider it by far the most intimidating part of the interview process. However, if you go in armed with some simple but useful analytical techniques, you'll have nothing to fear.

Your interviewer is not expecting you to have prepared an exhaustive discussion of, for instance, Renaissance sonnets and their Italianate influences in the 20 minutes or so you've had to look at the unseen poem before your interview; rather, the idea is that you can put forward your own ideas and claims about the way the poem works, and the effects it achieves.

XIX

*On Cupid's bow, how are my heart-strings bent,*
*That see my wrack, and yet embrace the same!*
*When most I glory, then I feel most shame;*

*I willing run, yet while I run repent;*

*My best wits still their own disgrace invent:*

*My very ink turns straight to Stella's name;*

*And yet my words, as them my pen doth frame,*

*Advise themselves that they are vainely spent:*

*For though she pass all things, yet what is all*

*That unto me, who fare like him that both*

*Looks to the skies and in a ditch doth fall?*

*O let me prop my mind, yet in his growth,*

*And not in nature for best fruits unfit.*

*Scholar, saith Love, bend hitherward your wit.*

Sir Philip Sidney, from Astrophel and Stella (1591)

The first thing to do is to ensure that you understand the literal sense of the poem: what is happening, who is speaking, what does he/she want, are there any narrative twists etc.? For this poem, you should first establish that the speaker is experiencing the agony of love as he attempts to write a poem for his beautiful beloved, Stella. Without a basic knowledge of what's going on, you won't be able to explore the poetic techniques the writer is using to express it.

Next, think about the form the poem is taking. This will help you to compare your expectations of the genre with how the poet is using that genre. Here, we have a Petrarchan sonnet (abba, abba, cdcd, ee), which, as is traditional with Petrarchan sonnets, has the torments of love as a theme. Knowing whether the poem is working with or against tradition will also help you to talk about its effect.

You should pay close attention to the words and groups of words used (the language or diction). This will lead us to consider imagery, mood and to develop our ideas on the theme. In this sonnet, the poet frequently creates pairs of contrasting words or ideas ('glory' and 'shame'; 'I willing run, yet while I run repent'; 'him that both/Looks to the skies and in a ditch doth fall'). The poet uses these contrasts to express the conflicting impulses and feelings involved in being in love – a mixture of joy and pain – and to put them across vividly to the reader. Be thorough with what you notice here – and back it up with examples from the poem – the more evidence you have, the more convincing your points will be.

All of this should lead you to your conclusion: a brief summary of your argument about what you think the poet is trying to achieve. Think of all the details you've picked up as weight for your argument. It's important that you conclude your argument, as it will prove that you're able to link textual details with the poet's intention in using them.

**Our advice for analysing unseen extracts**

Try to ground your impressions about what the poem means by pointing to the places in the text where you can find evidence for your assertions. If you see evidence of poetic techniques such as those mentioned above, use the technical terms, but make sure you're using them correctly. Perhaps study the definitions of frequently used literary terms like irony or satire before the interview. If you do use them, be prepared to say what they mean. And, finally, it's almost never valuable to say that a literary work is interesting. The natural response to that is, 'Why? What's so interesting about it?' Skip that step and get into the meat of what the poem or text is doing. The more specific you are, the more substantive things you'll have to say and the more you'll impress the tutor.

**Our advice for approaching broader questions about literature**

Interviewers may ask broader questions about some of the biggest debates in literature, such as 'What is a classic?' or 'Does literature have a moral purpose?' The key to answering a question like this well is to ensure you use concrete examples from literature you have read, rather than speculating vaguely. Apart from being a good opportunity to show off the scope of your reading, this will also help you put forward a clear and intelligent argument. Remember, the big questions don't necessarily have a right answer: the key is to make a claim and be able to justify it, especially when the tutor challenges you by offering a conflicting opinion.

# MODERN & MEDIEVAL LANGUAGES

## Questions to consider:

Could you say that an author is actually just another character in their novel or their play?

Do you notice any differences between English and European literature? If so, why might these be?

What do you think Voltaire meant by 'Il faut cultiver notre jardin'?

What is meant by subject and object?

Interviews for languages will assess your spoken ability in the language you are applying for, but they are also likely to include an element of literary analysis, as literature is a large part of the course. If you haven't studied literature as part of your AS or A Levels, don't worry, but you will need to show an interest in literature and an ability to think critically about literary ideas, language and styles. A good approach is to read a few different works of literature from authors or periods that you are interested in, preferably from the country you are hoping to study the language of, even if it is only in translation.

Consider the example question given in the English section of this chapter, as this is a helpful exercise to practice your critical approach to literature.

You may also be asked broader questions about the nature of language and/or its connection to literature, history or culture.

## What is the role of the translator?

In this question you are being asked to show an understanding of the applications of translation as well as the challenges. What makes one translation excellent and another mediocre, or simply inaccurate? What are the differences between different types of translation? Would we approach a poem differently to a piece of prose? Your ability to define, conceptualise, and think deeply about the relationship between language and meaning is what lies at the heart of this question. How do languages embody the unique concepts of a particular culture within their grammatical and idiomatic structures and how far can we transfer these concepts from one language to another whilst also preserving meaning?

There are two elements to tackling this question. Firstly, your definition of the 'role' of a translator, and secondly, how this can practically be achieved. You may also wish to discuss texts/excerpts you have read in translation and why some are more successful than others. The best answers will weave in examples from your own experience of texts in translation.

Firstly, outline your definition. A translator's role is primarily to enable a cross-cultural sharing of information, knowledge and concepts. To achieve this, one must initially unlock the overall meaning of the source text. The source text is then rendered into the target language, with the translator ensuring that the grammatical structures and cultural context of the target text are respected. The best translations do not appear to be translations, they convey the meaning and nuances of the source language using the lexicon and grammatical structures most appropriate to the target language. An excellent translation will take account of register, tone, target audience and time period and will find cultural equivalents for concepts in the source text that do not exist in the target language. The ultimate aim is for the target audience to access the inherent meaning of a text.

The more you can show knowledge of the technical terminology used in translation theory, the better. Examine and evaluate the different translation techniques: cultural borrowing calque, literal translation, cultural transposition, cultural equivalence and modulation.

**A note on joint schools**

If you are applying to read Modern Languages and another subject, the above still applies to the Modern Languages side. However, it might be a good idea to think about the links between your other subject and your chosen language. For example, if you are applying to read English and Spanish, you could consider the influence writers such as James Joyce, William Faulkner and John Dos Passos have had on Latin American authors, especially Mario Vargas Llosa and Gabriel García Márquez. Similarly, for History & French, you could think about the impact of French colonisation on writers such as Aimé Césaire and Patrick Chamoiseau. You will be interviewed in both subjects, but one of your interviewers may be interested to hear about the connections you have made between your two subjects and how you think the social, political and cultural developments of a country influence its literature.

## A note on studying a language ab initio

If you are applying to read a language ab initio you need to demonstrate a natural aptitude for languages and an ability to pick up languages and linguistic concepts quickly. To test your ability, you may be given something to read and comment upon in the language. You might prepare for this by engaging with the language as much as possible. Further reading can help: study the grammar and try to build up your vocabulary, perhaps by making a vocabulary list. It is a good idea to show that you have dipped into the literature and begun to develop an interest in a few authors or periods. You could apply the same strategy as described earlier: pick an author, a theme or a period, look at the literature and start forming your own opinion about your chosen area.

## Our advice

Prepare thoroughly for the literature aspect but don't go overboard – it is only one element of the interview. Focus on a few authors, themes or periods. Be aware of the wider context in which the literature you have read operates. Brush up on the grammar of your chosen language before the interview and make sure you are comfortable conversing on a range of different subjects. Re-read your personal statement and be prepared to answer questions on anything mentioned. Train yourself to respond instantly to ideas and arguments by reading passages from newspapers, novels or collections of poetry.

# Social & Political Sciences

## ECONOMICS/ECONOMICS & MANAGEMENT/PPE

### Questions you should consider:

Who do you think is the greatest economist?

What do we mean when we say someone deserves a reward?

What is the biggest economic problem facing Britain today?

Economics interviews often test your understanding of economic theory and current affairs. For the purposes of this exercise we have created four example questions, based on similar ones that have been asked in the past. The first is an example of a microeconomics question, the second a macroeconomics question, the third an example of a logical thinking question and finally a mathematics question.

### What factors could be expected to affect the price of houses in a free market?

At the core of this question is the interaction of supply and demand for houses. Given this, a logical way to answer the question, could be to work out the factors affecting supply and demand and then go on to explain how their interaction results in a final equilibrium price. To make your answer even stronger, it would also be good to consider what might affect the price of an individual house as opposed to what affects the price of houses in general in a free market.

Major factors affecting demand for housing include: the incomes of households in the economy, which affects the amount they are able to spend on housing in general, mortgage interest rates are key, as lower rates make houses in general more affordable and vice versa, likewise expectations of future house prices and future mortgage interest rates affect what householders might be willing to pay for housing.

The demand for a particular house rather than houses in general could be affected by the preferences of householders in the economy. For example, are Georgian houses in fashion or is there a fad for the clean lines of modern architecture? This factor might also apply to houses generally for example, if owning your own home is a sign of status in a society, this may increase willingness to pay across the economy. Other preferential factors include the size and nature of the house (e.g. a cottage, flat, bungalow, mansion, etc) and the location of the house. For example, is the house located in a densely populated urban centre where there are many jobs, or in a rural area? Is it near good schools and local amenities?

Meanwhile, housing supply is determined by the existing stock of houses, and the building of new houses.

The next step in answering this question is to draw a graph of supply and demand and illustrate the equilibrium price. One thing to note is that because a new building contributes only about 1.1 per cent to the existing stock each year, the supply of houses is relatively inelastic even over long periods. This means that the supply curve will be steep. In contrast, demand is relatively elastic because consumers are highly sensitive to house prices. This means the demand curve will be relatively shallow.

You could also demonstrate how changing demand or supply conditions would affect the equilibrium. For example, during the mid to late 1980s incomes grew rapidly, while financial deregulation in 1987 made mortgages cheaper and easier to obtain. This led to a rise in demand, shifting the demand curve up and right and causing a housing market boom.

### What effect would a tightening of monetary policy have on the value of government bonds in the bond markets?

The first step in answering this question is to define the various terms: 'monetary tightening' is a constriction of the supply of money by the central bank. 'Government bonds' are assets sold by the government to investors as a way of borrowing money. Investors hand over cash for the bonds to the government, in exchange for a promise by the government to repay this money at a specified future date. In the meantime, the investors receive interest payments from the government to compensate them for the amount of money they could have made by investing this cash elsewhere, and also for the risk that the government will go bankrupt and not repay the debt.

Next, a good answer would go on to explain how a central bank tightens monetary policy. It does this through 'open market operations' which work as follows: the central bank sells government bonds to investors from its own portfolio in exchange for cash. This reduces the supply of money the public holds. As we know from the law of supply and demand (see previous question), an increase in the supply of bonds in the market for a given demand will cause the price of the bonds to fall. One thing to note here is that this is equivalent to a rise in the interest rate because less money is needed today for a given value in the future. Bond prices, therefore, are inversely related to interest rates.

At this stage, a strong applicant would look to expand further on the results of this action on aggregate demand in the economy. The rate of interest on savings in the economy has increased so consumers may be encouraged to save rather than spend. If foreigners want to buy debt then they must first buy domestic currency: an increase in the interest rate will increase their demand for domestic currency which, as we know from the question above, will make domestic currency relatively more expensive. Exports become more expensive and imports cheaper. You will add another layer of dynamism to your answer if you show knowledge of the current interest rate set by the central bank, the Bank of England, and recent changes in interest rates.

### What is the angle between the hands on a clock at quarter past three?

This is a simple case of mental arithmetic. The best way to answer this question is to create a mental picture of a clock. Do NOT fall into the trap of thinking the angle is zero! There are 360 degrees in a circle and 12 hours on a clock face, so the angle between each hour is $360/12 = 30$ degrees. The minute hand is directly over the '3' marking. However, the hour hand will be a quarter of the way between the '3' and '4' markings. Therefore, the angle between the hands is $30/4 = 7.5$ degrees.

### Draw a graph of $y = \sin(x^2)$

As you will know from A Level Mathematics, the graph of $y = \sin(x)$ looks like this:

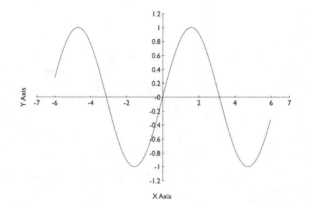

When working out how to draw sin($x^2$), think about the fundamentals of the graph, rather than trying to plot specific points: first, evaluate what the maximum and minimum values for y will be. Since the maximum value of y for sin(x) is 1, no matter how large x, the maximum value of sin($x^2$) will also be 1. Likewise the minimum value will also be -1, as this is the minimum for any value of x and thus $x^2$. Next, think about the frequency of oscillations. As x increases, $x^2$ increases exponentially, the rate at which y oscillates between 1 and -1 will increase. This will mean the gap between maxima and minima will decrease as x gets larger than zero or less than zero.

Finally, note that the graph of y = $x^2$ is symmetrical about the y axis, and thus so will the graph of y = sin($x^2$). Hence the graph will look as follows:

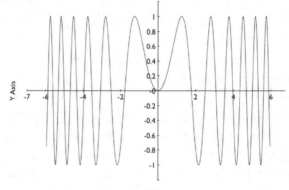

## Our advice

Have a glance through our glossary. Economics is full of jargon. This can seem tricky at first, but as your understanding of the subject develops it will become clear how useful it is to have words for very specific concepts. Here are some examples of vocabulary that an Oxbridge interviewer may use:

BUDGET DEFICIT/SURPLUS – the excess/shortfall of government spending over government receipts from taxation.

BUSINESS CYCLE – the short-term fluctuations in the economy's output around its trend path.

CENTRAL BANK – the institution responsible for implementing monetary policy (e.g. the Bank of England in the UK and the Federal Reserve in the USA).

CONSUMPTION – goods and services purchased by consumers.

ECONOMETRICS – the use of statistical techniques to quantify relationships in economic data.

ECONOMICS – the study of how individuals and societies allocate scarce resources.

ENDOGENOUS VARIABLE – one explained by the model.

EQUILIBRIUM – a state of balance between opposing forces, such as supply and demand in the market.

EXOGENOUS VARIABLE – one taken as given; assumed rather than explained in the model.

FISCAL POLICY – policy on government spending and taxation.

GDP (Gross Domestic Product) – the total income/production of the economy earned/produced domestically.

INFLATION – the rate of increase in the level of overall prices.

INVESTMENT – goods purchased by firms to increase their stock of capital.

MACROECONOMICS – the study of the economy as a whole; typical variables of interest include inflation, interest rates and exchange rates.

MICROECONOMICS – the study of individual behaviour with respect to consumers' and firms' decisions about the allocation of resources.

MONETARY POLICY – policy on the money supply and interest rates.

MONOPOLY – a market in which there is only one producer.

PROFIT – revenue minus costs.

REAL VARIABLE – a variable which has been adjusted for inflation (as opposed to a nominal variable).

UNEMPLOYMENT RATE – the percentage of the labour force without jobs.

You may be asked questions to test your comprehension of an article relevant to an economic topic. You may also be asked to talk about a couple of areas of the subject that especially interest you (such as economic growth in the third world), or an economist you admire (for instance John Maynard Keynes) and therefore it is helpful to think about how you might approach such questions. If possible, use your interview as an opportunity to talk about one or two books or articles you have read, particularly if they are mentioned in your personal statement. If you bring up a book, though, make sure you are able to talk in some detail about its ideas!

An understanding of mathematics is fundamental to economics and that is why Oxbridge Economics tutors deem Mathematics an important subject to have studied at A Level or equivalent. If you are new to the subject, your interviewers will naturally not expect you to know as much as your peers who have done Economics before and in this instance your interviewer will likely ask you more logic or maths-based questions. However, you should be able to show an initial understanding of key principles, to show you are committed and motivated to study the subject.

## GEOGRAPHY

### Questions you should consider:

What is the role of the media in Geography?

Describe a problem in your area which a geographer could solve.

What can we do to stop global warming?

How would you persuade an 11-year old to pursue Geography through GCSEs and beyond?

Geography is a multidisciplinary subject and the breadth of questions that applicants have been asked in past interviews reflects this. For the purposes of this exercise, our geographers have created some sample questions, based on similar ones that have been asked in previous years, to help you think about the subject a little bit differently.

**Should Physical and Human Geography be taught together and why?**

This question tests your grasp of the purpose and scope of geography in an academic context. A good answer to this question may begin by breaking the question down, in other words, explaining what is meant by the terms Physical and Human Geography. You might say Physical Geography investigates how the environment and natural habitats of earth operate. In contrast, Human Geography explores the spatial and temporal differences between human societies. The key point is that our physical and human worlds are mutually dependent and both Physical and Human Geography focus on exploring the links. You could then choose examples either from school work or wider reading e.g. volcanic eruptions to explain why such phenomena benefit from analysis of both the human and physical impact.

This would naturally lead to a conclusion (and it is important that you do reach one) that Physical and Human Geography must be taught together. You might then wish to elaborate, suggesting that one of Geography's greatest strength is its ability to bridge the arts, social and natural sciences. Geography enables us to consider and analyse complex problems using a broad lens.

At school, modules on Physical and Human Geography tend to be taught separately. At university the boundaries are more blurred, with topics such as climate change discussed from a human and a physical perspective. In fact, at Oxford and Cambridge, undergraduate courses contain compulsory modules of Human and Physical Geography, while at other universities there is often a very real division between the two. If you choose to argue in favour of an integrated approach then it is useful to mention that this element of the course particularly appealed to you. This shows you have done your research and are up to date with contemporary teaching debates. Interviews may focus on Human or Physical Geography, or you may be tested on both.

## What is more important, the economy or the environment?

This question tests your skills and how well you can structure a logical argument. A definitive answer would require subjectivity, however, before you reach your conclusion, the interviewer is testing your ability to think objectively and to use examples and your existing knowledge to support your points.

Firstly, break down the two terms – the economy and the environment. The first refers to relations of production, exchange and consumption of goods and services. It is regulated by human structures. Issues of scale are important. National economies now operate globally and are increasingly interconnected. The environment refers broadly to the natural habitats of earth: the landforms and processes that operate to renew our eco-systems and provide the tools necessary for human existence.

Once you have defined these terms, you then need to consider the value of each concept. But how can you measure this? The environment and the economy are integral to our lives, and are extremely complex concepts. In evaluating the importance of each we are ultimately asking: Which do humans rely on more? Could we exist without one? Ultimately both are fundamental to our existence. With a question such as this, is it possible to reach an unbiased conclusion? Admissions Tutors want to see evidence of your ability to interact with such a complex, macro idea and to have the confidence and intellect to ask these sorts of questions. This shows you have that ability to be flexible with your existing knowledge and are open to thinking and talking independently – exactly the qualities Admissions Tutors look for in successful applicants.

### Our advice

At the core of Geography are questions about place and space. Keep interested in these concepts and think about how they relate to you in terms of your reading, your studies and your daily life. One applicant was asked to talk about what they found interesting about their local area, another about what they thought made for an interesting geographic article in a magazine. You need to be interested and engaged with your subject, and in turn that will make you interesting.

In an interview you may be asked to analyse the key skills you have developed through fieldwork. The basis of your fieldwork investigation may be Human or Physical. Make sure, with this sort of question, you evaluate activities that you undertook during fieldwork, i.e. why something was particularly useful or why something was not. You may be asked factual questions. This is more likely to occur if you have mentioned a particular topic on your personal statement or have been given source material for the interview. Interviewers do not expect you to possess detailed knowledge on every geographic topic. Ensure you stay calm and use all the reading you have done before the interview to apply your knowledge to the question before you. Remain logical, think laterally and support your arguments.

## LAW

### Questions you should consider:

How important are jury trials?

When it comes to IVF treatment, should a male have rights equal to those of a female?

Do you think that anyone should be able to serve on a jury?

If A gave B £100 thinking it was a loan and B accepted the money thinking it was a gift, should he give it back?

At interview and throughout their degree, Law students are challenged to think analytically and this is reflected in the questions posed in interviews. For the purpose of this exercise, our legal minds got together and came up with this meaty law question, based on real past interview questions. The second question in this section is a real past question.

### Are judges really necessary since they don't always make the law certain?

This question does require you to understand the basics behind judge-made law. While Oxbridge interviews do not strictly require prior knowledge of the law, you should have a grip on the basics here, from your awareness of legal cases in the news.

In summary, law in England and Wales comes primarily from two sources – statutes that are passed by Parliament and from judges (common law). Unlike other regimes (notably, civil law systems), common law allows that judges not only interpret and apply the law but that they contribute to the evolution of the law by laying down precedent. Essentially, a ruling by a higher court on a point of law, as long as it does not run in the face of a statute, is binding on lower courts and they must follow that ruling. For example, if the Supreme Court rules that a 'mobile phone' includes a hands-free kit, then a lower court cannot overrule this and rule that a mobile phone does not include a hands-free kit.

An initial reaction to this question could, and should, be questioning that perhaps judges are necessary for other reasons anyway so that even if they don't make the law certain, they are still necessary. You may argue that judges are necessary in order to apply the law, to be neutral arbiters in disputes and to sanction appropriately those who act contrary to the law. Question what the state of a regime would be if judges didn't exist – who would decide who was right or wrong if there was a dispute?

Next, you should go on to assess the claim that judges don't always make the law certain. First, try to understand why the claim would be made. It could perhaps be because judges are allowed this law-making power and so they are able to make rulings that change the law. Secondly, assess the claim. You may agree that judges don't always make the law certain – for example, if a judge ruled that 'driving' includes sitting at traffic lights, questions would still emerge such as 'does it matter if the engine is on or off?' or 'does it matter how long you expect to be stationary?'

So the judge would not have made the law certain here, but perhaps you should question the state of the certainty of the law without this intervention. The law would be a lot less certain without a judge clarifying, to some extent, what 'driving' meant. So even though the judge did not make the law certain, s/he certainly went some way towards helping clarify the law and this may support the argument that judges are still necessary.

**Smith sees Jones walking towards the edge of a cliff. Smith knows Jones is blind but does not like him, so allows him to walk off the edge of the cliff. Is this murder?** (past question)

Obviously, murder has a legal definition. However, this question is not designed to test your understanding of the application of the law of murder to this situation (unless you have been given the law of murder and are expected to do this!). What it is really asking is whether Smith should be treated by the law in the same way as someone who commits a paradigmatic instance of murder, for example, a pre-meditated killing. Again, it is a normative evaluation testing your arguments justifying (or not) Smith's punishment. So your arguments should be on the issue of the moral blameworthiness of Smith and whether this blameworthiness is equal to that of a murderer.

In moral terms, it could quite simply be argued that if you know that somebody is going to die for certain, then you should stop them and prevent their death. However, this is obviously subject to various caveats which you should mention (or allow the interviewer to mention and respond to accordingly).

Is it certain that the person is going to die? In this case it seems from the facts that Jones is going to die for certain (especially bearing in mind that he is blind). This probably detracts from the moral culpability of Smith as he would be unable to prevent Jones's death even if he warned him. Perhaps if the risk of death is not high, then Smith has a greater moral responsibility to warn him e.g. if Jones was not walking towards the edge and only near the edge but aware of the drop.

How much do you need to do to prevent this death? In this case, if Smith is close enough to Jones that he could simply shout out to Jones to warn him then this is hugely morally blameworthy. Contrast this with the position whereby somebody is drowning in dangerous water – you should probably not be as morally culpable for failing to jump in to save that person as in Smith's case here. The fact that Smith knows that Jones is blind perhaps makes this even worse since he knows that Jones is less able to look after himself walking near a cliff. Although you could also say that perhaps Jones is not free of blame either – he should be aware of the dangers of walking close to the cliff edge, especially considering that he is blind. Should anyone be walking that close to a cliff edge?!

So you could conclude that Smith is extremely morally culpable if he could easily have prevented this death without much burden on himself. In addition, the fact that Smith does not like Jones perhaps makes this worse since it may imply that Smith consciously did not take any steps to warn Jones and so Smith somehow wanted his death to arise as opposed to just realising that it would be a consequence.

However, you should go the full stretch with this question and compare this moral culpability to that of a 'murderer'. Take the example of a pre-meditated shooting in the head. Is somebody who omits to warn someone of their death, no matter how certain it is, as morally culpable as someone who takes the active step of getting a gun, pointing at somebody's head and pulling the trigger?

You could argue that they are just as morally culpable or you could say that they are not – this is subjective. However, you could allude to distinctions such as omitting to do something versus taking practical steps or pre-meditation versus a sudden situation.

**Our advice**

Even if you do believe that you have some knowledge of the law in a certain area, ensure that you apply it with hesitance. Remember who you are conveying this knowledge to! Much of what is being asked is inherently subjective and there is no correct answer. Therefore, don't think that you may be 'wrong'. If you have a thought that sounds sensible then state it. The interviewers are looking to see your thought process so don't be afraid to think aloud and go through your thoughts step by step. Be receptive to contributions from the interviewers – they will help you formulate your views and your arguments but may also challenge any propositions. Take these on board and deal with them and remember that this doesn't necessarily mean accepting them. You are encouraged to think about what is said to you and challenge it if you feel that you can sensibly do so.

## POLITICS (FOR PPE AND HSPS)

**Questions you should consider:**

Is democracy the best system?

What would you say to someone who claims women have equal opportunities already?

Why do we need government?

Does the welfare state trap people into poverty?

Students applying for HSPS and PPE are likely to have at least one interview centred around politics. Politics interviews will often test your understanding of political theories, as well as your knowledge of political history and of current affairs. Some questions, such as the examples below, will be very broad, allowing you to bring in examples from your reading. Our politics graduates have demonstrated the kind of examples you might use in their answers to our practice questions.

**DO YOU THINK POLITICAL GROUPS CAN HAVE POLITICAL LEGITIMACY?** (past question)

To answer this question, you need to ensure that you are clear about what a political group is, what political legitimacy is and then how (if at all) this political legitimacy can be obtained by these groups.

When we think of a political group, the most obvious type of group is a political party, but there are also other groups which could be classed as political groups. For example, there are groups which exert political pressure such as trade unions, and lobby groups e.g Greenpeace, which can be seen as political groups.

Political legitimacy is the acceptance of a group as an authority, which has a right to rule. It is a basic condition for governing or exercising power as without it the exercise of power will struggle and collapse.

Political legitimacy can be created through the consent of those subjected to it, and the belief both by those exercising the power and by those subjected to it that the institutions and methods of ruling are the most appropriate ones for the society.

In your wider reading you may have come across two political thinkers – John Locke and Max Weber. Locke (regarded as one of the most influential Enlightenment thinkers) believed that political legitimacy is derived from general explicit and implicit consent. Max Weber (German sociologist and political economist) identified three sources of political legitimacy: charismatic authority, traditional authority and rational–legal authority. It is suggested that people may have faith in a particular rule because they have faith in the individual rulers (charisma), because it has been there for a long time (tradition), or because they trust its legality, this is the rationality of the rule of law (rational–legal).

If we use Weber's three descriptive sources of legitimacy, you can see how a group may be able to obtain political legitimacy.

A group could have charismatic authority if people have faith in the individual leaders of a group. Traditional authority could stem from people simply accepting the authority of a group as it has always exercised power over them, for example a trade union. A group may gain legitimacy from rational–legal authority because people trust its legality, perhaps because it has been appointed by the rule of law they support.

People do not agree on how political groups can have authority. While someone may give authority to a group because it has been there for a long time this may not make it legitimate for others. This benchmark of legitimacy may vary from person to person. Some may believe in democratic authority, where a group is legitimate if it is supported by the majority of people, while others might claim that authority could come from religion, such as a group that believe they are appointed by God to rule. Others may suggest that even usual democratic authority is not enough for political legitimacy, as the tyranny of the majority is not a legitimate way for a group to rule over everyone, for example, minority groups.

**Are there always winners and losers in politics?** (past question)

To answer this question, we must look at what the different actors in politics are hoping to achieve. We can then see how they can win and lose.

For politicians in elections, it could be said that there is always a winner and a loser, lasting for the length of a political term. However counter arguments to this could be that the politicians are not actually winners or losers in an election but it is the will of the people, expressed through the election, which is always the winner.

A politician who is placed second or third in an election, although not entering office, then has won if they believe in the democratic system. Furthermore, even from a selfish political point of view it may be beneficial to have not entered office in that election (due to political or economic turbulence) but to have participated in the democratic system with the possibility of entering in office after the turbulence.

In many political systems they also result in differing political parties having to work together, at both a local and national level. Whilst coalitions are common in more proportional electoral systems such as Germany and Italy they are not unknown in the UK.

In such a coalition system it may be possible for the politics of compromise and consensus to overcome the partisan nature. It may be difficult however to avoid having winners and losers – it is unlikely that a coalition will include all parties and therefore there will still be losers, even if it could be argued that there are no winners, due to the members of the coalition compromising.

Aside from the politicians, ordinary individuals in the distribution of public funds or taxation may be seen to be winners and losers, with some individuals paying higher taxes than others whilst receiving lower benefits and vice versa. It is difficult to see how there could be winners without losers.

With a question like this, draw on any extra reading you may have done and dip into your current affairs knowledge for pertinent examples to back up your arguments.

**Our advice**
Come prepared with opinions but remain respectful to established political theorists' views to avoid seeming dogmatic and arrogant.

# Physical, Chemical & Mathematical Sciences

## CHEMISTRY / NATURAL SCIENCES (BIOLOGICAL AND PHYSICAL)

### Questions you should consider:

What makes a material hard?

Explain how catalysts work.

How many atoms are there in a Brussels sprout?

Name a reaction in which a bond is made.

### Do you think O-H and O-D (deuterium) bonds differ in strength? (past question)

At any stage of the interview, do not be afraid to ask for help as you work through the questions. This is a purely theorising question. You are not really expected to know the answer but the interviewer will want to see how you approach it.

Start by thinking about what you know about deuterium, i.e. the fact that it has a significantly greater atomic weight to hydrogen. It is twice as heavy so you should be able to theorise that the bonds will be very different.

### Assuming the bonds do have different strengths, how will this affect the rate of exchange of hydrogen or deuterium ions in an aqueous solution? For example in a carboxylic acid? (past question)

Begin by thinking about what you already understand about dynamic equilibriums and how activation energy affects reaction rate. Based on this you can draw a reaction diagram of each dynamic equilibrium (one being the O-H equilibrium, the other being the O-D). Consider the reaction speed in both directions as well as how this affects the rate of exchange.

Don't be afraid to ask if you can draw diagrams as it will help you think clearly and follow through with your ideas. Drawing diagrams is also an essential part of the Chemistry tutorials and supervisions you will be having in the future.

**Given different rates of exchange, how will this affect the equilibrium point and therefore the acidity of the non-deuteriated and deuteriated forms?** (past question)

You could start by explaining the formula for an equilibrium point based on reaction rates:

$K_p = K_1 / K_2$

where $K_p$ is the equilibrium at constant pressure. Based on what you know about the different reaction rates for the hydrogen and deuterium exchange you can predict the different equilibrium points. This will then allow you to go on to explain the different concentrations of H+ and D+ and how this affects acidity.

If this interests you, you can go further by reading about the Kinetic Isotope Effect.

**a. How does the radius of an ion affect the strength of its interaction with water?** (past question)

You may already know that small ions are strongly polarising and will therefore have a strong interaction with water because their charge is more densely concentrated.

**b. How do cation and anion radii affect the ionic bond strength in an ionic lattice? For example NaCl.** (past question)

You may know from your school work that ionic lattice bond strength is affected by ionic radius and ionic charge. Greater ionic radii increase the distance between the ions in the lattice, and the strength of interaction is a function of $1/r$.

**c. What does the graph of 1/r² (r squared) look like?** (past question)

You are being asked this as a precursor to the next question. You will be able to use this graph to show that as the ionic radii increase there is a sharp drop off in the strength of the interactions.

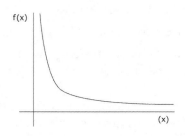

**Given the answers to a, b, c how would you explain solubility trends in the series NaF -> NaCl and AgF -> AgCl?**

This is the culmination of the answers you have given in the first three parts. You know the factors affecting the bond strength in the ionic lattice, and the strength of the cation and anion interactions with water. Using your knowledge that $Na^+$ is a relatively small anion and $Ag^+$ is a relatively large anion, you need to theorise about how the solubility trends down the halide group will differ. Drawing a Hess's Law diagram for this reaction would be a useful way of working through this analysis. You can use all of the knowledge and skills from your schoolwork and apply them to the question.

Hopefully you've seen from this that you can work through what seems like a complex problem by building on what you already know. If at any point you get stuck in your interview, you can ask for help. Even if you do end up with the wrong answer or make mistakes along the way, it doesn't matter too much as long as you've been thinking intelligently as you work through the problem.

Budding Chemists should also check out the questions in both the Maths and Physics section.

## COMPUTER SCIENCE

### Questions you should consider:

Tell me about binary searches. What about their efficiency?

What are the possible ways of making a secure transfer?

How do you understand Newton's Laws?

'The game of chess will be played perfectly by the computers of 2025.' What is the meaning of this statement and is it likely to be true?

We spoke to a number of Oxbridge Computer Scientists, who experienced a range of interview questions, some mathematical or logic-based, while others tended to focus on the science of computers. We take a look at these types of questions.

### If you have a sorted array of numbers, how would you find number n? (past question)

In other words, if you have a random array of 100 numbers, in ascending order, how would you find the number 38? The challenge is to answer this question out loud using logic. You might initially think to look at each number sequentially, but that would be inefficient. The tutor might suggest other starting points. What about the middle number? What if the middle number is bigger than n? What if the middle number is smaller? In these cases, which portions of the array might be sensible to focus on? What the tutor is looking for is for you to work with them. So really take on board their advice, articulate what you are thinking and why. They are there to help you get to the right answer (as they might do in the future with a successful candidate during their time at the university).

### What is the one fundamental difference between a spreadsheet and a database, as surely both hold information? Perhaps there is no fundamental difference? (past question)

A good place to start here would be to acknowledge that both a spreadsheet and database hold information, but the way in which they hold information differs. A spreadsheet is a flat file document that stores each line of information in serial. There is a list of attributes, or columns that each record has a piece of information in. The spreadsheet can be searched for values and calculations can be made using information in certain columns, or fields, but without the use of macros and higher order coding, not much else can be done. In contrast, a database is more intelligent in the way it stores information. Moreover, the user must be more aware of the relationships between the data they are to store. Rather than just simply listing records, in a database there are different entities which each contain their own kind of record. There are relationships defined between these entities that ensure that data stored is correct – referential integrity ensures that related data is consistent e.g. `John Smith' is always referred to as `John Smith' and there is never the opportunity for `John Smiht' to be confused with `John Smith'.

In addition, you might add here that within the infrastructure of the database, inferences (otherwise known as queries) can be generated. These are smart, modifiable views of the data created by the user. In this way, a database can address a more complex requirement than a spreadsheet can.

A good conclusion will then come back to the initial question, stating that therefore, as illustrated, there is a fundamental difference between a spreadsheet and a database.

**What is the structure of URLs?** (past question)

Firstly, when answering a question such as this, it is always good to demonstrate that you understand the concepts to which the question is referring. In this instance, you should define a URL. URLs of the form http://my.example.com/page.html are pointers to a particular page on a website. They are unique, case insensitive and should make more sense to the user than the corresponding IP address.

You can then explain the major parts of the URL structure in more detail. URLs have five major parts as follows:

- The first http:// is the protocol being used to access the page. This may be https:// or even ftp:// if a file transfer is being done.

- Next is the subdomain. This is an optional part and is defined by the owner of the domain. It may signify a different section of the same site or simply forward to another URL.
- Then it is is the top level domain including the country code and/or organisation code. The suffix signifies the location of the organisation and its type. Options include .com, .co.uk, .org or even .edu.
- Next is the directory under the main domain. A homepage URL would not normally feature anything from this point onwards.
- Finally, consider the format of the file. Previously, this always featured html or .htm. Nowadays, it is optional.

**Our advice**

All aspiring Computer Scientists should brush up on their mathematics and physics as they often ask technical questions. Practise answering and articulating answers to maths and logic questions out loud. The interviewer needs to be able to understand and follow your train of thought and you need to be able to justify your problem-solving logic verbally. Don't fret about not getting an answer right in the interview – this will probably happen and it does not matter. Be aware that the interviewer is there to support you and help guide you to your answer – be responsive to their suggestions and interact with them.

## MATHEMATICS

**Questions you should consider:**

Can you prove that any natural number consists of prime factors or is a prime number?

You are given an infinite square grid where each square contains a natural number and is at least the mean of the four neighbouring squares. Prove that each square contains the same number.

**A body with mass m is falling towards earth with speed v. It has a drag force equal to kv. Set up a differential equation and solve it for v.** (past question)

To answer this question, you need to be comfortable with the integration and differentiation you have studied at A Level.

Try to work out which forces are involved, and draw a simple diagram to aid your understanding.

By Newton's Second Law of Motion we know that $F = m\dfrac{dv}{dt}$. This must be equal to the balance between the weight pulling downwards and the drag force against the motion.

Make sure you get the correct signs in the equation. The weight acts in the negative direction, and the drag force against it. Therefore, remembering that velocity is negative, mdv/dt = − mg − kv, where g is the acceleration due to gravity.

Dividing through by m we get $\dfrac{dv}{dt} = -g - \left(\dfrac{k}{m}\right)v$ . For clarity let z=k/m.

By separating the variables we find that $\int \dfrac{\delta v}{g+zv} = -\int \delta t$

At this point it is helpful to make the substitution u = g + zv, and so du = zdv.

Therefore $\left(\dfrac{1}{z}\right)\int \dfrac{\delta u}{u} = -\int \delta t$ which gives us $\ln\dfrac{|u|}{z} = -t + C$ , and so $\ln|u| = -zt + C$

Remembering log rules gives us $|u| = e^{-zt} + C = Ke^{-zt}$.

Substituting back in we get $|g + zv| = Ke^{-zt}$, and so v = − g/z + Ke^{-zt}

Don't worry if you make a calculation error, it is your general approach to the problem that is more important. A tutor will want to see if you can think carefully about the maths involved.

**If you pick 51 of the numbers 1-100, will they include: An even number? A multiple of 3? A square number? A square number plus a cube number? Two numbers, one of which is a multiple of the other? Co-primes?** (past question)

This question builds upon easier problems to reach more complicated ones, to help you settle into the interview. Don't be surprised if you get something quite simple earlier on, the harder parts will come later!

There are 50 even numbers in the integers from 1-100, and therefore if you pick 51 numbers you will definitely have an even number.

Comparatively there are only 33 multiples of 3, and so a multiple of 3 is not guaranteed.

Simply list the square numbers – 1, 4, 9, 16, 25, 36, 49, 64, 81, 100. It is possible to choose 51 numbers not containing these numbers.

There are 5 cube numbers to consider, namely 0, 1, 8, 27, 64. Since there are 11 square numbers in consideration (including 0), there are at most 55 numbers equal to a square number plus a cube number from 1-100. However more than 6 of these numbers are over 100, and so it is possible to pick 51 numbers from 1-100 without picking a square number plus a cube number.

The question now becomes considerably tougher, and it might be tempting to look to the earlier parts for a solution. However instead partition the numbers from 1-100 into different sets generated by the formula $k \times 2^n$ where k is an odd number (for instance $\{1,2,4,8,16,...\}$). There are 50 such sets, and all numbers from 1-100 are in one of these sets. Therefore if we choose 51 numbers between 1-100, one must be the multiple of another.

Co-primes must not share common factors. If no two numbers amongst our 51 are to be co-prime, it is clear they cannot simply all be multiples of a single number. Instead the most efficient way to make such a set would be for all members to have precisely two prime factors from $\{2, 3, 5\}$. However this set is smaller than necessary, and so we must have co-prime numbers.

There are a variety of ways to tackle this problem. Even if you cannot give a well-formulated solution, explain your intuitions to the tutor.

**Top tips for Mathematics interviews**

Make sure you are completely on top of all AS and A Level work. It may be an idea to move ahead of the syllabus, if you have the inclination, as this may give you more confidence.

Make sure you are comfortable with applying proofs and formulae to questions you haven't met before and be prepared to stand and write on a white board from the beginning of the interview. You may be asked to do this!

If you have forgotten a proof or a formula, do ask. Tutors are there to help you in tutorials and tend to be more excited by a mind that can apply information than a mathematician who can repeat rules they have learnt. That being said, do still revise so that you feel prepared and confident.

Remember not to neglect mathematics studied early in your AS level course and be prepared to answer logic questions using estimation and logic. In these cases, keep thinking about how numbers work. How can you show you think logically and how can you use numbers to illustrate your point? To be successful as a mathematician, you have to prove you can think with numbers.

# PHYSICS / ENGINEERING / NATURAL SCIENCES (PHYSICAL)

**Questions you should consider:**

Explain how an aircraft flies.

What is time?

Why do sausages split lengthways rather than around the circumference?

If you are on a boat with a hairdryer and a sail, and you blow the hairdryer into the sail what are the forces acting on the boat?

Our team of Engineers and Physicists have put together questions for this section, based on the types of questions they and other applicants had to answer at their interview. All the questions are suitable for the above subjects, and some will be also be suitable for Mathematics.

**Sketch the graph of** $y = \frac{A}{x^4} - \frac{B}{x^2}$ **, where A and B are constants.**

This is a fairly straightforward question that tests a range of A Level techniques. The only real subtleties lie firstly in identifying those techniques and how they are useful in graph sketching, and secondly in noticing that the nature of the constants A and B affects the shape of the graph.

Make sure you understand what you need to draw by calculating intersections, for example, before drawing your graph.

### A suggested approach to the problem

– Think about symmetries first. Is the function odd or even?

As all the powers of x involved in this curve are even (−4 and −2), the curve must be symmetric about the y axis.

– Then consider the x-intercept

The x-intercept occurs when y = 0, and can be found by solving the equation $\frac{A}{x^4} - \frac{B}{x^2} = 0$ for x (in terms of A and B). This gives $x = \pm\sqrt{\frac{A}{B}}$ at y = 0.

Notice that these intercepts conform to the symmetry deduced above.

– Now consider the y-intercept

Similarly, the y-intercept occurs when x = 0. We cannot substitute this into the given expression as that would involve dividing by zero, so we know that there must be an asymptote. Instead we can consider the behaviour as x → 0 ( x tends to 0), for example by trying small values of x, by taking limits, or by considering an expansion.

Trying x = 0.1 and x = -0.1 both give a value of y = 10000A – 100B, which is clearly large and dominated by the sign of the first term. Thus if A is positive (negative), y will go to positive (negative) infinity as x → 0, from either direction. This is symmetric about the y axis, as required. By limits, which may not be covered in the Mathematics A Level course (although keen students, or ones taking Further Mathematics, may well be familiar with their use!), the derivation proceeds as:

$$\lim_{x \to 0} y = \lim_{x \to 0} \left(\frac{A}{x^4} - \frac{B}{x^2}\right) = \lim_{x \to 0} \left(\left(\frac{1}{x^4}\right)(A - Bx^2)\right) =$$

$$= +\infty \text{ if } A > 0, -\infty \text{ if } A < 0$$

and we see that the same result is recovered. Notice that this limit depends on the sine of the constant A.

– Look at the behaviour at large x

The technique of taking limits is also useful here. However, we are now considering the different limit:

x → ±∞

Trying x=10 and x=-10 both give a value of y = 0.0001A – 0.01B, which is small and dominated by the sign of the second term. When B is positive, y will approach 0 from below, likewise when B is negative, y will approach 0 from above as x → ∞.

Formally taking limits:

$$\lim_{x \to \pm\infty} y = \lim_{x \to \pm\infty} \left(\frac{A}{x^4} - \frac{B}{x^2}\right) = \lim_{x \to \pm\infty} \left(\left(\frac{1}{x^4}\right)(A - Bx^2)\right)$$

$$= -0 \text{ if } B > 0, +0 \text{ if } B < 0$$

where '+/– 0' means '0 approached from above/below', and we see that the same result is recovered.

We now know enough to sketch the form of the graph:

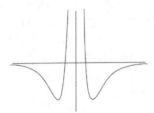

This is the form for positive A and B.

Note that we have not yet deduced that there are turning points. However, we know that this curve is symmetric, tends towards positive infinity as x tends to 0, and has only two x-intercepts, but the curve approaches 0 from below as x tends to either positive or negative infinity.

A complete sketch will have all the relevant points labelled, which we have not done here, so the final thing to do is to calculate the coordinates of these turning points. See if you can do this now.

– Turning points

We find the turning points by the usual A Level method: setting the differential to 0 and solving for x, then substituting these x values into the original expression to find the values of y at these points, thus finding the coordinates of any and all turning points. A common, although minor, mistake here is to forget to find the y values.

Performing the differentiation gives $\frac{dy}{dx} = -4Ax^{-5} + 2Bx^{-3}$. Setting this equal to 0 and solving for x gives:

$$-4Ax^{-5} + 2Bx^{-3} = 0$$

$$\Rightarrow \left(-\frac{2}{x^5}\right)(2A - Bx^2) = 0$$

$$\Rightarrow 2A = Bx^2$$

$$\Rightarrow x = \pm\sqrt{\frac{2A}{B}}$$

and our two values for x. Note that these two values of x obey the symmetry we discovered previously.

– Conclusion

Now we find the value for y at these x values. By the symmetry, the value for y will be the same for both values of x, so we only need to perform one calculation. For simplicity, we will take the positive root:

$$y = \frac{A}{\sqrt[4]{\frac{2A}{B}}} - \frac{B}{\sqrt[2]{\frac{2A}{B}}} = \frac{A}{\frac{4A^2}{B^2}} - \frac{B}{\frac{2A}{B}} = \frac{B^2}{4A} - \frac{B^2}{2A} = -\frac{B^2}{4A}$$

Notice that the negative root would be either squared or raised to the power of 4, and thus give the same value as the positive root – this justifies our statement that we only need to calculate the positive root.

Thus we have found the symmetries of the curve, the coordinates of the x-intercepts and the turning points, and deduced its behaviour as x → 0 and x → ±∞ and thus sketched the graph.

## Why do wind turbines have three blades?

A question that asks for why something is a certain size or shape, or as in this case has a certain number of something, is almost always the result of a compromise.

If asked a question like this, a good strategy is to look for two (or more) competing factors in the design, driving to opposite extremes. The model solution below provides a good example.

This style of question is popular because it requires interviewees to consider a problem from a number of different viewpoints and identify the important factors.

It also allows the interviewer to offer counter arguments to the 'correct' solutions, thus testing the student's scientific debating skills: whether they can defend a position and how they adapt to new ideas. Examples of this are given in the model answer below.

## A suggested approach to the question

There are a number of elements that influence wind turbine design, such as theoretically-tricky aerodynamics and practical considerations, for example cost. We can immediately see that there cannot be one dominating factor. If there were, this would drive the optimum number of blades to either a minimum (one) or a maximum (a fan-like structure).

A common early idea is to consider practical limitations, such as cost, availability of materials and so on. Whilst these are relevant issues, and mentioning them displays an awareness of the reality of commercial engineering projects (thus demonstrating that you have enough of an interest in the subject to know something about its practice), they do not display any scientific knowledge on the part of the applicant, and so should only be mentioned in passing. A student who focuses on these issues may, in the eyes of an interviewer, be doing so (either consciously or unconsciously) because they do not understand, or even recognise, the more fundamental physical issues.

For a wind turbine, the 'maximising' effect is a simple one – indeed, almost too simple, and could easily be overlooked: as the turbine wishes to extract as much energy from the wind as possible, it will be more effective if it can capture more wind. Thus, a high number of blades is preferable, to increase the surface area of the turbine.

A possible counter argument here would be to point out that adding more blades also adds more weight, and (assuming the blade design doesn't change) does not alter the surface area per mass. While more blades would capture more wind, the turbine would also now be heavier and require more force to move, negating the effect of the extra captured wind. While this sounds reasonable, a simple line of reasoning would deduce that each blade adds a given driving force to the turbine (in fact, the driving force will not be the same per blade, as discussed in the 'slipstream' argument below, but that is a different issue) otherwise the turbine would never move – each blade must capture enough energy from the wind to move, even with its weight taken into account, or the turbine would not work at all. Thus since each blade produces more than enough force to account for its own weight, adding blades adds to the total force produced.

This requirement is missed by a lot of students, and thus interviewers can use it to identify the applicants who are able to consider the 'big picture' and understand the question being asked, rather than diving straight into physics or maths without pausing to think carefully about the problem.

The 'minimising' effect is more subtle, and is a more straightforward test of the student's knowledge of physics. By the nature of a turbine, each blade follows the same path, and thus moves in the slipstream of preceding blades. At first this may appear to be a good thing – for example, in many racing sports (from speed skating to Formula 1) competitors prefer to race in the slipstream of their rivals, taking advantage of the reduced wind resistance, and thus move faster while using less energy. One may think that a blade moving in the slipstream of previous ones could move faster for less input energy, as with the racers, and thus turn the turbine more quickly and generate more energy. However, this approach shows some muddled thinking, and the analogy is not accurate. The turbine is not being powered from within with the aim of reaching a high speed, as with the racers. It is trying to extract energy from the air, so blades moving in slipstream (by definition, an area where there is little wind to affect the motion of the blade) will not be very effective at doing so. Each additional blade added to the turbine is less efficient at extracting energy than previous ones, so the most efficient option would be just one blade.

The above 'racing' analogy would be a good potential counter argument for an interviewer to use: it sounds plausible, and has a basis in physics that a student would recognise and is easy to explain and understand. However, it has flaws as explained above. A good student will examine the analogy carefully and spot not only that it is inappropriate for this situation, but also why, and use this to enhance their own understanding of the physics in the actual problem. Thus, we have two factors, one favouring a small number of blades, one a large. Balancing these two factors gives three as the optimum number of blades. However, deriving this quantitatively requires physical and engineering ideas and mathematics well beyond the scope of A Level students and possibly even undergraduates, and would not be expected. The point of this question is to explore qualitative arguments, and to test applicants' ability to consider and balance opposing viewpoints without recourse to explicit mathematical formulae.

**Integrate** $\dfrac{1}{1+\left(\dfrac{sin2x}{(1+cos\,2x)}\right)^2}$ with respect to x.

This is a straightforward question that shouldn't pose much of a problem to a serious candidate. Nevertheless, there are a couple of subtleties to mention. A Level students are taught a few methods of performing complicated-looking integrals, such as by parts or by substitution, and the interviewee will have to select the best option.

In fact, the best option here is not one of these integration techniques, but just to simplify the integrand before performing the integral. After the student has realised that this is the best method, the manipulation is simply a test of A Level ability. Some interviewers may also insist upon the inclusion of the integration constant (usually denoted c). This manipulation uses trigonometric identities with which the student should be familiar from A Level:

cos2x + sin2x = 1 the double angle formulae: sin2x = 2 sinx cosx and cos2x = cos2x − sin2x = 1 − 2 sin2x = 2 cos2x − 1.

The manipulation of the integrand, using these, is thus:

$$\frac{1}{1+\left(\dfrac{sin2x}{(1+cos\,2x)}\right)^2} \equiv \frac{1}{1+\left(\dfrac{2\sin x\cos x}{(\cos^2 x+\sin^2 x)+(\cos^2 x-\sin^2 x)}\right)^2}$$

$$\frac{1}{1+\left(\dfrac{2\sin x\cos x}{2\cos^2 x}\right)^2} \equiv \frac{1}{1+\tan^2 x} \equiv \frac{1}{\left(\dfrac{1}{\cos^2 x}\right)(\cos^2 x+\sin^2 x)} \equiv \cos^2 x$$

$$\equiv \frac{1}{2}(1+\cos 2x)$$

and the integral is now easy to perform:

$$\int \frac{1}{1+\left(\dfrac{sin2x}{(1+cos\,2x)}\right)^2}\,dx = \int\left(\frac{1}{2}+\frac{1}{2}\cos 2x\right)dx = \frac{1}{2}x+\frac{1}{4}\sin 2x + c$$

**Our advice**

Ensure that you make your assumptions explicit to the interviewer at all times. What is constant? What is changing? What simple concepts and formulae can be applied to the problem in front of you? (While the problem may look difficult, if you break it down into simple chunks, it should be possible for you to make sense of it, if not reach a firm conclusion). Ask questions! Many interviewees are wary of asking questions of the interviewer and remember that physics is a discourse, it is not just questions and answers. It is about ideas and communicating these ideas clearly. Make sure that you clarify terms of the question if they confuse you. And finally, think before you speak, especially with regard to mathematics problems and sketching graphs. Do not sketch prematurely!

# Medical & Biological Sciences

## BIOLOGICAL SCIENCES / NATURAL SCIENCES (BIOLOGICAL)

### Questions you should consider:

How does insulin function?

What is a mitochondrion? Why do you only inherit mitochondrion genes from your mother?

Why may a drug not have the same effect on a human as on a dog?

How do we know that species become extinct if we don't know that they exist?

### What happens during PCR? (past question)

A good way to approach this question is to first state what PCR stands for – Polymerase Chain Reaction. Of course, if you do not know what PCR stands for, ask the interviewer to clarify. If you know what PCR is, a good next step would be to summarise it clearly: PCR is a technique used to amplify a single or few copies of a piece of DNA to generate thousands to millions of copies.

After summarising, a good approach would be to highlight the details of the technique: PCR is used to amplify a specific region of a DNA strand. PCR uses two primers which are complementary to the `3′ (3 prime) ends of the sense and anti-sense DNA strands. A DNA polymerase (enzyme) is used to replicate the DNA between the two primers. The PCR mixture is first heated – this causes denaturation and separation of the sense and anti-sense strands so that the primers and polymerase can reach the nucleotides and allow replication. The mixture is then cooled slightly to allow the primers to anneal (bind) to the single strands of DNA. The mixture is then heated to the optimum temperature for the polymerase. The heating cycle is then repeated as many times as the user wants amplifications of the DNA, i.e. the first cycle turns one copy of DNA into two, the second cycle turns two into four, and so on.

In your conclusion, you can discuss its practical uses: **Amplification** of small amounts of DNA to a volume that is large enough to be analysed. This is useful in forensic analysis when only trace amounts of DNA are available. **Isolation** of a particular DNA sequence by selective amplification. This is useful to quantitatively assess levels of gene expression for genetic fingerprinting and screening for cancer. **Identification** of a particular DNA sequence in a genome, i.e. PCR will only be successful if the chosen DNA sequence is present. This is useful in screening of bacteria following insertion of DNA sequences (recombinant DNA).

In the case that you have not studied PCR, the interviewer may instead provide you with information on the first two points above, and ask questions aimed to test your logical and lateral thinking skills, such as: `How do you think PCR works?′ In this case, you must use what you know about DNA replication and enzymes, applying it to explain how amplification of a DNA strand could be achieved.

**What possible uses can you see for PCR?**

In this case, you must use what they have told you about the process and think laterally. PCR is amplification of DNA volume – in what circumstances would you need more DNA? Only the specific piece of DNA is amplified –

in what circumstances would you want to target specifically one piece of DNA?

**Imagine a frequency graph of three different viruses over a 30 year period. One gradually increases and decreases, one peaks every other year and one peaks three times within a 30-year period. Why?** (past question)

With a question like this, the information comes in graphical form but you are not actually supplied with a graph. A good approach would be to draw the graphs, as follows:

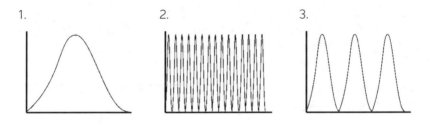

1.        2.        3.

It would then be wise to check with the interviewer they agree that the graphs represent the information given. Do not be afraid to ask for clarification and if you need more information, ask the interviewer.

Next, outline the factors that could affect frequency of viral infection in a population: **climate** – changes in temperature, humidity, seasons etc, **mutation of the virus** – could improve transmission, give resistance etc, **other viruses** – competition or symbiosis (e.g. infection with the influenza virus weakens the immune system and increases chance of other infections), **the discovery of a vaccine or other control methods.**

A good approach would then be to look at each graph in turn and apply the above factors to each situation, asking the question 'what could cause the change seen in each graph?' As far as possible, use examples to illustrate your hypotheses:

1. Discovery of a vaccine could explain graph 1. An example of a virus dramatically affected by the invention and implementation of a vaccine

is smallpox. Another possible explanation of graph 1 is environmental change affecting a virus. For example, if the UK climate warms to the extent that malarial mosquitoes can survive here, this would introduce an upsurge in the disease which might only be tackled by a strong response to the virus.

2. A virus that recurs biannually could be due to mutations that increase infection rates coupled to a constantly evolving treatment – for example, the influenza virus mutates every year and humans produce a new vaccine every year. A biannual recurrence might be caused by a slightly slower mutating virus.

3. It could be the same factor that occurs three times in 30 years, such as three particularly harsh winters or wet summers. It could also be three different factors causing three independent recurrences.

**How would you go about setting up a blood bank in a developing country?** (past question)

Please note: a question like this would not be out of place in an interview for Medicine or Biomedical Sciences. With a question like this, you are being asked to use your biological knowledge in conjunction with geographical, sociological and economic factors. As an interviewer you will be looking for a coherent plan-of-action that takes into account anything you know about blood donation systems in the UK or abroad.

To start, you might want to clarify the meaning of the term 'blood bank,' and once again, if you are unsure, ask your interviewer to clarify. A blood bank is a store of blood or blood components gathered from donations for later use in transfusions.

You can then move onto listing the factors you would need to consider in planning your approach: set-up and running costs; how to get donations; staff; safety of donating blood; location and logistics of storage; and transportation.

A good applicant would then move on to consider each factor in more detail:

SET-UP AND RUNNING COSTS: there will be a large initial cost associated with acquiring the necessary facilities needed, however, it would be equally important to consider how the project would be funded in the long-term. You might suggest approaching the government, WHO and charities for funding.

HOW TO GET DONATIONS: the National Blood Service in the UK relies on charitable donations, however other countries pay people for their donations. You could propose establishing a service in return for a donation. Due to the shortage of healthcare in many developing world countries, an effective strategy could be to offer a free health check-up to blood donors.

LOCATION: the National Blood Service in the UK has multiple static and mobile facilities. The majority of developing countries have less well-developed infrastructures and fewer hospitals. Therefore, although mobile teams would make donating more accessible, you might consider multiple static teams working from existing hospital facilities across the country.

STAFF: setting up the blood bank will provide new jobs for nurses, transport workers, administrators, etc.

BLOOD SAFETY: there are two safety aspects to consider – donation safety and blood safety. Donation safety is vital so that nurses receive proper procedural and safety training. Any blood that may be used in a blood transfusion must be clean from transfusion-transmitted diseases. In the developing world, the main culprit is HIV/AIDS, although malaria, hepatitis B and C and many more are also present. As many developing countries have tropical climates and poor living standards, the frequency of many of these diseases is higher. A blood donor would first need to be questioned and then tested for all of the diseases relevant to that area/country.

TRANSPORTATION: a storage site would have to be acquired and fitted with refrigeration/climate control systems. It would have to be manned. The location should also be within easy access of the hospitals that will require blood for transfusions. The transportation of blood would require refrigerated trucks.

You might also go one step further and suggest that the blood bank is used to gather information about the population's health, as well as using blood for transfusions. A good way to end this question would be to give a brief conclusion, stating that safety is the most important factor to consider, although all factors would need research before a comprehensive plan could be formulated.

**Our advice**

It's very important that you know your A Level syllabus as answers may require/benefit from factual knowledge you have already acquired. Be prepared to discuss species that you have not encountered before and in these instances, apply knowledge that you have as well as lateral thought. Many successful applicants find watching nature documentaries and regularly visiting the Scientific American and New Scientist websites helpful to keep abreast of their subject and its wider context. As one graduate said, 'there's nothing like a bit of David Attenborough to inspire you!'

## EXPERIMENTAL PSYCHOLOGY/PSYCHOLOGY, PHILOSOPHY & LINGUISTICS

**Questions you should consider:**

Who is the most intelligent: the straight-A Oxbridge candidate or the young mechanic living in Africa who left school at 14?

How do we test memory in animals, and can we apply the findings to humans?

Can you teach creativity?

What use is psychological study for society?

**Why do we have handedness?** (past question)

Questions like this, that contain unknown material, invite you to speculate, so make sure you are clear that you are indeed speculating rather than stating your opinions as fact. The interviewer may prompt you to aid debate, don't think that this is a negative action or that you are not saying enough, they just want to understand better how you think or the method behind your reasoning. Strong answers to questions like these would clearly take one or two approaches to psychology, attempting to explain how handedness can be explained by them, and then weigh up the two approaches against one another.

The biological or physiological approach to psychology may suggest that handedness occurs to conserve energy. If only one side of the body has to develop higher levels of dexterity to perform tasks efficiently then there seems to be little benefit in both sides of the body developing to the same and complex degree. It may also be that because language is located in one side of the brain – the left hemisphere – this part of the brain already has in place more complex neural connections, and therefore has a better capacity to form the dominant hemisphere. This is supported by the fact that the majority of people are right handed (which corresponds to having a dominant left hemisphere).

On the other hand, the question of handedness can also be explained from a behavioural perspective. There are two ways of explaining this. Firstly, modelling behaviour could occur when an infant sees their caregiver using one particular hand to do certain tasks; they copy this. Secondly, conditioning may play a part. Perhaps, an infant uses a certain hand to pick up a cup of juice because it is on one side of their highchair. They then drink the juice and are rewarded by the good taste. The action of using this hand and being rewarded are linked in a form of classical conditioning.

You then might conclude that although both of these approaches have valid points, the biological approach punches more weight. It has been proven that handedness is linked to a particular cerebral hemisphere, and therefore seems logical that only one side of the brain should hold the capacity for handedness.

### How would a psychologist measure normality? (past question)

'Very strong answers would include ways of measuring more than one type of normality,' says one Oxford Experimental Psychology graduate. They would also then give an opinion of which approach they feel is superior and why.

As we learn in mathematics, deviation from statistical norms is measured using the bell shaped curve of normal distribution (see image). The x axis shows the frequency/level of a behaviour/characteristic, and the y axis the proportion of people in the population displaying that frequency/level. Arbitrary norms are set for the lower and upper limits, and a person outside of these norms is considered to be abnormal. An example would be levels of anxiety. Very high levels of anxiety are abnormal, and may lead to a diagnosis of an anxiety disorder. Very low levels of anxiety may also be indicative of a mental health problem.

Another method of measuring normality is to define abnormal as causing distress to self/others. Whereas two people might engage in the same level of behaviour, for example checking their watch frequently, one may do this as part of their routine because they like to know the time, and are not overly distressed if they cannot access the time. The other may find it crucial to check their watch, infringing on their day to day happiness, and experience great distress/panic if for some reason they cannot check the time. This would be measured by a self-report diary, where the individual charted their feelings alongside their day to day experiences. It could also be measured through observations.

You might argue that monitoring the distress caused to self or others is a better way of measuring normality. This could be because it takes into account personal experiences of the sufferer, and therefore forms more of a basis for identifying and treating the condition. However, the statistical approach allows larger numbers of people to be more quickly identified, which could be advantageous.

**Our advice**

Ask questions: some interviewers will want you to assume certain things to formulate your answers, whereas, for others, part of the exercise will be for you to ask the correct questions to find out more about the situation. By asking a preliminary question you will be able to determine which of these situations you are in, and not deprive yourself of useful information. In answering questions, try to show logical development throughout your answer. Use terms commonly used in Psychology if they help you. For example, if looking at the question 'why would a 5-year old refuse to speak with you?', you could frame your answer by looking at factors which are internal (due to the child), external (due to the environment), stable (a problem that is always there), or unstable (a problem that is only due to this situation). Try to include a variety of factors in your answer. Perhaps also try to include a biological, physiological, social or behavioural factors. Do try to show your breadth of knowledge at all times.

# HUMAN SCIENCES

**Questions you should consider:**

Are human beings still evolving?

Are there too many people in the world?

What is the purpose of religion?

Should gorillas have human rights?

Human Sciences blends creative and scientific thought. For the purposes of this exercise, we asked Human Sciences graduates to create different types of interview questions, based on their experiences of the interview.

**What makes HIV/AIDS an interesting disease from the perspective of a Human Scientist?**

A good answer to this question would be one that, in the first instance, addresses the biology of the disease. You could start by mentioning the fact that HIV/AIDS affects the immune system and renders the person more vulnerable to infection from other diseases. You could also mention that it's difficult to treat because of the ability of the virus to develop resistance to drugs rapidly. Don't be afraid to ask about the biological aspect of HIV/AIDS if you don't know the science of the disease because the tutors will appreciate a demonstration of your interest.

To address the question from another angle, you could discuss where geographically HIV/AIDS is a significant problem (giving your definition of significant in your answer). Sub-Saharan Africa currently has a high number of HIV/AIDS cases as do parts of Asia. In these countries, the disease is often transmitted via sexual networks which include prostitutes and drug users. Transmission of the disease has been linked to poverty in the countries which have high prevalence rates. As an example, women driven to prostitution may be unable to refuse sex because it may be their main source of income. If condoms are unavailable or considered undesirable, these women may be at great risk because of cultural or religious factors.

HIV/AIDS creates problems within societies because it leaves orphans in its wake when parents die of the disease. Further, the disease may be transmitted to babies during pregnancy creating HIV positive children at birth. This means that governments need to find ways of caring for orphaned HIV positive children, who require general everyday care and treatment for the disease.

There are interesting instances of misinformation about transmission of HIV/AIDS. For example, some men believe that their disease can be cured by sexual intercourse with virgins, an act which may infect the women that they have sex with. Also, the use of condoms is avoided by certain people because they are associated with the infection itself. HIV/AIDS is stigmatised in many communities and, therefore infection is often traumatic both for the patient and their family.

With your answer it is a good idea to show that you understand that HIV/AIDS is more than a biological disease; it has much wider social, cultural and economic implications which play an important role in the transmission, treatment and prevention of the disease.

## What is the difference between marriage and mating?

This question tests your ability to identify ways in which human behaviour might differ from that of animals because of the existence of culture within human society.

You could answer this question by explaining that mating is natural, and likely to be driven by physiological desires which you could say are genetic or 'innate'. These desires are likely to be influenced by natural selection, and, consequently, behaviour which improves the reproductive fitness of an individual (the number of offspring they produce) is likely to spread within the population.

You could then go on to say that marriage in humans is determined by culture. Although men and women might have natural or innate preferences, the people they actually mate with are largely determined by who they marry. Rules about what makes a good marriage partner are often subject to cultural preferences, so for example in the West a woman may choose a marriage partner who has good levels of education, whereas in a more 'traditional' society a good marriage partner might be a man who is good at hunting. Another good point to add would be to raise the question of whether or not humans are still subject to natural selection because of the fact that our culture determines our behaviour?

It is important to demonstrate in your answer that humans are different to other animals, and that human behaviour is difficult to study because our culture influences our behaviour.

## Our advice

You may be presented with graphical information in your interviews. If the graphs demonstrate a correlation between two variables, it's important to remember not to jump to a conclusion which assumes a causative relationship. Two factors can be associated without any real connection between them. For example, ice cream sales are high in July. However, July does not cause a peak in ice cream sales; it is the hot weather in July which drives the purchase of ice cream.

Keep reading the news so that you are aware of developments such as the sequencing of the Neanderthal genome, which has revealed that humans interbred with this extinct hominin species. The BBC news website has a great, trustworthy science section, so you can get some excellent talking points from there.

You may be asked to explain the purpose or function of an object shown to you in the interview. Remember that the interviewers may be assessing your ability to analyse objectively without assuming that objects have the same meaning for you as for people in other cultures. Objectivity is a skill which is essential in anthropology. Tutors aren't expecting you to have any specific knowledge about the object in question.

## MEDICINE

**Questions you should consider:**

What is the purpose of DNA?

How would you design a brain?

What are ulcers?

Why do we see things in the colours we do?

Having spoken to many successful Medical applicants, interviews for Medicine tend to be a mix of scientific and ethical questions. Our medical minds have therefore created some sample questions below, based on their own interview experiences, which they believe would be helpful to any aspiring Medicine applicant to think about in advance of their interview.

### If there was only one bird flu vaccine left, who would you give it to between you and me?

A good way to start this sort of question is to mention briefly what the bird flu vaccine is and what you know about the potential consequences of not receiving it. For example 'the majority of healthy people are able to recover from having the flu having experienced only normal flu-like symptoms such as a mild fever etc.'

You could then start looking at who should get this vaccine. Consider whether the person asking you the question is, for instance:

- In a position of having a lowered immune system so less able to cope without the vaccine if he or she contracted the flu: pregnant, elderly, on any other medication, suffering from any other illnesses such as AIDS.

- A person who has already recovered from the flu before and would be in a much better position to recover from the flu again. You could perhaps slip in here your knowledge of the primary and secondary immune response.

- A person who has dependents who would be affected if the person was to suffer from flu: children or a disabled person for whom they are caring.

- A person who spends/has spent/will spend a lot of time in a high-risk environment for the flu or around people who have, perhaps in a country where there is an epidemic at the moment.

- Suffering from any condition that may affect his or her life expectancy.

Having considered these factors you can reach a conclusion. With a question like this, however, it is very difficult to reach an informed decision, and a number of our medical graduates do believe it would be acceptable to conclude that 'without further information about your health and general circumstances I could not make an informed decision'.

In contrast, however, if you are one who would rather not sit on the fence, you could equally say that 'assuming that we are both of the same health and have the same circumstances, then, I may give it to myself because I am younger than you'.

### If you were the new Secretary of Health, how would you want to improve the NHS?

Questions like this are very common, and Admissions Tutors are looking for an awareness of the problems currently facing the NHS, as well as the proposed reforms, which would radically change the way the NHS operates.

One issue that all students should be aware of is the problem of the superbug MRSA and C-difficile. This is the sort of thing you could talk about here.

A good way to start this question would be to talk briefly about the problem caused by MRSA being resistant to antibiotics due to resistant strains mutating via natural selection etc., as well as talking about the problem this poses – patients come into hospital with a broken leg and may leave it with a deadly disease! The main problem with this is the lack of good hygiene in hospitals with visitors and staff not using the alcohol gels enough or properly as well as improper sterilisation of equipment used. As the Secretary of Health you may wish to improve training for the staff in hospitals to keep the environment clean and put more money into cleaning measures.

You might also say that you would like to put money into computerising a lot more of the work that doctors and their team do so that it is easily transferred and for safe-keeping. It is ALWAYS a good idea to mention something that you have picked up at work experience here. Be as specific as possible; drill down into detail.

One of the really big issues currently facing the NHS is the rise in obesity and its links to diabetes and coronary heart disease. Thus you might argue that more money should be spent on preventative measures to cost the NHS less in the long run. For example, increasing government campaigns to reduce childhood obesity by encouraging healthy eating and an active lifestyle – along the lines of what we are already seeing on TV and in the press at the moment. Again, you can strengthen your answer by referring to your work experience.

**Work experience**

Medical interviews tend to be different from other interviews because they are often carried out by practising doctors, rather than academics and therefore they expect you to be informed about the job of a doctor. Remember at the end of your course this is what you will be and your interviewer will partly be assessing your suitability for the role as well as for the course. Consequently, work experience is very important and it is highly likely that it will form part of any medical interview.

When it comes to asking about your work experience, questions tend to be along the lines of 'tell me about your work experience'. Many students can fall into the trap of simply listing all the different hospitals and surgeries they have visited, thinking that this sounds impressive. What's more interesting however is not the quantity of experience you have, but the quality. Tutors want to hear about an experience where you learned about what it means to be a doctor, and the relationship a doctor can build up with his/her patient.

Good students might therefore approach this type of question by mentioning their observation of the importance of good communication – seeing a doctor smiling as he/she greeted the patient, the tone of the voice used (which helped to make the patient feel more relaxed). Indeed, one of the many difficult aspects of being a doctor is to make the patient feel relaxed enough in a consultation to give you all the information that you may need to know. Initially, doctors often do not know what they are looking for and must rely on the openness of the patient. You may have also noticed how a doctor spoke in simple, layman terms, refraining from using medical jargon to ensure the patient understands what is going on at every step of their treatment to ease worry and stress.

It may be that during your work experience you observed how important the wider team of other medical staff are to the role of a doctor, for example nurse and radiographers and doctors and how essential it is that a doctor has the confidence to work independently but also as part of a team. You might have seen certain negative aspects of being a doctor, including the amount of paper work involved or the strain of having to deliver bad news to a patient. You may have seen how important it is that a doctor be able to detach him/herself emotionally from the case.

Your answer will very much depend on your experiences. Really think about what you learned, and how it changed, strengthened or indeed weakened certain viewpoints or opinions of the role of a doctor that you previously held.

**Our advice**
'From my experience,' says one Cambridge Medicine graduate 'students are best off knowing the whole A Level syllabus because Admissions Tutors may ask you about topics ahead of the level that your school may have got

to. This was certainly the case for me but won't apply to all applicants. Of course, if it is something that you have not covered yet you should always say you don't know something, but they may expect you to attempt the question anyway using logic, common sense and an application of the knowledge you already possess.' Be willing to give each question a go – show you are open and willing to consider new ideas.

## VETERINARY MEDICINE

**Questions you should consider:**

What do you think about kidney transplants in cats?

Why do animals have two ears (i.e. why not one or four)?

Is selective breeding tantamount to genetic modification?

Why do dogs behave badly?

**What is the time difference from sound reaching one ear and the other?** (past question)

The time difference between sound reaching the first and second ears is called the interaural time difference. The time difference varies depending on the location of the sound source. If the sound comes directly from in front of the face, say at eye height and equal distance from either ear, then there is no time difference in the sound arriving. We would describe this as sound arriving at a zero degree azimuth (the angle of the signal in relation to the head), the interaural time difference being zero also.

If the sound comes directly from the right or left (i.e. a 90 degree azimuth), then clearly the sound will arrive at the nearest ear first, having further to travel to the second ear, and the interaural time difference will no longer be zero.

It can be calculated as follows:

T = D/V

where

D = distance between the ears (probably in the region of 20cm or 0.2m)

and

V = speed of sound (roughly 343m/s)

So in this case the interaural time (T) would be
$0.2/343 = 0.00058s$

If the sound is coming from a smaller angle than 90 degrees (or between 90 and 180), there will be a smaller difference between the distances sound has to travel to either ear (i.e. D is smaller) and the time difference will be reduced. The variation in the interaural time differences does not seem large, but it is detected by the brain when processing sound and is a key source of information in sound localisation.

**How would you have solved the Foot and Mouth crisis?** (past question)

A good way to approach this question, is to firstly show to the interviewer that you understand what Foot and Mouth Disease is – it is a highly infectious viral disease which affects cloven hoofed animals such as cows, sheep and pigs. Next, you could refer to past Foot and Mouth crises – explaining how in the past, the virus has spread rapidly and beyond control, decimating the UK farming industry. It is therefore important to take the threat seriously and act quickly and decisively.

You can then move into the 'meat' of the argument (no pun intended). Assuming it has only been reported on one farm, you could suggest that the affected farm and the surrounding area be immediately quarantined and that the animals that had been in direct contact with any sufferers culled. The virus can be destroyed by heat, sunlight and certain disinfectants, but it can survive for long periods of time in the right conditions. Thus the affected farm would have to be completely gutted and disinfected before the farmer could even consider going back to normal. The virus does not affect humans, but can be spread on vehicles and boots and so on, so movement from affected to non-affected areas should be strictly limited.

Ideally any roads that neighbour the affected property should be shut until the virus has been controlled. Wild animals which could carry the disease between farms, for example deer, should be controlled (probably culled) if/ when they are seen.

When the Foot and Mouth crisis hit in 2001, farmers were hesitant to use vaccinations due to difficulties that would later arise in selling the animals overseas. However the rules have since been changed to allow vaccination as an emergency measure in the event of an outbreak. There are several strains of Foot and Mouth Disease, so once the strain has been identified, you could propose recommending the vaccination of all cloven hoofed farm animals in an even wider area than the quarantined area – say county-wide. Airborne spread is known, so if conditions are right (i.e. windy, not too hot) then animals should be kept inside.

As an outbreak of Foot and Mouth Disease can be so devastating, you might point out that you do not think you can overreact to another outbreak. As much as possible should be done to prevent the virus spreading, and if it does the affected farms need to be identified immediately. Clear information should be given to the press and to farming bodies with what to look for in affected animals and who you should call if you suspect you have found a new case. The emphasis is on speed of reaction, and on ensuring that the movement bans/quarantines/culls (if necessary) are strictly adhered to.

### Our advice

Make sure you know your personal statement inside out and that your knowledge is thorough and technical. If you don't know something, ask the interviewers – don't try to make up an answer. There is nothing worse than an interviewee desperately fumbling for an answer, after having claimed that they have understood something. Be honest about your ability and this will help the interviewer to assess your potential. You are not supposed to have all the answers now – that's why you are applying to university!

# 8 REAPPLICANTS

# How applicants can strengthen their application the second time around

If you apply to Oxford and Cambridge and are unsuccessful, this does not necessarily mean that Oxbridge is not for you. Many applicants are unaware that, should they choose to, they can wait until the following admissions cycle and reapply to either Oxford or Cambridge. If you choose to reapply to Oxbridge, you will need to take a gap year between applications, but many students find this to be a useful opportunity to explore their interests outside of full-time study.

Those considering reapplication should know that in general, reapplicants are more successful at gaining entrance to Oxbridge than first-time applicants. Reapplicants can have many advantages which contribute to their success – with their exams behind them there is no doubt as to whether they will achieve the required grades. They are also older, more mature, and have had more time to devote to reading around their subject area. Finally, they already have experience of the application process and how it works. Particularly for students who found the process nerve-wracking the first time, this added level of comfort can make all the difference.

Being a reapplicant says nothing of a student's capacity to do well at Oxbridge – often students just need an extra year to mature and expand their knowledge before they are fully prepared for the university system. However, reapplication does not suit everyone and you should not feel pressured to reapply if you do not want to. There are many brilliant universities which may offer better courses for your interests, and the skills and knowledge you have developed during your first application will help you to make a strong application wherever you go on to study.

## DECIDING WHETHER TO REAPPLY

Some students know immediately that they are going to reapply once they find out their application was unsuccessful. Some even find themselves successful only on the third try. For others, the decision to reapply requires time and consideration. If you are considering reapplying, there are some key things to ask yourself to decide if a reapplication is the right course of action for you.

### How did I find the process?

If you found the process overly difficult, stressful and unenjoyable, it is worth thinking about whether Oxbridge is right for you at all. Such an important application is always going to be a relatively stressful process, but if you did not at least enjoy finding out more about your chosen subject, it is likely you will not enjoy being at Oxbridge.

### Do I want a gap year?

For many students, the idea of a gap year is extremely appealing – it is an opportunity to have a break from education and gain new experiences, be that through work experience, volunteering or travelling. However, if you are against the idea of having a year out before you progress to university then this route is not for you. If you are applying for a subject such as Mathematics, you will need to demonstrate that you plan to maintain your mathematical knowledge and ability during the gap year, so that the tutors have confidence in your ability to work effectively when you return to full-time education.

### Am I happy to reapply to all of my universities?

If you choose to reapply to Oxbridge, you will lose any university offers you currently have – even if you have a deferred place – as you will need to begin a new UCAS application. The likelihood is that if you received an offer first time round you will be offered a place again, but this is never a guarantee.

## CHOOSING A COURSE, COLLEGE AND UNIVERSITY AS A REAPPLICANT

If you decide to reapply, you will have the same considerations you had in your first application as to the course, college and university you should apply to. There is no formula for reapplying more than there is when applying for the first time – but there are important factors to consider when making these decisions.

### Should I apply to the same university?

Which university you apply to is an important decision. While Oxford and Cambridge are similar in many ways, there are significant differences between the universities which would have influenced your initial choice when applying.

As a reapplicant, one of the main reasons you may choose a different university is because of your exam results. The benefit of being a reapplicant is knowledge of your actual, rather than predicted, grades. As such, you might be in a position to apply to Cambridge with a guaranteed 2 A*s and an A at A Level, whereas before you applied to Oxford on the basis of strong GCSEs but low A Level predictions. Considering how your actual grades compare to the grade requirements for your chosen course at both universities can help you make the decision of which university to apply to. Your decision may also be influenced by your experience of the Admissions Test or interview. It may be that you applied to Oxford and found the TSA difficult and would rather apply to Cambridge where you can sit a more subject-focused test, or you might just have found that Oxford did not suit you when you attended your interview. Equally, you might appreciate the smaller, community feel of Cambridge, and just can't imagine yourself at Oxford. This aspect of the reapplication is almost always down to preference. Will they know I've applied before?

Many students are worried that they will be at a disadvantage if they decide to apply to the same university, because the university will know they have applied the previous year. The fact that you have applied previously will not be used to measure your application. Based on the small pool of Admissions

Tutors for some subjects at individual colleges, it is, however, advisable to apply to a different college to avoid being interviewed by the same person who interviewed you previously. Reapplicants should also rewrite their personal statement to take into account the new knowledge they have accumulated over the course of the year.

## Should I apply for the same course?

Some students change courses when they reapply (particularly when changing universities), but this is by no means a necessity. In fact, if you are truly passionate about your subject, you are unlikely to want to change. It may be useful, however, to consider other courses that might be more suited to you. For example, if you applied for Mathematics and Philosophy but found you didn't particularly enjoy the Philosophy preparation, you could consider applying for Mathematics and Statistics, Mathematics and Computer Science, or Mathematics.

Notably, our survey of hundreds of Oxbridge applicants in 2016 indicated that reapplicants were most successful when applying for the same subject at the same university, followed closely by those who applied for the same subject but changed university. Reapplicants should therefore not be deterred from applying to the same course they were initially unsuccessful for.

"I reapplied to Cambridge because I had my heart set on reading French and Italian there. I knew that there was more work I needed to do to improve my linguistic proficiency and knowledge of the literary canon and wanted to prove I could do this the second time around."

Jen, Cambridge

## MAKING A STRONG REAPPLICATION

Now we have established the factors reapplicants should consider, the next steps involve elevating your second application from your first. With this second opportunity, you should look to develop your strengths and use your gap year effectively.

### What should I do with the extra year?

As a reapplicant, you will need to ensure that your application is of a high standard. Admissions Tutors will be considering your application alongside those without the additional year of preparation and so the key to making a good reapplication is to make the extra year count. Firstly, work hard to ensure you achieve strong results in your exams. You need to be at least meeting, if not exceeding, the standard offer for your subject; for Cambridge this is at least 1 or 2 A*s at A Level and for Oxford this is a minimum of 3 As. The benefit to applying as a post-qualification applicant is that you remove an uncertainty in your application as your grades are known, but this does also mean that you will be competing against students predicted a full set of A*s, and so your grades need to be competitive.

Secondly, use your spare time and especially the summer to read around your subject area. As a reapplicant, your interviewers will expect you to have read more, particularly outside of your school syllabus. If you're not sure what to read, talk to your teachers for suggestions or explore the reading lists on our website (www.oxbridgeapplications.com).

Finally, plan what you are going to do in your gap year. For some subjects (Medicine and Veterinary Medicine in particular) you should be using this period between school and university to do work experience in your chosen field. Those applying for Law could also take this opportunity to shadow a barrister or watch some court cases, and applicants for PPE or Economics could strengthen their application by organising work in economic research. However, even for the less obvious subjects you can find relevant things to do in your year off. For example: an applicant for Spanish may plan to do a language course in Spain; Classics applicants may arrange to visit the classical cities of Athens and Rome; Archaeology and Anthropology students might decide to attend an archaeological dig; Chemistry students could arrange work in a lab, and so on. Although it is not necessary that everything you do in your gap year relates directly to your degree, it is good to show the university that you plan on keeping up your interest in the subject. The best thing about a reapplication is the extra time it gives you – use it wisely.

**How should I use my feedback?**

Unsuccessful applicants have the opportunity to ask for feedback from the college they applied to. Even if you are unsure about reapplying, it is a good idea to put in the request as there is a time limit on how long colleges retain this information. This feedback will usually outline the strengths of your application against the weaknesses in respect to other candidates. Although the length of this feedback varies from college to college, it is important to read it thoroughly and look back over the process with it in mind.

The feedback is a real gift to help you make the strongest possible reapplication as it allows you to direct your focus on the areas in which you underperformed. If you performed significantly poorer than other applicants in the Admissions Test then you need to ensure you spend time practicing and improving your grade. If the Admissions Tutors felt that your interview wasn't strong enough, you should try and organise some mock interviews, or look over old interview questions and consider how you could answer them, even those that you have no knowledge of.

Even if you do not agree with what the feedback says, it is important to take it on board if you hope to succeed in your reapplication. Remember that the tutors see thousands of applicants every year and they know what they are looking for. Use the feedback to your advantage – you have several months to work on the weaknesses they have highlighted and can use it to strengthen your reapplication.

In sum, reapplicants are well-positioned to make a competitive application to Oxbridge if they adhere to their strengths and develop the weaknesses highlighted by the first application. If you make good use of your gap year and continue to develop your subject interest and knowledge, you will maximise your chances of making a successful reapplication.

# 9 LIFE AFTER OXBRIDGE

## THE CAREER PATHS OF RECENT OXFORD AND CAMBRIDGE GRADUATES

# The career paths of recent Oxford and Cambridge graduates

Studying at one of the best universities in the world, and to be enriched by the experiences on offer both academically and socially, ensures that Oxbridge-graduates go on to a range of interesting, challenging, and diverse career paths upon graduation. We talk to recent Oxford and Cambridge graduates to find out what they have achieved since leaving university and how their undergraduate degrees have influenced their career choices.

### LUCY, Oxford Law graduate

"Since university I have done a lot of academic stuff – two sets of graduate courses, both law-related. I'm currently working in medical law, which I really do find interesting. I love my subject, and although in practice, law is very different to studying it as an academic discipline, I can't imagine myself working in any other field. So my degree really has influenced my career choices. It is also a good degree for forcing you to learn how to deal with a large workload, think logically, argue persuasively, and problem solve – all valuable life skills.

My advice to prospective Law applicants would be: if you are really interested in working as a lawyer in the future, but you don't enjoy the academic side of law, an undergraduate Law degree might not be for you. You would be far better off doing an undergraduate degree in a subject that you know will interest you, and then converting to law in the future – only around half of all currently practicing lawyers completed an undergraduate Law degree.

You do need to be quite stubborn and determined to make it through a Law degree at Oxford as well as in the legal profession today. Having a close circle of non-lawyer friends has also definitely helped keep me sane over the years of exams!"

## JACK, Oxford History graduate

"I spent most of my time at Oxford (aside from socialising) acting in plays and performing as part of an improvised comedy troupe. On leaving Oxford, I acted in a Noel Coward play for 5 months with Robert Bathurst. I am now a producer at Channel 4 News, specialising in politics and Europe. My History degree taught me to weigh evidence, treat most things with scepticism and how to write a story – all very useful skills for a journalist."

## JEREMY, Cambridge Physical Natural Sciences graduate

"After leaving Cambridge, I completed my PGCE at Oxford, before spending two years teaching at a state comprehensive in Wembley followed by more teaching at a private school in Ealing, where I currently work. I'm also doing a part-time masters in Social Research Methods.

Doing a broad base of sciences at Cambridge is really useful when you walk into a school and have to teach general science. It's also given me flexibility – I'm actually now a Physics teacher despite my Chemistry degree. I also instinctively use mathematics and logic to solve problems, with varying degrees of success.

My advice to people considering a career in teaching is: don't be a teacher just because you can't think of anything else to do. Teachers have one of the most important jobs in the world – you need to really want to do it. If it is actually something you want to do, go and visit some schools. If it's still what you want to do, train, get a job and do it. It is the best job in the world. I found what I wanted to do by trying it (I've been tutoring since I was 17, then did some work experience in a school and knew teaching was for me) so I guess trying lots of things out and seeing what works for me has been useful. I'm pretty sure some of the stuff I did whilst an undergrad has been useful – when you've been heckled off stage by 200 people at a May Ball 30 teenagers aren't going to scare you."

## MICHAELA, Cambridge Economics graduate

"After graduating, I started working at the Financial Services Authority (now the Financial Conduct Authority). Whilst there, I spent my free time as a member of a semi-professional dance troupe and I also spent a lot of time working as a mentor in Tower Hamlets and helping to establish a mentoring programme for local schools. I left the FSA and started working part-time in the House of Lords for a Baroness and for two Conservative Party organisations. I began tutoring A Level Economics as well and I became the Governor for a Special Needs school in my local area. I also joined the Management committee for the Conservative Friends of India. I joined the board of a large charity promoting female and child empowerment and I started writing political and economic blogs and opinion pieces for newsletters and websites.

In July 2013, I began working as an Economic Advisor for a Member of Parliament and I continued to work for one of the political organisations – Women2Win which promotes women in Parliament and Public Life. In December 2013 I became an approved member of the Candidates' List for the Conservative Party.

My degree has instilled in me a solid work ethic and a strong interest in how politics and economics interact. It also gave me great practice at juggling various commitments and at dealing with deadlines.

My advice to anybody wanting to pursue a career in politics would be to make sure you're informed about political and economic events and try and gain work experience through your local MP. Try and read about issues from different news sources so that you understand all points of view, even if you strongly disagree with them. Consider all routes in, whether that's through your local MP or joining APPGs (All Party Political Groups), working for a political think-tank or even simply joining your local association."

311

## TOM, Oxford Engineering Science graduate

"I followed my final year with a four month placement as a research assistant at the Chinese University of Hong Kong, and am currently studying a PhD in Biomedical Engineering at Imperial. A lot of my success has been due to trying things outside my comfort zone, persevering if something sounds exciting and worthwhile even if it may be very difficult. You may regret not taking chances! I use my degree every day for my research, not only the theory but also ways to approach problem solving and collaborating across disciplines. I would advise Engineering applicants to try to gain as much work experience as possible, and keep an eye on engineering developments in the news and on the internet – it's a rapidly changing and exciting field!"

## CAROLINE, Oxford Philosophy, Politics and Economics (PPE) graduate

"After graduating, I worked at Oliver Wyman as a management consultant for 18 months. I then worked at The Economist for two years, before moving to Germany to join a start-up, where I'm currently working. I'm also in the process of setting up my own business.

My time at Oxford benefitted me hugely: the friends and connections I made, the confidence I gained that even if something seems really hard I can manage it, and widening my horizons to aspire to things that seem very ambitious but are attainable if you try.

Most of my "organised" spare time activities were in second year, e.g. JCR Overseas Officer, rowing in the college team, peer support training. Other than that I loved going to the Oxford Union and other societies' speech events, drinks events and college balls! I did an internship at a small management consulting firm between my first and second year, an internship at Oliver Wyman between my second and third year, and volunteered in India and Niger – the latter with TravelAid.

I think my success has been down to hard work and doing things I enjoy. Enjoying your work makes it so much easier, and making sure to do things that relax you in your spare time also makes you more effective when you do work. My advice to PPE applicants would be read widely and have a genuine passion for what you do."

## ALEX, Cambridge English graduate

"I have worked as an actor and filmmaker for the last four years. Whilst at university, I spent most of my time acting in plays, running the college drama society and going to poetry readings and conferences. The friends I made at Cambridge and the ambition of everyone I was around helped me to believe in my potential and meant there were always exciting people to work with and turn to for advice and help. That has continued out of Cambridge and also helped me to believe in my own value and take risks that maybe I would not have otherwise taken.

The work ethic you develop as an undergraduate is probably the key thing I've taken away from university. Learning to concentrate on a variety of tasks for 12 hours a day, being able to shift focus quickly, and to set your own goals and priorities is something that comes from navigating your way through a Cambridge literature degree. Those are invaluable for beginning a career as a freelancer or entrepreneur. Also the English degree teaches you to question and reformulate everything around you whilst maintaining an eye for detail. It teaches you to problem solve and bring things together that you usually might not see as compatible. These are invaluable in a creative industry where a lot of the time you are trying to make something from nothing.

My advice to prospective applicants is take as much as you can from university. It is a unique time to make mistakes and try things out. If you are thinking about directing films, get some other students together and make one. There are usually societies that you can join that support student projects and if there isn't then start one. Universities are such supportive places for people trying to be creative and they have the money to allow you to experiment and you have the people around you with whom you can collaborate. Don't miss that opportunity. If you want to act, produce, direct, design, be an agent, or run a company you can do that in miniature at university and see if it's for you, As long as you balance some of that with hard-time in the library, you'll probably be ok."

## REBECCA, Oxford Music graduate

"Upon leaving Oxford, I joined a small education business which gave me some experience in presentations, events management, marketing and sales. From there I went into a brand new Marketing and Brand agency, where I worked for two years to grow it into a team of five and clients including National Geographic and No7 (Boots). I then decided I wanted to go into a business rather than work across a number of different clients so I am now Marketing Manager at the UK's leading art supplies retailer.

My advice to graduates would be to always be willing to support small ventures – there is so much pressure out of university to go for the most well-paid job. The smaller the organisation, the more responsibility you will have from day one and the more you will learn. It makes you all the more employable in jobs two and three.

Music was essentially a course around the History of Music, studying context, reception and audience reaction to music. It really does define how I think about the customer today, and I think I am a better Marketer for the tutorial-based system at Oxford where you take the time to think of multiple ways to tackle a question. I was a Choral Scholar in Lincoln College Chapel Choir, Secretary of Turl Streets Arts Festival two years in a row, and directed two musicals in college with a university-wide cast. It was managing the festival, coordinating its launch ball and creating all the posters etc. for the musical that first got me into marketing.

If you're thinking about applying for Music make sure you know the course you are applying for. Oxford and Cambridge are very different. Cambridge is based more around the aural and practical skill you have when you apply, whereas Oxford looks at your basic analytical skills and how they could be enhanced on the course. If you are then looking to go into Marketing, be aware – if you promote any event via social media, write copy for a student paper, or organise events and problem-solve how to get people to turn up – then you are already getting experience in Marketing."

# Glossary of Terms

Definitions of commonly used Oxbridge jargon to familiarise you with the language of the universities.

**ADC** – Amateur Dramatic Club. A university-wide drama society in Cambridge, as well as the name of the theatre where the society performs most of their plays.

**Battels** – the Oxford term for your college bills.

**Bedder** – the Cambridge term for the cleaner in the college rooms.

**Blue/half blue** – the name given to someone who plays sport for the university team, more specifically if they play in the Varsity match between Oxford and Cambridge. A full blue is awarded to those who play some sports (usually the most prominent, such as rugby and rowing) and a half-blue is given for others.

**The Bod** – the Bodleian Library, Oxford's university library.

**Bop** – a college party, which is themed and often involves fancy dress.

**Bumps** – a Cambridge inter-collegiate rowing race that takes place in Lent and Easter terms, where boats race each other in single file with the aim of catching and 'bumping' the boat in front. Similar to Summer Eights in Oxford.

**Collections** – exams set by Oxford colleges to assess what you have learnt the previous term. They do not count towards your final grade, but you are expected to pass them.

**College** – smaller communities that make up the universities as a whole. They function as halls of residence, the base for your academic study, and pastoral support, and are generally the centre of your student life.

**College parents** – a system run by many colleges where first year students are allocated two or more students from higher years (usually second years) to look after them and introduce them to university life.

**COPA** – Cambridge Online Preliminary Application. A form that must be filled out in addition to the UCAS application, for students applying from overseas or for an organ scholarship.

**Court** – the term for 'quad' in some colleges; an area in college, usually a square or rectangular area of grass or paving, enclosed by college buildings (e.g. 'my room is in Tree Court').

**Crew date** – dinner between two or more colleges or university societies at Oxford. Usually held at Formal Halls or a nearby restaurant.

**Cuppers** – inter-collegiate sports tournament which happens every year for most sports.

**Dean** – a senior fellow at a college (sometimes the Head of the College), with advisory and disciplinary functions.

**Don** – an academic professor or lecturer at the university.

**DoS** – pronounced 'doss', this stands for Director of Studies at Cambridge. Your Director of Studies is a fellow in your subject who is your first port of call for any academic concerns. They oversee your learning and organise supervisions with fellows outside of college, and advise you on which lectures to attend and papers to take.

**Easter** – the third and final term of the academic year in Cambridge.

**Ents/Entz** – short for 'entertainment', this refers to college events and the team that organise them.

**Fellow** – an academic professor or lecturer (including visiting professors) employed by the university or college. Often fellows are involved in the governing of the college. Some colleges also have honorary fellows who are usually distinguished alumni.

**Formal Hall** – dinner in the college hall. Usually involves a gown and/or formal attire and a three-course meal.

**Gyp-room** – Cambridge term for the kitchens in college halls.

**Hilary** – the second term of the academic year in Oxford.

**JCR** – Junior Common Room. This is a communal area in college for all undergraduates. Sometimes used to describe the individual college student unions.

**Lent** – the second term of the academic year in Cambridge.

**Master** – some colleges' term for the Head of the College.

**May Ball** – Cambridge term for the large scale, black or white-tie events held, confusingly, in June by various colleges. Often themed, May Balls generally go on all night and involve lots of food, drink and live music.

**May Week** – the week after all exams are finished in Cambridge (mid-June), before the end of term. Filled with garden parties and May Balls.

**Michaelmas** – the first term of the academic year in Oxford and Cambridge.

**Norrington Table** – an annual ranking of Oxford colleges based on the fraction of final year undergraduates achieving each degree classification.

**Nought week** – the week before term officially starts, when lots of students arrive to settle in before lectures begin.

**Pidge** – nickname for your pigeon hole, which is where all of your post and university notices will be delivered.

**Plodge** – nickname for Porters' Lodge, where the porters reside. Usually at the front of college, the plodge is the place to go with queries, and often a popular meeting point.

**Porter** – guardians of the college, the porters are the first people you will meet on arrival at the college.

**Pooling** – a system by which Oxford and Cambridge share applicants amongst colleges, in an attempt to ensure that all deserving students receive an offer.

**Prelims** – contraction of preliminary examinations, taken in Cambridge by students of courses that do not have official examinations until the end of second year. They do not count towards your final degree classification.

**Punting** – a popular activity for both students and tourists in Oxford and Cambridge. A flat bottomed boat or 'punt' is propelled down the river using a pole which is pushed against the river bed.

**Quad** – an area in colleges, usually a square or rectangular area of grass or paving, enclosed by college buildings (e.g 'my room is in the main quad').

**SAQ** – stands for Supplementary Application Questionnaire, an electronic form that must be filled in by all Cambridge applicants after the UCAS deadline.

**Scout** – the Oxford term for the cleaner in the college rooms.

**Sub fusc** – academic dress, including a gown, which must be worn in Oxford for exams and all formal university ceremonies.

**Summer Eights** – similar to 'bumps', this is an Oxford inter-collegiate rowing race that takes place in Trinity term, where boats race each other in single file, with the aim of catching and 'bumping' the boat in front.

**Supervision** – the Cambridge name for a one-to-one or small group session with an academic in a specific paper. Usually takes place once a week.

**Swaps** – dinner between two or more college or university societies at Cambridge. Usually held at Formal Halls or a nearby restaurant.

**Tab** – short for 'cantab', refers to a graduate of Cambridge. Also used by Oxford students to refer Cambridge students generally.

**Tompkins Table** – an annual ranking of Cambridge colleges based on the fraction of final year undergraduates achieving each degree classification.

**Torpids** – similar to 'bumps', an Oxford inter-collegiate rowing race that takes place in Hilary term, where boats race each other in single file, with the aim of catching and 'bumping' the boat in front.

**Trashing** – the term used to describe the tradition of covering students with food and drink as they leave their final exam to congratulate them on finishing.

**Trinity** – the third and final term of the academic year in Oxford.

**Tripos** – the Cambridge term for the undergraduate course.

**Tutorial** – the Oxford name for a one-to-one or small group session with an academic in a specific paper. Usually take place once a week.

**UCAS** – University and College Admissions Service. This is the website through which you will submit your application to all UK universities.

**The UL** – the Cambridge University Library. A copyright library.

**The Union** – short name for The Cambridge Union Society and The Oxford Union Society. The societies also regularly host famous speakers.

**Varsity** – sports matches between Oxford and Cambridge (e.g. varsity rugby). Also the name of a Cambridge student newspaper.

# Further Resources

For more information on the Oxbridge admissions process, we recommend the following resources:

For more information about Admission Tests, including registration, FAQs and past papers, see the Admissions Testing Service Website
**http://www.admissionstestingservice.org/**

For in-depth course and college information, and general details on the admissions process, see the University of Cambridge website (and individual faculty/college websites)
**https://www.cam.ac.uk**

For in-depth course and college information, and general details on the admissions process, see the University of Oxford website (and individual faculty/college websites)
**http://www.ox.ac.uk/**

For more reading lists, mock tests, subject blogs and more, see the Oxbridge Applications' website
**www.oxbridgeapplications.com**

For features and tips on all areas of the application process, see the Oxbridge Applications' section of the Telegraph
**http://www.telegraph.co.uk/sponsored/education/oxbridge/**